D0294701

THE GOOD COOK

Soups

by
THE EDITORS OF TIME-LIFE BOOKS

TIME-LIFE BOOKS·AMSTERDAM

TIME-LIFE BOOKS
EUROPEAN EDITOR: Kit van Tulleken
Assistant European Editor: Gillian Moore
Design Director: Ed Skyner
Photography Director: Pamela Marke
Chief of Research: Vanessa Kramer
Chief Sub-Editor: Ilse Gray

THE GOOD COOK
Series Editor: Windsor Chorlton
Series Designer: Douglas Whitworth
Series Co-ordinator: Liz Timothy

Editorial Staff for *Soups*
Text Editor: Marguerite Tarrant
Anthology Editor: Markie Benet
Staff Writers: Gillian Boucher, Norman Kolpas
Researcher: Sally Crawford
Sub-Editors: Jay Ferguson, Nicoletta Flessati, Katie Lloyd
Permissions Researcher: Mary-Claire Hailey
Design Assistants: Mary Staples, Adrian Saunders
Editorial Assistant: Molly Sutherland

EDITORIAL PRODUCTION FOR THE SERIES
Chief: Ellen Brush
Quality Control: Don Fragale
Traffic Co-ordinators: Pat Boag, Joanne Holland
Picture Co-ordinator: Philip Garner
Art Department: Julia West
Editorial Department: Anetha Besidonne, Debra Dick, Margaret Hall

© 1979 Time-Life Books B.V.
All rights reserved. Fifth European English language printing 1986.

No part of this book may be reproduced in any form or by any electronic or mechanical means, including information storage and retrieval devices or systems, without prior written permission from the publisher, except that brief passages may be quoted for review.

ISBN 7054 0594 X
TIME-LIFE is a trademark of Time Incorporated U.S.A.

THE ENCHANTED WORLD
LIBRARY OF NATIONS
HOME REPAIR AND IMPROVEMENT
CLASSICS OF EXPLORATION
PLANET EARTH
PEOPLES OF THE WILD
THE EPIC OF FLIGHT
THE SEAFARERS
WORLD WAR II
THE GOOD COOK
THE TIME-LIFE ENCYCLOPAEDIA OF GARDENING
THE GREAT CITIES
THE OLD WEST
THE WORLD'S WILD PLACES
THE EMERGENCE OF MAN
LIFE LIBRARY OF PHOTOGRAPHY
TIME-LIFE LIBRARY OF ART
GREAT AGES OF MAN
LIFE SCIENCE LIBRARY
LIFE NATURE LIBRARY
THE TIME-LIFE BOOK OF BOATING
TECHNIQUES OF PHOTOGRAPHY
LIFE AT WAR
LIFE GOES TO THE MOVIES
BEST OF LIFE
LIFE IN SPACE

Cover: The first ladleful of a mixed vegetable soup (*page 42*) is lifted from a steaming casserole. The rosy hue of the soup comes from tomatoes that have simmered to a purée. The other vegetables have been added in stages according to their different cooking times—potatoes and onions first, courgettes and shredded cabbage last.

THE CHIEF CONSULTANT:

Richard Olney, an American, has lived and worked since 1951 in France, where he is a highly regarded authority on food and wine. He is the author of *The French Menu Cookbook,* and the award-winning *Simple French Food,* and has contributed to numerous gastronomic magazines in France and the United States, including the influential journals *Cuisine et Vins de France.* and *La Revue du Vin de France.* He has directed cooking courses in France and the United States and is a member of several distinguished gastronomic and oenological societies, including *L'Académie Internationale du Vin, La Confrérie des Chevaliers du Tastevin,* and *La Commanderie du Bontemps de Médoc et des Graves.*

THE PHOTOGRAPHERS:
Tom Belshaw was born near London and started his working career in films. He now has his own studio in London. He specializes in food and still-life photography; undertaking both editorial and advertising assignments.
Alan Duns was born in 1943 in the north of England and studied at the Ealing School of Photography. He specializes in food photography and has undertaken many advertising assignments. His work has appeared in major British publications.

THE INTERNATIONAL CONSULTANTS:
Great Britain: *Jane Grigson* was born in Gloucester and brought up in the north of England. She is a graduate of Cambridge University. Her first book on food, *Charcuterie and French Pork Cookery*, was published in 1967; since then, she has published a number of cookery books, including *Good Things, English Food* and *Jane Grigson's Vegetable Book.* She became cookery correspondent for the colour magazine of the London *Observer* in 1968. **France:** *Michel Lemonnier* was born in Normandy. He began contributing to the magazine *Cuisine et Vins de France* in 1960, and also writes for several other important French food and wine periodicals. The co-founder and vice-president of the society *Les Amitiés Gastronomiques Internationales,* he is a frequent lecturer on wine and a member of most of the vinicultural confraternities and academies in France. **Germany:** *Jochen Kuchenbecker* trained as a chef, but worked for 10 years as a food photographer in many European countries before opening his own restaurant in Hamburg. *Anne Brakemeier,* who also lives in Hamburg, has published articles on food and cooking in many German periodicals. She is the co-author of three cookery books. **The Netherlands:** *Hugh Jans,* a resident of Amsterdam, has been translating cookery books and articles for more than 25 years. He has also published several books of his own including *Bistro Koken, Koken in een Kasserol* and *Vrij Nederlands Kookboek,* and his recipes are published in many Dutch magazines. **The United States:** *Carol Cutler,* who lives in Washington, DC, is the author of a number of cookery books, including the award-winning *The Six-Minute Soufflé and Other Culinary Delights. Shirley Sarvis,* a freelance food writer and consultant in San Francisco, is the author and co-author of a dozen cookery books. The late *José Wilson* was food editor of *House and Garden* magazine for 15 years and wrote many books on food and interior decoration, including *American Cooking: the Eastern Heartland* in Time-Life Books' Foods of the World series and, with Arthur Leaman, *The Complete Food Catalog.*

Valuable help was given in the preparation of this volume by the following members of Time-Life Books: *Maria Vincenza Aloisi, Joséphine du Brusle* (Paris), *Bona Schmid, Maria Teresa Marenco* (Milan).

CONTENTS

INTRODUCTION 5 Cuisine's kindest course/A versatile resource/Broth, bouillon, stock and consommé/A further vocabulary of soups/Serving wine with soup/Basic broths: the foundations of good soups/ Diverse ways to embellish a soup

PURÉES 23 **1** Smooth harmonies of flavour/Vegetables that provide their own thickener/ Adding body to puréed vegetables/Eggs and cream for velvet smoothness/ Combining leftovers for a fresh-tasting purée/Finely ground crayfish shells to enhance a bisque/Pounding chicken for a sumptuous soup/A game purée thickened with lentils/Puréeing requirements at a glance

COMPOUND BROTHS 41 **2** Hearty and nourishing/Soups from two vegetables or from many/Making a pistou/A substantial blend of mutton and barley/ Two more ways to use meat/A tripe soup thickened with natural gelatine/Fish soups with a Mediterranean flavour/ Serving clams in their own juice

BREAD SOUPS 55 **3** Time-honoured staples/ Variations on the simplest bread soup/Two classic onion soups/A pumpkin soup served in its shell

COLD SOUPS 63 **4** Creations for summer/Clarifying broth for a jellied consommé/Soups that need no cooking/Fish and vegetables assembled in a refreshing liquor/Kvas: a Russian home brew/ Hot spices blended in a bland liquid/Fruit soups: a balance of sweet and savoury

WHOLE MEAL SOUPS 75 **5** Stuffed chicken and beef poached in a pot/Bacon and beans: warming winter staples/ A fish soup with a lively garlic sauce/The solid goodness of a vegetable soup/A borscht on a grand scale/ A refreshing way with leftover borscht

ANTHOLOGY OF RECIPES 87 Simple broths 88/ Garnishes 90/Purées 93/ Compound broths 105/Bread soups 134/ Cold soups 141/Whole meal soups 147/ Standard preparations 163

RECIPE INDEX 168

GENERAL INDEX AND GLOSSARY 171

RECIPE CREDITS 173

ACKNOWLEDGEMENTS AND PICTURE CREDITS 175

Cuisine's Kindest Course

Originally, soup was basic sustenance—a daily pot of warming nourishment that brought the family together in communion around the hearth in which it was made. Soup was a meal in itself; and although nowadays it is more often served in small quantity at the beginning of a meal, soup continues to represent the main body of a meal for many people. It may be a bacon and bean soup (*left*), a Scotch broth, a *garbure*, or a seafood chowder; or it may be the primordial soup for which there can be no recipe—a blend of foods chosen with common sense and a bit of discretion from whatever may be in the larder and cooked with a few fresh vegetables and herbs.

In its etymology and popular usage from one tongue to another, the word "soup" gives insights into the way our eating habits have evolved. The word itself derives from "sop"—originally the bread over which a pottage, broth or other liquid was poured. "Sup" and "supper" share the same root: no doubt, in rural tradition of comfortable but unsophisticated eating, a sop moistened with a broth represented the archetypal evening meal. In some regions of France, *la soupe* still refers to the crust of bread with which the liquid—*le potage*—is served. Indeed, bread is an inseparable accompaniment to soups ". . . et trempez votre soupe". These words wind up many a soup recipe in French cookery books, both old and recent. Literally, they mean ". . . and moisten your soup", but they should be interpreted to mean: ". . . and pour [the soup] over your bread". The phrase is an incantation out of ancestral memory. It entreats one never to forget the sacred role of bread; it reminds one of the criminality of waste, of the luxury of being able to take pleasure in simple things—and it embodies ritual, which in cooking, as in all things, magnifies meaning and pleasure.

More sophisticated concepts of dining have altered the role of soup, but the memory of soup as basic nourishment lingers on in the popular tongue. "Soup's on!", a familiar cry to Anglo-Saxon ears, means "The meal is served"; a French mother remonstrates with a child who dawdles over its food by saying "Mange ta soupe"; professional cooks in France, be they short-order purveyors of *steak-pommes-frites* or stars in the Michelin firmament, speak affectionately of members of their trade as *marchands de soupes*—"soup pedlars".

Restaurant chefs, in fact, have particular cause to acknowledge the culinary influence of soups. The first eating establishment to be known by the name of restaurant was opened by a Parisian soup vendor, M. Boulanger, in 1765, and served soups exclusively. The establishment, and all its successors, took its name from a motto inscribed in Latin above the entrance: *Venite ad me omnes qui stomacho laboratis et ego restaurabo*—"Come to me all of you whose stomachs cry out and I will restore you."

Now, as then, the restorative powers of soup have been justly praised. Louis P. De Gouy, a European-born chef who worked in the United States during the first half of this century, sums up the appeal of soup in *The Soup Book*, published in 1949. "Soup is cuisine's kindest course," De Gouy wrote. "It breathes reassurance; it steams consolation; after a weary day it promotes sociability . . . there is nothing like a bowl of hot soup, its wisp of aromatic steam making the nostrils quiver with anticipation."

A versatile resource

Although soups are part of the foundations of our cooking traditions, they are not always treated in today's kitchens with the respect they deserve. Many cooks, seduced by the plethora of tinned, packaged and dehydrated products that pass under the guise of soups, have forgotten how delicious the real thing is. But anyone who can cut up a vegetable can make a soup in only a little more time than it takes to open a tin of soup and heat it up. A perfect example is the leek and potato soup demonstrated on page 42. It is ready to serve 20 minutes after the water has been put on to boil. The fact is that fresh vegetables cooked in clean water count among the sublime things in this world; only a crust of bread and a last-minute dab of sweet, fresh butter is required for such a soup to be equally at home at the table of an aristocrat or as the principal element in a farm-house supper.

This volume starts with the premise that soups are the most versatile and variable item on the menu. Served hot, they will banish the cold on a winter evening; served chilled, they will refresh the palate on a summer afternoon. They can be made with every category of food—meats, poultry, fish, fruits and vegetables. And they encourage the cook to experiment with the entire range of herbs, spices and seasonings. The demonstrations on the following pages will teach you how to give rein to all of these possibilities, and they will enable you to execute all of the recipes in the Anthology that makes up the second half of the book. These recipes present the best soups from 24 national cuisines; between them, they provide both an introduction and a guide to an elemental aspect of cookery.

Broth, bouillon, stock and consommé

Most of the names by which different types of soup are known date only from the mid-19th century and are frequently misapplied. In particular, a murky confusion surrounding the terms broth, bouillon, stock and consommé has led many people to believe that each must be different from the others. In fact, so far as mode of preparation is concerned, they are all one and the same thing: any differences between them resides in their respective roles and strength of flavour.

A broth is a clear, savoury essence drawn from a combination of meats, aromatic vegetables and herbs that are simmered in water and then strained out when they have yielded their flavours. A broth makes a delicious soup in its own right and can also be used as the moistening agent in other soups. Bouillon is merely the French word for broth.

The predominant flavour of a broth may come from beef, chicken, game, vegetables or fish; but for all general purposes, a broth is made with beef, often supplemented with chicken, sometimes with veal. Chicken contributes a soft—almost sweet—flavour that, in effect, rounds off the robust flavour of the beef; and the veal lends a mellow flavour and a gelatinous body to the fragrant liquid.

A stock is simply a broth that is employed as a braising medium or a sauce base. Used for these purposes the liquid should have a somewhat less assertive flavour than a broth and a higher proportion of natural gelatine. A gelatinous stock is designed to give richness and body to a preparation without masking or altering the flavours of the basic ingredients. Since the flavours of beef or chicken would tend to overpower those of other ingredients, a broth that is meant to serve specifically as a stock might be made with gelatinous cuts of veal to the exclusion of other, and more distinctive meats.

These definitions are necessary for a precise understanding of broth and stock, but they apply more to the world of highly refined restaurant cooking than to the practical demands of day-to-day living. The prototypal broth is that furnished by a pot au feu (*recipe, page 149*), a whole meal soup that Auguste Escoffier praised as a "comfortable and thoroughly bourgeois dish that nothing may unseat". The meats used for pot au feu do not surrender all their flavour; they are served as a main course after the broth. And any broth that is left over from the meal is reserved as stock or as the liquid for another soup.

A consommé is a consummate, or perfectly prepared, beef broth: it should be richly flavoured and completely clear. It is made with the same ingredients as a basic broth, but its flavour may be intensified by simmering the meats in a previously prepared broth rather than in water; in this case, it qualifies for the title of "double consommé". And whereas a few pearls of fat glistening on the surface of a pot au feu are in keeping with the homely nature of the dish, a consommé must be cleansed of every trace of fat. In addition, it should be only delicately gelatinous and perfectly limpid. (To some people, a broth that meets all of these qualifications will never quite be a consommé unless it is served from the white-gloved hands of a butler.)

Many old cook books, and more than a few modern ones, insist that a consommé cannot be brought to the required degree of clearness unless it is clarified by adding egg whites and finely chopped beef and vegetables. These ingredients attract the tiny particles that may cloud a broth, and are then strained out. However, even though the chopped meats and vegetables are added in the interest of greater succulence, a consommé's initial delicacy of flavour is always lost in the process.

In fact, clarification is not necessary to convert a basic broth into a consommé. A faultlessly clear consommé can be produced simply by taking care in the cooking of the broth: the meats and carcasses are placed on a shallow grid to keep them from sticking on the bottom of the pot; they are covered with cold water and brought very slowly to the boil; the liquid is skimmed repeatedly of all traces of scum before the aromatic elements are added, then scummed again; the heat is adjusted precisely so that, with the lid kept always ajar, the barest murmur—not quite simmer—disturbs the liquid's surface.

Nevertheless, accidents do occur: a moment of inattention, or a well-meaning guest seeing the lid of the pot askew and placing it squarely on the pot, may result in a rolling boil and a muddy broth. The liquid may serve passably as a stock, but it must be clarified if it is to be represented as a consommé. Accordingly, the technique of clarification is demonstrated in this book; however, to underline the importance of avoiding the technique where it should not be necessary, it is not presented in the demonstration of a basic broth (*page 10*), but in the demonstration of a jellied *madrilène* (*page 64*), a chilled consommé that is clarified to remove the tomato pulp which gives the soup its distinctive hue.

A crystalline consommé, unlike a basic broth, is not poured over bread crusts. It is a symbol of elegance and is garnished accordingly. It may be enlivened by jet darts of truffle, pastel-coloured custards or a filigree of chervil leaves—or by any of the hundreds of other classic garnish combinations, many named in honour of a celebrity. La Belle Otéro, a celebrated turn-of-the-century music hall artiste, has been immortalized by the addition of frogs' legs, rice and little peas to her consommé. Her contemporary and rival, lovely Polaire, receives a raw egg in her consommé. George Washington's memory has been rather amusingly honoured in the form of diced skin of calf's cheek and a truffle *julienne* garnish.

A further vocabulary of soups

In addition to the clear broths, there are the thick or opaque soups (which may, of course, incorporate broth as a moistening agent). The various categories within this larger group are often named for the way they are made. Purées, for example, whether based on vegetables, poultry or fish, are reduced to a uniform consistency by means of a sieve or other processor.

Cream soups are simply purées with cream added; if the main ingredient is shellfish, however, such a soup may be called a bisque—a term that was originally applied to game and poultry soups in addition to those made from shellfish. Veloutés, from the French word for velvet, are based on a velouté sauce—a broth thickened with flour—that is enriched with egg yolks and cream.

In this volume, the term compound broth has been given to soups in which the solid ingredients are cut into pieces and served with the liquid. Included in this category are Scotch broth, minestrone, chowders—soups that are akin to stews.

Bread soups, or *panades*—from the French word for bread—are a category of soups that use bread not just as a garnish or for supplementary thickening, but as a central ingredient.

Many of the compound broths are nourishing enough to make a meal in themselves. In this volume, though, the term "whole meal soup" is reserved for preparations—such as *poule au pot*, *garbure* and borscht—that provide two courses from a single pot: a broth and a meat or fish course. All of the soups in this grouping share the simple, yet bountiful, spirit of a pot au feu.

A few rules

On the whole, soup-making is a relaxed process mercifully free of rules and dictums. A broth that is correctly set to simmer needs only to be left undisturbed; it will tend to itself. Indeed, many a soup has been ruined in the name of improvement. Vegetable soups, in particular, are the victims of unnecessary refinements: the traditional beliefs that vegetables should be pre-cooked in fat and simmered in beef broth have been responsible for masking and altering many a fresh garden flavour.

Another familiar mistake is salting and peppering a soup when it is first put to cook. Common sense dictates caution when adding salt: an amount barely sufficient to season a full pot may be far too much when the liquid has reduced by the end of cooking. Pepper should never be added at the start of any long cooking process. Ground into a soup at the last moment, its clean, spicy

perfume accents the flavour of the other ingredients; but if pepper is cooked in the liquid for any length of time, its perfume dissipates and its taste becomes harsh and acrid.

The role of soup in a meal

"Soup is to dinner what the portico or the peristyle is to an edifice. That is to say, not only is it the first part, but it should be conceived in such a way as to give an exact idea of the feast, very nearly as the overture to an opera should announce the quality of the whole work." The author of these words was Alexandre-Balthazar-Laurent Grimod de la Reynière, a 19th-century French lawyer who spent his entire life pleading the case for intelligent and enlightened gastronomy.

Not everybody agreed with de la Reynière's assessment. Another contemporary, the Marquis de Cussy, aide to Napoleon I, acknowledged that soup was the preface to dinner, but noted that a good work can do without a preface. When the great chef Antonin Carême heard of this attack, he replied, with some puzzlement: "Why should the Marquis de Cussy wage war on soup? I cannot understand a dinner without it. I hold soup to be the well-beloved of the stomach."

During the lifetimes of these luminaries, the structure of a menu was, to say the least, an "edifice" of astounding complexity, often made up of more than a dozen courses. But Grimod de la Reynière's message is none the less relevant to the simpler menus of today. Imagine the cacophony if one were to follow a truffled consommé with a pot of Boston baked beans, or preceded a delicate turbot in champagne with a garlic-flavoured *soupe au pistou*. And consider the dullness were a macaroni gratin to follow upon the heels of a pasta-laden minestrone.

Escoffier cites Grimod de la Reynière in *Le Guide Culinaire* and goes on to say: "We agree with the illustrious gastronome. . . . Of all the elements that compose a menu, soups are those which demand the severest attention and the most delicate perfection, for the success of the rest of the dinner depends largely on the impression, good or bad, that they have produced on the guest." This is not to suggest that you can be careless in the preparation of other courses, but it is a psychological certainty that a brilliant opener will favourably prejudice your table companions towards the body of the meal to come.

Serving wine with soup

Soup and wine are rarely associated. Most people hold the idea that a liquid should not accompany another liquid. If you believe, however, that one of the precepts of civilized dining is that one's guests' glasses should never be empty, there is no reason why you should not serve a wine with the soup course. If champagne or a dry white wine has been served as an aperitif, it is logical to continue the same service with most soups; if wine has not been served, the first wine on the menu may be served with the soup.

Consommés—in particular, game consommés—are often perfumed at the last moment by the addition of a few drops of fortified wine—perhaps a fine, dry, old sherry. In such a case, a glass of the wine used to flavour the soup would be the most appropriate accompaniment.

Most of the whole meal soups are rustic in spirit and robust in flavour; young, uncomplicated but assertive wines—such as a St-Joseph, a Gamay or a Valpolicella—are most comfortable in their presence. The exuberant and garlicky Mediterranean whole meal fish soups are usually accompanied by a dry white or rosé wine; but a cool, young red wine—Bandol, Côtes-du-Rhône, Bourgeuil, Chianti or Zinfandel, for example—will be as complementary. Most white wines would be annihilated by a *garbure*: a rough, country red wine is the best choice in this instance—a Gigondas, perhaps, or a Cahors. A *poule au pot* is equally at home with a sumptuous Chardonnay, a six-month-old Beaujolais or a venerable wine from one of the great vineyards of the Médoc.

These wines are suggestions only. As in all things associated with the table, make your decisions after you have judged with your own palate—and always be wary of rules, be they imposed by tradition or by today's prevailing culinary fashions.

Richard Olney

The Foundations of Good Soups

There is no mystery attached to the making of broths. The basic method is the same, whether you make the broth with meat, poultry, vegetables or fish: simply simmer the ingredients in water until they have yielded their flavours to the liquid. In each case, the fragrant broth that is produced can either be served as a soup in its own right or used as the foundation of another soup.

Indeed, broths are so fundamental to soup-making that you should choose only the best ingredients and exercise scrupulous care in their preparation. The ingredients for a meat broth (*below, left; recipe, page 164*) should contribute a mellow flavour and a smooth body to the liquid. The main ingredient must be a stewing cut of beef, such as shin, which has flavour to spare and enough natural gelatine to thicken the broth slightly. Additional flavour and gelatine are provided by a fresh, leftover chicken carcass, some chicken trimmings, a piece of veal flank and a veal knuckle bone. Some recipes call for the inclusion of beef bones, but these, unlike veal bones, would add little extra flavour or gelatine, while taking up valuable space in the cooking pot.

Aromatic vegetables and a mixture of herbs round out the flavour of the broth. The proportion of vegetables to meat is a matter of personal choice. Some cooks add a single carrot and an onion for discreet aromatic support; others prefer the fuller flavour and perceptible edge of sweetness that is contributed by additional vegetables. If you wish to add garlic to the broth, use unpeeled cloves or a whole, unpeeled head; peeled garlic cloves would cook to a purée that would make the broth cloudy.

To perfume the liquid, stick two or three whole cloves in the onion and add the classic herb combination of parsley, bay leaf and thyme. Since broths are strained after cooking, you can leave the herbs loose. Or for easy retrieval, wrap them in muslin, celery stalks or leek leaves to form a bouquet garni.

To make a chicken broth (*below, centre left; recipe, page 164*), replace the mixture of meats with a trussed boiling fowl; a roasting chicken lacks both the flavour and gelatine of the older bird. A vegetable broth (*below, centre right; recipe, page 163*) includes the usual aromatic vegetables, but is supplemented with leafy vegetables such as lettuce and cabbage, for extra flavour. Chop or slice the vegeta-

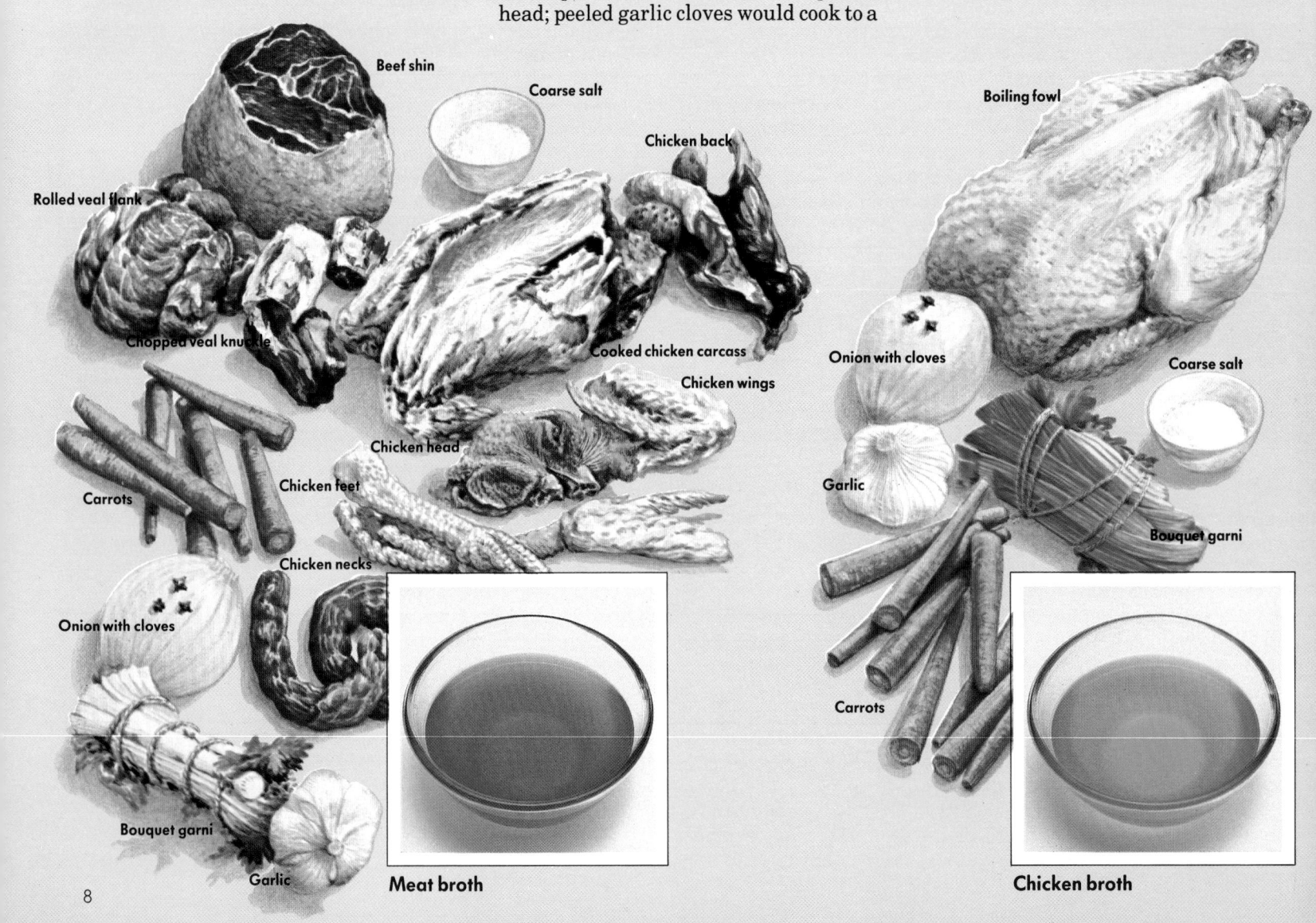

Meat broth

Chicken broth

bles so that they will yield the maximum flavour in a relatively short cooking time.

A fish broth (*below, right; recipe, page 163*) derives most of its flavour from the carcasses and trimmings of lean fish. The finished liquid will be less clear than a meat or vegetable broth, and it will have little body unless it is made with turbot or angler-fish, which are among the few fish that yield substantial amounts of gelatine. Supplement the basic herb mixture with chopped fennel leaves, whose anise flavour marries especially well with fish.

The actual cooking of broths is demonstrated overleaf, using meat broth as an example; the preparation of chicken, vegetable and fish broths differs only in detail. In each case, make the broth in a heavy pan that will hold the ingredients snugly—an oval one is best for a fowl. Since the aim is to produce a broth rich in flavour, add only as much water to the cooking pot as necessary; the closely packed ingredients should be covered by no more than about 4 cm ($1\frac{1}{2}$ inches).

When meat is heated in water, it precipitates albuminous proteins that will cloud the broth if they are not removed. The water should therefore be heated very slowly to draw out the impurities, which form a scum on the surface where they can be spooned off. Only after the skimming process is completed are the aromatic vegetables added.

All broths are cooked at a bare simmer: boiling would cause the solid ingredients to disintegrate and muddy the liquid. During the first 30 minutes' cooking, look at the broth frequently and adjust the heat, if necessary, in order to prevent the broth from boiling too vigorously.

Once the simmer has been established, 5 to 6 hours' cooking are required to draw out the flavour of meat. You can, however, make a meat broth in little more than an hour if you cut up the ingredients very finely (*page 10*), thus increasing the surface area through which flavour can escape. A chicken broth should be simmered for $1\frac{1}{2}$ to 3 hours, depending on the age of the bird. Only 30 to 40 minutes cooking is needed to produce a vegetable or fish broth: longer cooking would not draw significantly more flavour from the fish or vegetables.

After the cooking, the solids will be exhausted of flavour and should be discarded. You can, however, produce both a broth and a main course (*page 76*) by poaching meat or chicken just long enough to flavour the liquid.

Vegetable broth

Fish broth

A Classic Meat Broth Rich in Flavour

1 **Packing the pot.** To prevent the meats from sticking, arrange them on a wire rack in a large pot. Add the bony pieces first—here, a cooked chicken carcass and some chopped veal knuckle. Pack in the large cuts of meat—beef shin and rolled veal flank. Then insert the small pieces—chicken feet, necks, head and back. Add cold water to just cover.

2 **Cleansing the liquid.** To encourage the meat to precipitate albuminous scum, heat the liquid very slowly, without stirring: it should take 1 hour, or more, to reach the boil. Remove the grey scum that collects on the surface as it comes to the boil. This task is simplified by using a ladle with a shallow, tapered bowl (*above, left*). Pour in a cup or so of cold water (*above, centre*) to encourage more scum to rise. Ladle off the second, cleaner, scum that forms as the broth returns to the boil (*above, right*). Repeat, until the scum is replaced by a white froth.

A Short Cut to a Meat Broth

The more finely meat and vegetables are cut up, the more surface area is exposed and the more quickly they will yield their flavours to a liquid. Only 1 hour of cooking is required for this meat broth (***recipe, page 89***), but it makes a good substitute for the classic broth (***above***).

This broth does not require scumming, since the finely chopped meat has the capacity to reabsorb the coagulated albumin particles that it releases. All you need to do is stir the broth as it heats up, to prevent the pieces of meat from clumping together. The albumin that is released clings to their many cut surfaces. When the broth is strained, the albumin is filtered out with the meat.

The flavour of the broth is good and fresh; but the broth does not have much body because it is made without bones and trimmings, which require long cooking to yield their gelatine.

1 **Chopping the ingredients.** finely cut up some aromatic vegetables—here, carrots, and leeks. Finely chop or mince lean stewing beef. If you prefer, ask the butcher to mince the meat for you, but be wary of butcher's mince prepared in advance: it can be very fatty.

2 **Bringing to the boil.** Put the meat and vegetables in a pan and cover with cold water. Add herbs and salt. Slowly heat the water, stirring to keep the pieces of meat apart. Stop stirring when the water approaches the boil: this is when further stirring would cloud the liquid.

3 **Adding the vegetables.** In the gaps left between the meats, tuck in the vegetables: an onion, stuck with 2 or 3 cloves, carrots, an unpeeled head of garlic and a bouquet garni. Salt and remove any fresh scum that rises as the broth returns to the boil. Partly cover the pan (*above*), so that steam does not build up and overheat the broth.

4 **Cooking and straining.** Simmer the broth gently, undisturbed, for its entire cooking period of 5 to 6 hours; stirring would release particles that could cloud the broth. Dampen a doubled square of muslin so that it will hold back fat as well as small particles. Line a colander with the muslin and strain the broth through it into a bowl.

5 **Removing the fat.** Discard the solids strained from the broth. Let the broth cool, then blot up the remaining liquid fat by placing several layers of folded paper towel on the broth's surface. If you do not intend to use it the same day, refrigerate the broth and later spoon off the solidified fat from the surface.

3 **Cooking the broth.** Put the lid on the pan ajar and adjust the heat so that the liquid simmers gently. Leave the broth to cook, undisturbed, for 1 hour. By the end of the cooking period, the liquid will be perfectly clear (*above*).

4 **Straining through muslin.** Pour the broth into a bowl through dampened muslin draped inside a colander or sieve. Remove any fat from the surface of the broth (*Step 5, above*).

Freezing Broth in Neat Packages

Freezing in bags. Although broth is most flavourful when freshly prepared, convenience prompts most cooks to make a large amount at a time and freeze what is not needed immediately. Plastic storage bags make convenient containers. Support each bag in a straight-sided vessel while you ladle in the broth (*above*). When you thaw the broth, place the bag in a pan of warm water until the broth begins to melt.

Diverse Ways to Embellish a Soup

Displayed below, adorning 12 servings of the identical consommé, is a selection of the soup garnishes whose preparation is demonstrated on pages 12-21. All of the garnishes that follow will complement the clean, full flavour and amber clarity of a carefully nurtured broth (*pages 8-11*), but many can also be served with purées or other thick soups.

Herbs are the simplest, most universal garnish. You can add a sprinkling of fresh parsley or chervil to any soup; or choose fresh herbs that will marry with the flavours of individual soups. Snippets of chives, for example, will give a subtle onion flavour to an avocado soup (*page 66*), anise-flavoured fennel goes well with most fish soups; and the sweet-sour scent of dill weed is a perfect finishing touch for chilled borscht (*page 86*). If you use sizeable whole leaves—some tarragon to garnish a carrot purée (*page 24*), for instance—wilt them by dipping them briefly into boiling water. Because wilted leaves are less rigid than freshly cut ones, they will float on the surface of the soup, and blanching them before adding to the soup will brighten their colour as well.

Vegetable garnishes (*page 14*) add texture as well as flavour; in one form or another, they are suited to all savoury soups. Leaf vegetables—especially cos or round lettuce, endive, spinach and sorrel—make light, refreshing garnishes when sliced into thin strips. In this form, they are called a *chiffonade*. Firm aromatic vegetables—such as carrots and turnips—should be cut into thin strips, known as *julienne*, or into small cubes, called *brunoise*, and then parboiled to soften them slightly. Sweet red, green or yellow peppers, which add a flourish of colour to soups, should be roasted or grilled whole to loosen their skins, then peeled and seeded before being cut into *julienne* or *brunoise*.

Egg garnishes—whole eggs, egg threads and custards (*page 15*)—are best appreciated in clear broths. A poached egg, trimmed into a neat circle, then slipped into the broth, makes a beautiful and nutritious addition to each serving.

Egg threads (*recipe, page 165*), made from a thin batter of eggs and flour, cook in the soup as they are dribbled into it. Custards, made from a mixture of egg yolks and broth (*recipe, page 167*), require more elaborate preparation. The custard mixture is cooked in a water bath, cooled, and then cut into decorative shapes.

Crusty bread (*recipe, page 165*) is a cardinal accompaniment to soups. Leftover bread, a few days old and slightly

Spinach noodles

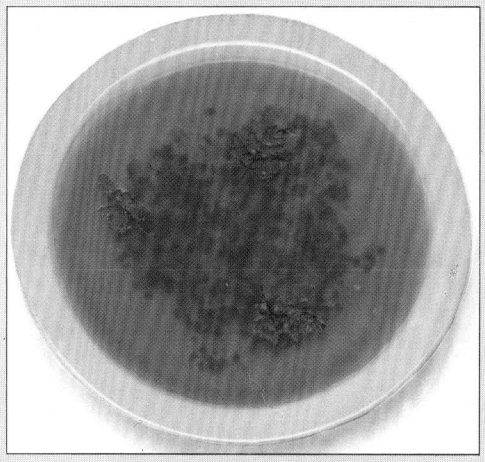

Carrot and turnip *brunoise* with chervil sprigs

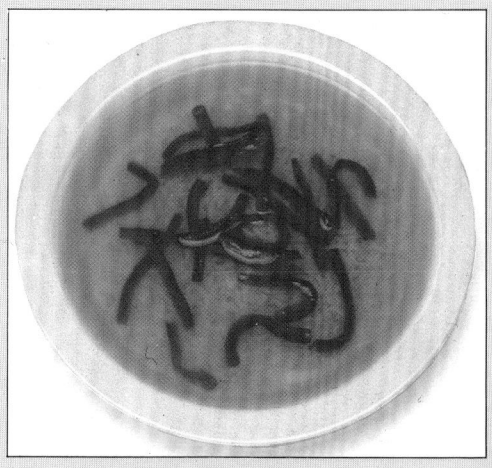

Sweet red pepper *julienne* with rice

Stuffed pasta

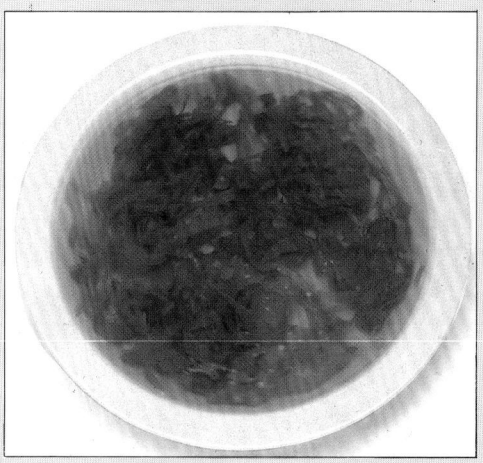

Lettuce *chiffonade*

Julienne of carrots, turnips and leeks

dry, can be sliced thinly, toasted and topped with some grated cheese (*page 16*). From a narrow French loaf, you can fashion small hollowed crusts and fill them with puréed aromatic vegetables extracted from a broth or *poule au pot* (*page 76*). And a dense-crumbed white loaf can furnish crisp, cube-shaped croûtons to garnish a broth or a purée: fry them in butter or olive oil scented with a crushed garlic clove.

From Italy to the Orient, pasta is used as a soup garnish. Good quality commercial pastas are available in a myriad of miniature forms—stars, wheels, shells, letters of the alphabet—that are made specially for soup. But the freshness and fine flavour of pasta made at home, either by hand or with a pasta machine, will justify the time spent in preparing it. A basic pasta dough (*page 17; recipe, page 165*) can be flavoured and coloured with dissolved saffron or with puréed spinach or chard, and it may be sliced to any width. You can cut square or circular wrappers from the dough to make ravioli or tortellini; fill these with a savoury mixture, such as *ricotta* cheese, spinach and egg yolks (*recipe, page 90*).

Dumplings (*page 18*) can turn a light broth into a substantial first course. The most basic dumplings are made with flour, puréed potatoes or breadcrumbs mixed with fat and seasonings; but you can replace some or all of the starchy or fatty ingredients with either minced meat or beef marrow.

Quenelles (*page 20; recipe, page 165*), a light form of dumpling, are made from pounded raw veal, poultry, game or fish, mixed with egg whites and double cream, and then poached. As they cook, quenelles acquire a light, airy texture. They are a traditional garnish for clear soups, but also make a luxurious addition to game purées (*page 36*) and other rich soups.

Small pastries—such as the crescent-shaped *pirozhki* (*page 21; recipe, page 90*) that traditionally partner borscht—are a separate accompaniment to a soup rather than an integral garnish. You can make them from shortcrust, puff or yeast pastry: fill them with stuffings based on minced meat, cheese or vegetables, and bake or deep fry them.

Paper-thin French crêpes can be used as a garnish that is added directly to a broth. Start with a basic thin pancake batter (*recipe, page 166*) and add chopped parsley or other fresh herbs (*page 21*). Roll the finished pancakes and slice them into narrow strips: they will unfurl like ribbons in the liquid to make an attractive cream and green mosaic.

Mixed vegetables and chicken *julienne*

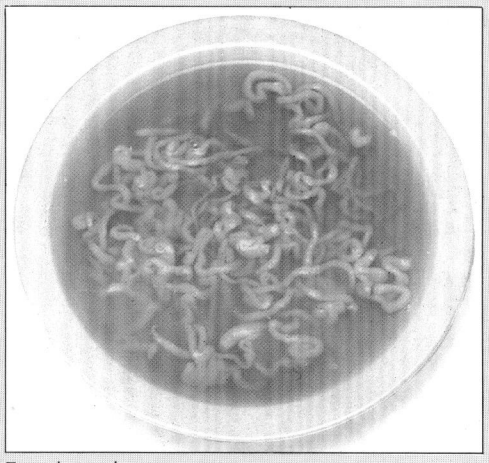
Egg threads

Dumplings of flour, egg and parsley

Egg-custard cubes with truffle *julienne*

Poached egg on toasted French bread

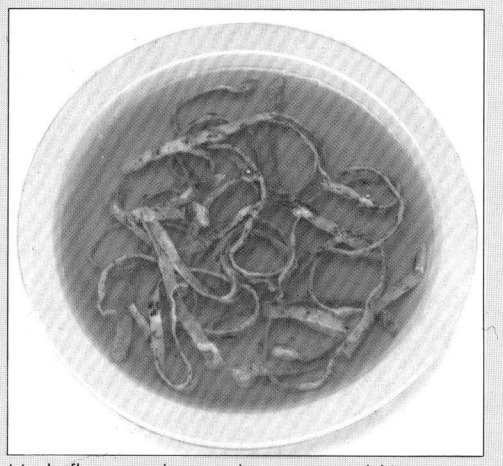
Herb-flavoured pancakes cut into ribbons

Vegetables: Adding Colours and Textures

Cutting a Chiffonade

1 **Preparing spinach or sorrel.** Discard any leaves that are not fresh and green. Fold each leaf—sorrel, in this case—in half, with the ridged rib outermost. Pull the rib away down the length of the leaf.

2 **Rolling and slicing.** Stack several leaves on top of each other and roll them up lengthwise. With fingertips turned slightly under for safety, steady the roll with one hand and slice it into strips.

3 **Softening the chiffonade.** Bring the soup to simmering point. Gather up all the shredded leaves and drop them into the soup. Leave them to soften for a few seconds before serving the soup.

Cutting Julienne and Brunoise

1 **Slicing.** Cut vegetables—here, carrot and turnip—into thin slices. To make *julienne*, stack several slices and cut them into strips. For *brunoise*, cut the strips into dice.

2 **Cooking.** Drop the cut-up vegetables into boiling salted water or broth and parboil them for about a minute. The vegetables should remain slightly firm.

Skinning Sweet Peppers

1 **Peeling.** Grill the peppers at a fairly high heat, turning them so that the skins blister evenly. Leave to cool, covered with a damp cloth. Strip off the skins and pull out the stems.

2 **Seeding and slicing.** Pull open the peppers at their stem ends. With a teaspoon, remove the seeds. Slice the flesh lengthwise into strips. Cut across the strips to make dice.

A Vegetable Medley

1 **Slicing.** Trim each vegetable to make small, evenly shaped pieces. Here, carrots, beans and skinned, seeded tomatoes are cut to the size of the smallest vegetable—peas.

2 **Cooking.** Leave tomatoes raw. Parboil the other vegetables separately by lowering them into the pan in a strainer. Reserve the vegetables in cold water.

Eggs: Simple and Sophisticated Enrichments

Poaching an Egg

Tipping in the egg. Break the egg into a saucer. Bring salted water to the boil, then turn off the heat and slip in the egg. Cover and let the egg sit for 3 minutes until set. Lift it out with a slotted spoon.

Making Egg Threads

1 **Making the batter.** In a bowl, whisk flour and eggs together—1 to 2 tablespoons of flour for each egg. Add a little salt. Pass the batter through a fine sieve to remove any solid bits of egg.

2 **Cooking the threads.** Hold a large perforated spoon over a pan of simmering broth. Ladle the batter into the spoon. It will drip into the broth in fine streams and cook in 3 to 4 minutes.

Colouring and Cutting Out Custards

1 **Mixing the custard.** In a bowl, whisk egg yolks and whole eggs—3 yolks to each whole egg. Whisk warm—not hot—broth into some of the whisked egg and sieve the mixture to remove solids.

2 **Adding purées.** Dilute separately puréed vegetables—here, tomatoes and peas—with a little broth. Make flavoured custards by whisking a portion of the whisked egg into each purée.

3 **Baking.** Pour the plain and flavoured custards into well-buttered moulds and set them on a wire rack in a pan of hot water. Cook, covered, at 180°C (350°F or Mark 4) for 15 to 20 minutes until firm.

4 **Unmoulding.** Firm up the custards in a dish filled with ice. To loosen the custard, run a small knife round the inside of each mould. Invert it over a plate and tap it sharply to turn out the custard.

5 **Cutting to shape.** Cut each custard into slices. Slices from small moulds may be used whole as individual garnishes; larger square or rectangular slices should be cut into small strips or dice.

6 **Cutting decorative shapes.** Occasionally you may like to garnish a soup with custards of more fanciful shapes. Use small biscuit cutters to stamp the custard garnishes from larger slices.

Bread: a Traditional Accompaniment

Three Garnishes from a French Loaf

Toasting bread. Cut a narrow, slightly dry French loaf into thin slices. Place the slices on an ungreased baking tray and colour each side in turn under a slow grill.

Topping with toasted cheese. Slice a loaf thinly. Brush one side of each slice with melted butter, sprinkle on grated Parmesan cheese, some cayenne pepper, and grill.

Stuffing crusts. Cut a loaf into 5 cm (2 inch) lengths, then halve each length. Hollow out each half, brush it with melted butter and fill with mashed vegetables from a broth.

Baked Bread Flavoured with Garlic and Olive Oil

1 **Drying the bread.** Cut thin slices from a narrow French loaf. Put the slices on a baking tray in a slow oven and dry them out without browning them.

2 **Rubbing with garlic.** Peel a large clove of garlic and cut off the root end. Rub one side of each toast slice with the cut surface of the garlic clove.

3 **Sprinkling on olive oil.** Dribble olive oil over the toast. You can regulate the flow by pouring the oil from a bottle with a cork in which a groove has been cut.

Croûtons: Bread Cubes Fried in Butter

1 **Slicing the bread.** Cut slices from a stale, firm-crumbed loaf; remove the crusts. Cut each slice into fingers and cut across the fingers to make cubes.

2 **Heating the bread cubes.** In a sauté pan, melt plenty of butter over a very low heat. Add the cubes in a single layer, so that they soak up the butter evenly.

3 **Tossing the croûtons.** Fry the cubes gently so that they become crisp all the way through. To ensure even browning, toss them frequently.

Pasta: Mixing, Shaping and Filling

Making Your Own Noodles

1 **Mixing the ingredients.** Make a well in a mound of sifted plain flour. Into the well put salt, olive oil and beaten egg. Mix the ingredients with your fingers, working the flour towards the centre.

2 **Kneading the dough.** Knead the dough on a floured surface: with the heel of your hand, spread the dough out, then fold it over and give it a half-turn. Repeat until it is smooth and elastic.

3 **Rolling out the dough.** Lightly flour a marble slab or pastry board and the surface of the dough. With a rolling pin, roll out the dough firmly and evenly until it is 2 mm ($\frac{1}{16}$ inch) thick.

4 **Rolling up the dough.** Dust the top surface of the dough with fine semolina flour. Loosely fold over 5 cm (2 inches) of dough on opposite sides of the sheet; continue folding until the rolls meet.

5 **Slicing the noodles.** Slice the rolled-up dough into strips—wide or narrow, as you prefer. To unfold the noodles, slip the flat of the knife into the middle of the slices and lift (*above*).

6 **Pre-cooking the noodles.** To prevent the noodles' floury coating clouding a broth, pre-cook them in boiling, salted water for about 2 minutes. The noodles should be soft, but still slightly resistant.

Cutting Pasta Rings for Stuffing

1 **Cutting the pasta.** Prepare and roll out a noodle dough as above. Cut out circles with a pastry cutter or a glass, and stack to keep them from drying.

2 **Shaping.** Dab stuffing—here spinach and cheese—on to each circle. Moisten the edges, fold in half and pinch edges together. Join the ends to form a ring.

3 **Parboiling the stuffed pasta.** Drop the tortellini into boiling salted water. Cook for about 4 to 5 minutes, lift them out with a wire strainer and let them drain.

Dumplings: a Choice of Mixtures

Rolling and Cutting Potato Dumplings

1 **Cooking and puréeing.** Peel, cut up and boil the potatoes. Drain in a sieve. Rest the sieve over a mixing bowl and press the potatoes through with a pestle.

2 **Adding flavour.** Stew some chopped onion in butter until soft. Add the onion, some chopped parsley, salt and pepper to the potatoes and mix.

3 **Thickening and binding.** Stir in semolina to thicken the mixture and raw egg to bind it. Sprinkle in enough flour (*above*) to make the mixture firm.

Moulding a Marrow, Breadcrumb and Herb Dumpling

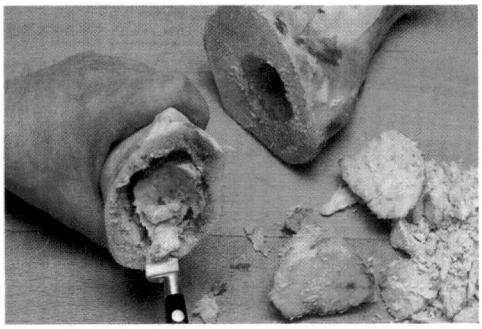

1 **Removing the marrow.** Buy beef marrow bones sawn into 8 to 12 cm (3 to 5 inch) sections. With a small knife prise out the marrow (*above*). Chop it finely.

2 **Mixing.** Put the chopped marrow in a bowl. Add salt, pepper, mixed herbs, chopped parsley, an egg and some breadcrumbs. Mix thoroughly.

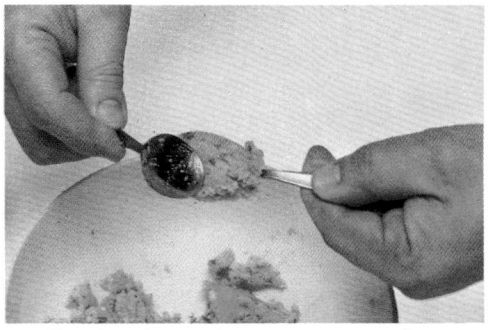

3 **Shaping.** Leave the mixture in a cool place for a few minutes to let the flavours mingle. Use two teaspoons, dipped in cold water, to mould smooth dumplings.

Shaping Meat Dumplings by Hand

1 **Preparing the ingredients.** Finely chop lean meat—here, veal—and beef kidney suet. Soak crustless white bread in milk and squeeze out the excess liquid.

2 **Combining the mixture.** Put the meat, suet and bread into a large bowl. Add chopped onions, eggs, a grating of nutmeg and a little cream. Mix well.

3 **Pounding.** For light dumplings that will cook evenly, pound the mixture, a little at a time, in a mortar until absolutely smooth; or use an electric processor.

4 **Rolling out the mixture.** Place a handful at a time of the mixture on a well-floured surface. Roll the mixture into a sausage shape about 2.5 cm (1 inch) thick.

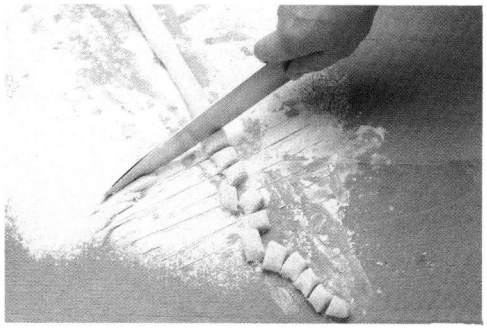

5 **Cutting the dumplings.** With a sharp knife, slice the roll diagonally into individual dumplings, 2.5 cm (1 inch) long. Put them on a floured dish.

6 **Cooking.** Refrigerate the dumplings for 30 minutes to firm them. Poach them in simmering water for about 10 minutes, or until they float. Lift out and serve.

4 **Unmoulding the dumplings.** Use the underside of one teaspoon to gently push the dumpling off the other teaspoon and on to a plate (*above*).

5 **Poaching the dumplings.** Bring a pan of water to the boil; adjust the heat to maintain a simmer. Slip the dumplings one by one into the simmering water.

6 **Draining the dumplings.** Cook the dumplings until they float, and then a few minutes longer: about 15 minutes in all. Lift them out with a slotted spoon.

4 **Shaping dumplings.** Wet your hands. Roll a teaspoonful of mixture between your palms to form a ball. Place each ball on a plate of fine, toasted breadcrumbs.

5 **Coating with breadcrumbs.** When the plate is half filled, shake it gently with a circular motion so that the dumplings pick up an even coating of crumbs.

6 **Poaching.** Poach the dumplings in boiling water until they float, then a few minutes more—about 15 minutes. Remove with a slotted spoon.

Quenelles: an Airy Purée of Meat or Fish

Piping and Poaching Quenelles

1 **Pounding the flesh.** Trim raw meat or fish—here, partridge breasts are used—of all skin, fat and sinew, and cut it into small chunks. Pound the flesh to a paste in a mortar. Add egg white and pound (*above*) until it has been incorporated. Season lightly with cayenne pepper.

2 **Sieving the mixture.** Using a flexible piece of plastic, press a spoonful of the purée at a time through a drum sieve. Scrape the purée from underneath the sieve and transfer it to a metal bowl. Cover the purée closely, embed the bowl in ice and refrigerate for 1 hour.

3 **Adding cream.** With the bowl still set on ice, beat double cream into the purée, a spoonful at a time. Spoon the mixture into a nylon icing bag or, as here, into a bag improvised by rolling a sheet of greaseproof paper into a long cone.

4 **Piping the quenelles.** Butter the base of a wide-bottomed sauté pan. Clip off the tip of the paper piping bag and then squeeze the bag from the top to form tiny quenelles in whatever shape you fancy.

5 **Adding water.** Pour boiling water into the pan until the quenelles are submerged. To avoid disturbing the uncooked quenelles, pour the water through a funnel placed at one side of the sauté pan (*above*).

6 **Poaching the quenelles.** Bring the water to a bare simmer. Cook, covered, until the quenelles float to the surface—2 to 3 minutes. Lift them out with a slotted spoon (*above*). Place the quenelles in a tureen and pour soup over them or reserve them in a warmed, covered dish until ready to serve.

Shaping and Filling Crescent-Shaped Pastries

1 **Cooking the stuffing.** Sauté chopped onion and garlic in oil; add chopped spring onion, mushrooms, lemon juice and seasonings. Cook until the liquid evaporates. Add chopped cooked egg.

2 **Mixing flour and butter.** In a mixing bowl, put roughly equal quantities of plain flour and chilled, cubed butter. Rub the flour and butter together (*above*) to a coarse, crumbly consistency.

3 **Binding with soured cream.** Make a well in the centre of the bowl and spoon in some soured cream. Combine the soured cream with the flour and butter by cutting through the mixture with a knife.

4 **Gathering up the pastry.** After enough soured cream has been mixed in to bind the pastry, gather the dough together into a mass (*above*). Place the dough on a floured surface and roll it out.

5 **Forming the pies.** Cut out circles of dough. Put some stuffing on one half of each circle and brush the edge of the other half with beaten egg. Fold the pastry over and press edges together.

6 **Baking the pies.** Preheat the oven to 220°C (425°F or Mark 7). Place the pies on a greased baking tray and brush them with beaten egg. Bake for 12 to 15 minutes, until the glaze is golden.

Herb-Flecked Crêpes, Sliced into Ribbons

1 **Pouring the batter.** Make a crêpe batter (*recipe, page 166*) and add a chopped herb—here, parsley. Melt enough butter to make a thin film. Pour in batter, tilting to distribute it thinly.

2 **Turning the crêpes.** Cook each crêpe until its edges colour and curl up slightly. Slip a spatula beneath it and turn it over. Cook the other side of the crêpe for a few seconds, then remove to a plate.

3 **Cutting the ribbons.** Stack the finished crêpes and cover them with plastic film to keep them moist. Before serving, roll up each crêpe and slice it thinly: lightly toss the strips to unfold them.

1

Purées

Smooth Harmonies of Flavour

Last-minute enrichments of cream or butter
Thickening with potatoes or flour
Blending eggs and cream for a classic velouté
Transforming vegetable leftovers
Extracting flavour from crayfish shells
Thickening with lentils

Characterized by a more or less uniform texture and a spoon-coating consistency, purée soups are made by breaking up the solid ingredients into minuscule fragments that are suspended in the soup liquid. You can make smooth-textured purées—blends of cream with chicken, shellfish or asparagus, for example—to grace the most formal meal. Or you can make rough-textured ones—such as the leek and potato soup illustrated on the opposite page—for family suppers.

Purées often include only one or two main ingredients. If you add more, the flavours merge with each other, producing a soup of indeterminate origins. In addition to the main ingredient, purées include some liquid, an enrichment of butter or cream and a starchy element that will thicken the mixture and bind the solid ingredients in a stable suspension. Without the presence of starch, the purée would be thin and the solids would separate out from the liquid. Unless you are using naturally starchy ingredients, such as potatoes or pulses, you must add a thickener—flour or bread, for example. Endless combinations of main ingredients, liquid, thickeners and enrichment are possible; the chart on page 38 will guide you in devising your own purées.

Coarse purées are best prepared in a food mill. The food is forced through a disc pierced with holes; the size of the holes determines the texture of the soup. Fine-textured purées are made by pushing the ingredients through a sieve. A close-meshed drum sieve gives the smoothest result, since it not only breaks up solids into very small pieces but also holds back every scrap of fibre or membrane, such as the skin of peas. A nylon or stainless steel sieve is required for some foods—for instance, vegetables such as artichokes, celeriac and salsify which react with most metals, blackening and acquiring an acrid taste.

Electric food processors are invaluable for puréeing the resistant flesh of game and of molluscs. A food processor or blender can be used to make either a fine or coarse purée, but the machine's speed makes it difficult to control the soup's texture precisely. In the case of fine purées, a further drawback of these machines is their inability to keep out fibres or membranes. But if you want to make a smooth purée with the minimum of effort, first use a food processor, blender or food mill to break up the ingredients, then use a sieve to filter out any tough fragments.

A purée of leeks and potatoes is finished by stirring in a chunk of butter. The soup's granular texture is achieved by puréeing the cooked ingredients through a food mill; a smoother leek and potato soup, puréed through a wire mesh sieve, is demonstrated on page 26.

Vegetables that Provide Their Own Thickener

Firm vegetables such as carrots, mature peas, broad beans or celeriac have a high proportion of cellulose or starch that adds substance to a purée soup. Used in ample quantity, one of these vegetables, newly picked if possible, can be transformed into a purée soup base with marked sweetness and intensity of flavour (*recipes, pages 94-95*). Herbs and aromatic vegetables can be added to lend support, but their flavours must remain subordinate to that of the main vegetable. Young peas, leaves and other vegetables without much body may be suitably sweet, but are too soft to form a firm-textured purée.

As indicated by the two demonstrations on these pages, different vegetables may call for slightly different techniques in the making of this kind of purée. For example, carrots (*right*), which are strong tasting, can be given a preliminary stewing with aromatics to let them soak up flavour. A mild broth—veal, chicken or vegetable—can be used as a cooking liquid to add still another flavour element.

By contrast, fresh peas are delicate in taste. In a pea purée (*right, below*), plain water is used as the cooking liquid to preserve the purity of the peas' flavour. Lettuce and leeks lend appropriately mild aromatic support.

No matter what the vegetable, it should be cooked long enough to be tender, but still a little firm. The next step—puréeing—will vary, however, according to the vegetable. One that is soft throughout after cooking—such as carrots or celeriac—is generally best puréed by a single passage through a food mill or sieve. A vegetable that has a tough skin—peas or beans—will need to be sieved twice. In either case, sieving will be easier if you moisten the vegetables with a little broth as you go. Afterwards stir in more liquid to bring the soup to an appropriate consistency: a common proportion is one part purée to two parts liquid.

You may choose a garnish to add textural contrast to the purée—fried croûtons, for example. Or you can decide to echo the flavour of the soup. For either of the purées demonstrated here, you might sprinkle over some fresh leaves of the flavouring herbs, or add a few whole peas or some carrot curls.

A Simple Purée of Carrots

1 **Combining carrots with aromatics.** Melt butter in a heavy pan over a low heat, then add a thick layer of chopped onions, and sprigs of herbs—tarragon is used here, but mint or parsley could be substituted. Simmer gently until the onions begin to release their juices, then add peeled and sliced raw carrots (*above, left*). Cover the pan tightly and let the carrots cook undisturbed for 15 minutes or so. The moisture rising from the aromatics will penetrate the raw slices, serving both to soften and perfume them.

The Fine Texture of Twice-Sieved Peas

1 **Preparing a base for the peas.** Finely slice lettuce leaves and leeks. Add chopped herbs—here, mint and savory. Stew the mixture in melted butter over a low heat until the leaves wilt and begin to sweat their juices. Then add a generous quantity of shelled peas.

2 **Cooking in water.** Because the peas will keep more of their colour if they cook in minimum time, boil the water before adding it to the pot. Add enough water to cover the peas (*above*), and simmer until they are tender. The timing will vary with the age and size of the peas, but start testing them after 5 minutes.

2 **Adding liquid.** Add enough hot liquid—in this case chicken broth—to cover the pieces of carrot. Simmer them in the liquid, uncovered, for about 20 minutes, until they are just tender.

3 **Puréeing the vegetables.** Remove the cooked carrots from the broth with a perforated spoon. Pick out and discard the sprigs of herbs. Press the vegetables through a sieve or food mill. As you work, ladle a little broth over them to speed the puréeing process. If the resulting purée is too thick to stir easily, dilute it with more broth, milk or cream.

4 **Finishing.** Taste for seasoning, add a spoonful of white wine or lemon juice if the carrots are too sweet, or a pinch of sugar if they are not sweet enough. Pour in enough double cream (*above*) to give the soup the desired consistency, then return the soup to a low heat, bring it to simmering point, and serve.□

3 **Pulping the peas.** To achieve a smooth-textured purée without overcooking, sieve the peas twice. First pass them through a coarse sieve or food mill (*above, left*) to separate the internal flesh from the skins, adding a little of their liquid to moisten them. Then force the roughly pulped flesh through a fine-meshed sieve (*above, right*). With some of the cooking liquid, dilute the resulting thick purée to the desired consistency and taste for seasoning.

4 **Finishing with butter.** Gently reheat the purée before serving, stirring regularly to prevent sticking. Remove the soup from the heat before it boils. Stir in chunks of butter (above) to enrich the soup without dimming its emerald colour.□

Adding Body to Puréed Vegetables

Unless it features an ingredient with a high starch or cellulose content such as peas or carrots, a purée will need a supplementary thickener to give it the dense body and smooth consistency characteristic of this type of soup. Cooked rice, breadcrumbs, potatoes and flour are all useful as thickening agents (*chart, page 38*). But while crumbs or rice can simply be added to a nearly finished soup, potatoes and flour must be cooked with the soup.

Potatoes have a particularly wide range of applications in heavy-textured purées because they serve simultaneously as a thickener and a main ingredient—as in the leek and potato soup demonstrated on the right (*recipe, page 105*). For any potato-thickened purée, start with a mealy potato variety. As they simmer in the cooking liquid, mealy potatoes will break up more readily than waxy, yellow-fleshed ones, and when puréed afterwards they will be dispersed more evenly in the soup. Before cooking, cut up the potatoes so that they will be done at the same time as the other ingredients. Here, both potatoes and leeks are sliced thinly to cook in 15 minutes. But the heartier leek and potato soup on page 22 simmers for much longer; the leeks can be cut in large chunks and the potatoes halved or left whole—after the extended cooking, both vegetables will purée quite easily.

For lighter-textured purées, flour can provide an unobtrusive support to the main ingredient. Because flour requires long cooking to eliminate its raw taste, it should be added directly to the soup only if the other ingredients can withstand a lengthy simmer—as with the onion soup demonstrated here (*recipe, page 99*). The onions for this soup are sliced and precooked in butter to soften them; flour is then sprinkled on and stirred in thoroughly. When milk, water or broth is added, the starch is completely incorporated into the liquid. During 40 minutes of slow simmering, any taste of flour vanishes, and the soup reduces to a rich creaminess.

When the main ingredient is too delicate to withstand long cooking, a thickening sauce of flour, butter and liquid, such as velouté (*page 28*), can be made in advance and combined with the main ingredient shortly before serving.

Thickening with Potatoes

1 **Cutting up the vegetables.** Trim away the roots and coarse, dark green leaves of each leek. Slit the tender green leaves lengthwise, rinse to remove grit, then cut the leek crosswise into thin slices. For vichyssoise (*recipe, page 105*), use the white parts only, to ensure a pale soup. Quarter peeled potatoes and slice thinly.

2 **Cooking the leeks and potatoes.** Melt butter in a saucepan over a low heat. Add the sliced leeks, cover the pan and cook for 4 to 5 minutes—until the leeks are soft but not coloured. Add the sliced potatoes (*above*) and stir with a wooden spoon to combine them with the leeks.

Thickening with Flour

1 **Preparing the onions.** Peel the onions and halve them vertically. Cut the halves lengthwise into thin slices of equal size that will cook evenly. Melt butter in a saucepan small enough so that the onions will fill it about half way. Add the onions (*above*), cover and cook them over a low heat, diffused by a fireproof mat, and stir the mixture occasionally.

2 **Adding flour.** After about 30 minutes, the onions will be soft but still pale, and reduced to less than a third of their original volume. Sprinkle plain flour over the onions (*above*), and, with the pan still over a low heat, stir with a wooden spoon to combine the onions and flour thoroughly to make a smooth mixture.

3 **Adding liquid.** Pour hot water, milk, or, as here, a meat broth into the pan (*above*). Salt lightly. Simmer gently, uncovered, skimming off any frothy scum that rises to the surface. Cook for about 15 minutes, until the potatoes are soft enough to crush easily when pressed against the side of the pan with a spoon.

4 **Puréeing.** Drain the vegetables by pouring the soup into a wire mesh sieve over a bowl. Then hold the sieve and its contents over the pan in which they were cooked. With a wooden pestle, press the vegetables through the sieve. When they become too dry to sieve easily, moisten with their liquid (*above*).

5 **Finishing the purée.** Gradually add the cooking liquid to the pan, stirring to incorporate it, until the soup reaches the desired consistency. Enrich with cream if you wish, then reheat gently. (To serve as vichyssoise, thoroughly chill the cooked soup without enriching it, then add cream at serving time.)□

3 **Adding liquid.** In a separate saucepan, warm some water, broth or, as here, milk. Add the liquid all at once to the pan containing the mixture of onions, butter and flour (*above*). Raise the heat and stir continuously until the soup comes to the boil, then reduce to a simmer. Season with a grating of nutmeg.

4 **Sieving and serving.** Gently simmer for about 40 minutes over a fireproof mat, occasionally stirring so that the mixture thickens gradually without sticking to the pan bottom. Pour the soup through a sieve into a bowl and push the onions through with a pestle (*above*). Reheat the soup, stirring it well. Add cream, if you like, and serve in warmed plates (*right*).□

Eggs and Cream for Velvet Smoothness

A velouté is a sauce made by cooking stock with the flour and butter mixture known as a roux. But the term velouté is also applied to a roux-thickened soup, that is further thickened by the last minute addition of beaten egg yolks and cream.

The velouté foundation and finish are especially helpful to thicken purées of vegetables that contain little starch. The mushroom purée shown on the right is a classic velouté (*recipe, page 100*).

Since the purée is already somewhat thickened, only a dilute mixture of egg yolks and cream is necessary: a mixture of 10 cl (4 fl oz) of double cream and 2 or 3 yolks for 1 litre (2 pints) of soup.

Where an egg yolk and cream *liaison* is the sole thickening agent for a purée, more egg is required. In the sorrel-based *potage germiny* demonstrated below (*recipe, page 100*) 6 egg yolks in 10 cl (4 fl oz) of cream are added to 1 litre (2 pints) of soup. When so much egg is used, the mixture should first be warmed with a ladleful of purée to avoid it curdling in the hot soup.

Making a Classic Velouté

1 **Making a velouté base.** Melt butter in a saucepan over a low heat; stir in flour (*above, left*) and cook, stirring constantly, for about 3 minutes, until the roux turns golden. Whisk in hot broth (*above, centre*), raise the heat and continue to whisk until the mixture comes to the boil. Reduce the heat and barely simmer for 40 minutes to 1 hour, to eliminate the floury taste. Regularly skim off the skin of butter that forms on the surface (*above, right*).

Blending Egg Yolks into a Sorrel Purée

1 **Cooking.** Remove the stems from sorrel leaves, then rinse and drain the leaves well. Mass the leaves into a compact bunch and slice them into coarse shreds. Melt butter in a saucepan and toss in the shredded leaves (*above*). Cook over a low heat, stirring occasionally, until the sorrel is very soft—about 15 minutes.

2 **Sieving the sorrel.** To extract any fibrous sorrel ribs, pass the cooked leaves through a sturdy, fine-meshed sieve set over a bowl (*above*). Discard the fibres that remain in the sieve.

3 **Adding liquid.** Return the puréed sorrel to the saucepan and moisten it with broth (*above*); chicken broth is used here. Stir the mixture to combine the sorrel and broth thoroughly; adjust the heat to maintain the soup at a bare simmer.

2 **Mixing in the mushroom.** Purée raw mushrooms in a food mill or food processor; add a little lemon juice to preserve their colour. Melt butter in a sauté pan and cook the mushrooms over high heat, stirring and tossing until their liquid has evaporated. Add the mushrooms to the velouté (*above*).

3 **Adding egg yolks and cream.** In a mixing bowl, blend egg yolks with double cream; season lightly with nutmeg. Stir this mixture into the soup (*above*); immediately remove the pan from the heat and whisk to amalgamate the ingredients. The egg yolks will cook in the hot velouté and will thicken the soup.

4 **Finishing the soup.** Still off the heat, enrich the soup further by whisking in chunks of butter until they melt. Ladle the velouté into warmed soup plates (*above*) and garnish with slices of raw mushroom that have been drenched in lemon juice. The juice adds a refreshing acidity to the rich soup.□

4 **Thickening the soup.** Blend 6 egg yolks with 10 cl (4 fl oz) of double cream in a mixing bowl. Stir a ladleful of the warm—but not boiling—soup into the bowl (*above, left*) to heat the mixture gently. Add the warmed and diluted egg and cream mixture to the soup (*above, right*), whisking constantly as you pour.

5 **Serving the soup.** Continue whisking the soup as it thickens, taking care to keep the heat so low that the liquid does not approach a simmer. Cook and whisk until the soup is creamy, with sufficient body to just coat a spoon. Remove the soup from the heat and whisk in small pieces of butter. Serve garnished with a sprinkling of chervil leaves (*above*).□

Combining Leftovers for a Fresh-Tasting Purée

Puréeing techniques, which are designed to amalgamate flavours and textures, can be applied successfully to a collection of leftover vegetables to make a fresh-tasting soup that quite belies its humble beginnings. Since most vegetables combine well, the contents of your larder or refrigerator can determine the recipe; the soup demonstrated here is made from both cooked and raw leftovers.

If the cooked vegetables for a soup of leftovers were tossed in butter for their first appearance at table, scrape off as much of the butter as possible before adding the vegetables to the soup. Any remaining butter will rise to the surface of the liquid during cooking and should then be skimmed off.

The outer leaves of lettuce or cabbage—usually sound but not quite tender enough for a salad—make good raw ingredients for such a soup; so do large, starchy peas or asparagus stalks whose tender tips have been served separately. Do not use discoloured vegetables, however, or any salad ingredients that have dressing on them.

Two essential ingredients are raw aromatic vegetables, which help to unify the flavours, and a starchy element to stabilize the purée. Onions, celery, garlic, leek greens or spring onions in any combination will provide a strong aromatic flavour base. The starchy element may be leftover cooked potatoes, pulses, rice or pasta; in the absence of these, thicken the soup with a handful of fresh breadcrumbs or some croûtons.

Do not overcook the soup. Start by simmering raw aromatic and leaf vegetables, since they need the longest cooking. Next, add any quick-cooking raw vegetables—such as the peas here—together with firm-textured cooked vegetables. Add puréed vegetables—mashed potatoes or spinach, for example—at the last minute.

After puréeing the soup you can add an enrichment of fresh butter or cream.

1 **Gathering the ingredients.** Assemble the leftovers—here, the selection includes boiled carrots, turnips and mange-tout; mashed potatoes; macaroni with tomato sauce; spinach purée; sautéed mushrooms; and asparagus stalks. Supplement the leftovers with some raw vegetables, including aromatics cut into small pieces.

2 **Starting the soup.** Put the raw leaves and aromatics—here leek, onion, spring onion, garlic, fennel and outer leaves of cabbage and lettuce—into boiling water or leftover vegetable water.

3 **Adding more vegetables.** Simmer the mixture for 15 minutes, then add the pasta, carrots, turnips, mange-tout, asparagus, mushrooms and any quick-cooking raw vegetables, such as peas.

4 **Cleansing the soup.** Both scum and any butter present will rise to the surface after you add the vegetables. Remove the impurities with a ladle or large spoon as the soup returns to the boil.

5 **Adding the purées.** Simmer for about 15 minutes more, until all the vegetables are tender. Add any cooked puréed ingredients you have—leftover mashed potatoes and spinach, in this case.

6 **Puréeing the soup.** Press the soup through a sieve, or purée it in a food mill. This soup was coarsely puréed so that the different vegetables would retain some of their original texture.

7 **Seasoning and enriching.** Add salt sparingly: many of the soup ingredients will have been salted during their first cooking. Reheat gently, grind in some pepper and enrich the soup with butter (*left*) or a little cream, before serving in warmed soup plates (*below*).□

Finely Ground Crayfish Shells to Enhance a Bisque

A purée based on shellfish—which may be anything from oysters to lobster—is generally known by its French name, *bisque*. Like most purées, a bisque requires a thickener—a few tablespoons of cooked rice or a handful of breadcrumbs—to give it just the right velvety body.

If the basis of the soup is a crustacean—whether crab, prawns, crayfish or a small lobster—the consistency can be further enhanced by the shells and their contents. By breaking up the emptied shells and other discarded parts of the body and simmering them in the soup, every tiny crevice containing meat and juices will offer up its substance; additionally, the shell particles will give the soup an extra depth of flavour and colour.

Such bisques taste freshest if you use live crustaceans rather than pre-cooked meat. In this demonstration (*recipe, page 102*), live crayfish are dropped into a shallow, simmering bath of white wine and brandy, flavoured with herbs and diced aromatic vegetables. The heat of the liquid (fish or chicken broth would also be suitable) kills the crayfish swiftly, and cooks them in less than 10 minutes.

After cooking, pry open the tail section of the crayfish—this is the meatiest part—and remove the flesh. Do not bother to remove the dark thread of intestine from the tail meat: the digestive tract automatically gets rid of its bitter-tasting waste matter almost as soon as the crayfish is caught.

A mortar and pestle are the simplest equipment for breaking up the head section, or carapace, and the tail shell. After brief simmering with the soup, most of the inedible shell is removed by passing the mixture through a food mill, which both extracts more juices from the crayfish and traps most of the shell debris. After thickening, strain the soup through a fine sieve, to amalgamate the ingredients and filter out any remaining shell fragments, leaving the bisque with a luxurious, satin texture.

1 **Cooking the crayfish.** Melt butter in a frying pan over a low heat. Add the chopped vegetables and mixed herbs and cook, stirring frequently (*top*), for about 15 minutes until the vegetables are soft but not coloured. Add wine and brandy, turn up the heat and bring to the boil. Drop in the crayfish and stir (*above*) until they turn red. Cover the pan, reduce the heat and simmer for 7 to 10 minutes; transfer the pan contents to a colander set in a large bowl.

2 **Shelling the tails.** When the crayfish are cool enough to handle, twist each tail free from the carapace (*above*), and put the carapace into a large mortar. Using your thumbs, split open the underside of the tail to remove the meat (*left*); put the shell into the mortar, and reserve the meat. Put the vegetables and strained liquid into a saucepan.

3 **Pounding the crayfish.** With a pestle, pound the carapaces and tail shells into coarse fragments in the mortar. Then add them to the vegetables and cooking liquid (*above*). Add more liquid—here, fish broth—and a little cayenne pepper.

4 **Extracting more flavour.** Simmer, uncovered, for 2 to 3 minutes. Add a little more broth if the mixture seems too thick, then pass it through a food mill set over a large bowl. (*above*). Discard the shell fragments that remain in the mill.

5 **Thickening the bisque.** Return the milled pulp and its liquid to the saucepan, and set the pan over a moderate heat. Add white breadcrumbs (*above*) and cook, stirring to distribute them evenly, until the bisque comes to a simmer.

6 **Sieving the bisque.** To smooth the soup and remove the inedible pieces of shell, pour the mixture into a fine-meshed, heavy-duty sieve set over a large bowl. Press the mixture through the sieve with a broad, heavy pestle (*above*). Discard the fragments that remain in the sieve.

7 **Serving.** Return the soup to the pan, set it over a moderate heat, and stir in double cream as you bring the bisque back to a simmer. Combine the reserved crayfish tail meat with the soup, and serve from a warmed tureen (*left*).□

Pounding Chicken for a Sumptuous Soup

It takes time to transform poultry flesh into a smooth purée, but generations of cooks have found that the *potage à la reine* (*recipes, page 104*) amply rewards their efforts. This classic soup shown here blends chicken breast with almonds, lemon peel, hard-boiled egg yolks, a broth-soaked thickener of bread and cream.

To ensure a fine, even consistency, the solid ingredients should be pounded in a mortar. This gives the cook close control over the results—which is essential in a purée composed of a variety of ingredients all of which have different textures. Steady pounding, with attention paid to each of the elements, yields a purée that is uniformly fine and perfectly combined.

The breast meat that dominates the soup should come from a whole, slightly under-roasted bird just out of the oven; not only will such flesh have maximum flavour and juiciness, but the puréeing will be easier if the meat fibres are still soft from the heat. If you wish, you can reserve some of the breast meat to garnish the finished soup.

You can vary the soup, while retaining its essential character, by substituting the breast meat of partridge, pigeon or other small birds for the chicken.

1 **Puréeing the solids.** Assemble the more resistant ingredients in a mortar: skinned almonds, strips of lemon peel and the breast meat of a chicken. Break the meat into small pieces by hand, removing any skin or connective tissue. Pound the ingredients to merge them into a fine purée; the almonds will require the greatest effort. Add hard-boiled egg yolks when the pounding of the other ingredients is almost complete.

2 **Adding bread.** Drop a trimmed chunk of coarse white bread into simmering chicken broth (*top*). After a minute or so, lift the bread, a spoonful at a time, from the pan into the mortar (*above*) and thoroughly blend each spoonful into the chicken mixture with the pestle. The warm, broth-soaked bread will smooth and thicken the pounded mixture.

3 **Incorporating liquid.** Transfer the purée from the mortar to a large mixing bowl. Pour in double cream (*above*)—the main liquid of this rich soup—and stir well to mix it in. Carefully add chicken broth, a little at a time, to dilute the soup to the desired consistency.

4 **Sieving the purée.** Ladle the diluted purée into a fine-meshed nylon or stainless steel sieve placed over a pan. (An aluminium sieve could discolour the egg yolks.) Use a broad pestle to force the purée through the sieve. If any solid residue remains, return it to the mortar for additional pounding, then mix it with a little of the soup and sieve it again.

5 **Serving the soup.** Taste for seasoning before serving. Quails' eggs, soft-boiled and peeled, make both a creamy and unusual garnish (*left*) for this soup; other suitable choices include diced chicken or skinned and chopped pistachio nuts.□

A Game Purée Thickened with Lentils

Although logic would seem to decree that velouté soups always include a velouté sauce (*page 28*), there are exceptions. A few purées—including those based on game—traditionally bear the name velouté even though they are thickened by other means. For example, the partridge velouté demonstrated here gains its body and texture from lentils, a legume also used to flavour many other game purées, from pheasant (*recipe, page 104*) to rabbit.

Like the chicken prepared for the *potage à la reine* (*page 34*), the partridges are roasted underdone so that their breast meat—the basis of the soup—will be juicier and, therefore, both easier to purée and more flavourful. During their brief roasting, the partridges are carefully protected from the oven's dry heat: thin strips of pork fat cover their breasts and the birds are trussed compactly to prevent any loss of moisture.

Cooked in this way, the partridge breasts should be sufficiently tender to be puréed with a mortar and pestle. Alternatively, their flesh can be broken into fragments in an electric food processor. As with the mortar and pestle method, this is done in two stages. First the flesh alone is broken up; then the lentils—which have been simmered in water with aromatic vegetables—are added and pulping is continued. Finally, the amalgam is sieved to make a fine purée.

The partridge carcasses and the meat remaining on them are used to enrich the soup's liquid by simmering them in a basic meat or chicken broth (*box, right*), along with a light aromatic support: a small onion, a piece of carrot and a bouquet garni. Additional flavour for the broth can be obtained by deglazing the solidified juices in the roasting pan. Pour off any fat and place the pan over a moderate heat on top of the cooker; add a glass of wine, broth or water and, as the liquid comes to the boil, stir and scrape the fragments with a wooden spoon to dissolve them. Pour the juices into the broth.

Once strained, the enriched broth is used to dilute the puréed game and lentils. If any liquid remains, serve it on another day as a clear broth, perhaps garnished with finely sliced mushrooms.

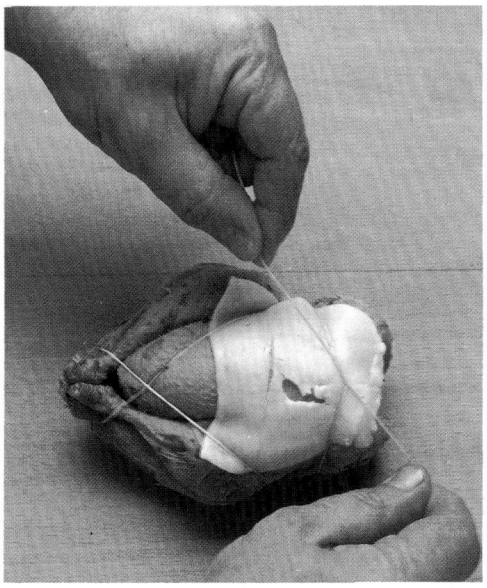

1 **Barding and trussing.** Cover the breast of each partridge with thin strips of pork fat. Position the bird breast uppermost; slip the centre of a 60 cm (2 foot) piece of string beneath the tail and cross the ends over the bird's feet. Pass the ends along the thighs, round the back and over the wings to meet at the centre of the breast (*above*); knot securely.

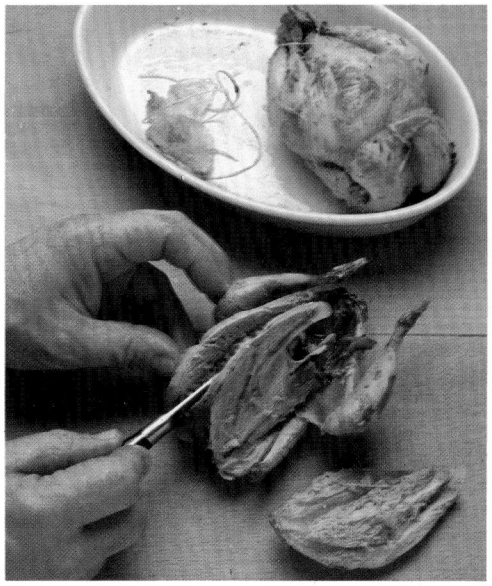

2 **Roasting the partridges.** Place the birds in a baking dish and roast in an oven preheated to 240°C (475°F or Mark 9); 15 minutes should suffice to undercook them slightly. Remove the string and barding. With a small, sharp knife, slice along either side of the breastbone to remove the meat (*above*). Use the carcasses for the broth (*below*).

Transforming Broth into a Game Consommé

1 **Assembling the ingredients.** Put the partridge carcasses in a heavy saucepan and cover them with hot chicken or meat broth (*above*). Place the pan over a moderate heat; skim off any scum that collects as the liquid comes to the boil.

2 **Cooking the broth.** Reduce the heat so that the broth merely simmers, then add aromatic vegetables. Cook the combined ingredients for at least 2 hours to extract all their nutrition and flavour. Strain the broth through muslin (*above*).

3 **Puréeing and sieving.** Skin the partridge breasts; if you like, set aside a little of the meat for garnish. With a food processor or by hand, reduce the remaining meat to a coarse pulp. Add cooked, drained lentils (*above, left*), and reserve the liquid. Process the lentils and meat to a smooth purée. Press the purée, a few spoonfuls at a time, through a fine sieve (*above, right*); moisten it regularly with the lentil cooking liquid.

4 **Adding the broth.** Transfer the purée to a heavy saucepan. Place the pan over a moderate heat and pour in enough game-enriched broth (*above*) to dilute the purée to a light, creamy consistency.

5 **Finishing and serving.** Bring the soup to a bare simmer, then remove it from the heat and stir in small chunks of butter (*above*). Serve in warmed soup plates (*right*), garnished with quenelles (*page 20*) or with fine strips of partridge.□

Creating Your Own Purées

Almost any food can become the base for a purée soup, providing it is cooked with a complementary liquid and thickened—if necessary—with a suitable starchy element, then puréed with appropriate equipment and finally enriched.

The chart on the right is a guide to the wealth of purée-making options. For each of 57 foods that may serve as the main ingredient of the soup, it shows what liquids, thickeners, puréeing equipment and last-minute enrichments are fitting.

Several choices are given for every main ingredient. Since all produce good results, the selection is mainly a matter of personal preference. However, you should bear in mind a few points. If you select flour as your thickener, for instance, remember that the flour must be incorporated into a sauce and thoroughly cooked if it is not to remain sticky in texture and starchy in taste. Make a roux from flour and butter, incorporate the roux in the chosen liquid and simmer for at least 40 minutes. If the main ingredient needs lengthy cooking, it can be cooked in the sauce (*page 26*); otherwise it should be simmered separately.

Of the other thickeners, potatoes or pasta can be simmered to tenderness and puréed with the main ingredient. Pulses need such long cooking that they should be simmered on their own.

Although many ingredients can be puréed with just one device, others require two or three kinds of equipment, used successively (*pages 32-35*).

Butter, cream and a combination of egg yolks with cream are the most versatile enrichments for purées; but, for variety, soured cream goes well with beetroot and bean purées, and olive oil with pumpkin and pulse soups. If you like, add more than one enrichment: velouté soups, for example (*page 28*), often include butter as well as egg yolks and cream.

How to use the chart. Locate your main ingredient in the row at the top of the chart. Choose a liquid, a thickener and one or more enrichments from the possibilities shown by dots in the column below the main ingredient. In the equipment section, numbers signify stages of puréeing: (1) indicates all the devices suitable for the first—or only—stage of puréeing, (2) and (3) show equipment to which you can proceed to eliminate skins, fibres or shells for a finer purée. For example, you would first pound crustaceans in a mortar (1), next use either a food mill or a food processor and finally a sieve (3).

		Leaf Vegetables							Thistles	The Cabbage Fa				
		Chard	Chicory	Endive (curly or batavian)	Lettuce	Sorrel	Spinach	Watercress	Artichokes	Broccoli	Brussels sprouts	Cabbage (green or white)	Cauliflower	Kale
Basic Liquid	Water	●	●	●	●	●	●	●	●	●	●	●	●	●
	Milk												●	
	Meat or chicken broth	●	●	●	●	●	●	●	●	●	●	●	●	●
	Vegetable broth	●	●	●		●	●	●	●	●	●	●	●	●
	Fish broth													
Additional Thickener	Flour	●	●	●	●	●	●	●	●	●	●	●	●	●
	Bread or breadcrumbs	●	●	●	●	●	●	●	●	●	●	●	●	●
	Croûtons		●	●	●	●	●		●	●			●	
	Pasta	●								●	●	●	●	●
	Rice	●		●					●	●	●	●	●	●
	Potatoes	●		●		●		●	●	●	●	●	●	●
	Haricot beans	●								●	●	●		
	Lentils													
Puréeing Equipment	Mortar and pestle								1					
	Masher								1				1	
	Metal sieve	2	2	2	2		2	2		2	2	2	2	
	Nylon sieve								2					
	Nylon drum sieve					1			2					
	Food mill	1	1	1	1		1	1		1	1	1	1	1
	Electric food processor	1	1	1	1		1	1	1	1	1	1	1	1
Final Enrichment	Butter	●	●	●	●	●	●	●	●	●	●	●	●	●
	Cream	●	●	●		●	●	●	●	●	●	●	●	●
	Egg yolks and cream	●	●	●		●	●	●	●	●	●	●	●	●

	Roots and Tubers										The Onion Family		Fresh Pods and Seeds						Pulses						Mushrooms	Vegetable Fruits			Squashes		Stalks and Shoots					Fish and Shellfish			Poultry and Game		
	Beetroot	Carrots	Celeriac	Jerusalem artichokes	Parsnips	Potatoes	Salsify and scorzonera	Swedes	Sweet potatoes	Turnips	Leeks	Onions	Broad beans	Chestnuts	French beans	Peas and mange-tout	Runner beans	Sweetcorn	Black beans	Chick peas	Haricot beans	Kidney beans	Lentils	Peas	Mushrooms	Cucumbers	Sweet peppers	Tomatoes	Courgettes (summer squash)	Pumpkin (winter squash)	Asparagus	Cardoon	Celery	Fennel (bulb)	Seakale	Crustaceans	Fish	Molluscs	Chicken	Game birds	Hare and Rabbit
		●	●	●		●	●	●	●	●	●	●	●	●	●	●	●	●	●	●	●	●	●	●		●	●	●	●	●	●	●	●	●	●						
						●	●					●		●				●							●					●											
●	●	●	●	●	●	●	●	●	●	●	●	●		●			●	●	●			●		●	●	●	●	●	●	●	●	●	●	●	●				●	●	●
●	●	●	●	●	●	●	●	●	●	●	●	●		●			●	●	●	●	●	●	●	●	●	●	●	●	●		●	●	●	●	●	●	●	●	●	●	●
																																				●	●	●			
			●	●	●		●	●		●	●	●			●		●	●							●		●	●	●		●	●	●	●	●	●	●	●	●	●	●
		●	●	●	●		●	●		●	●	●			●		●	●							●	●	●	●	●	●	●		●	●	●	●	●	●	●	●	●	●
			●		●					●																			●	●	●							●				
											●																●	●	●	●					●			●				
		●									●				●												●	●	●	●				●	●		●	●	●			
●		●		●				●		●	●	●					●											●	●								●					
																																								●	●
																																				1	1		1	1	1
1	1			1			1	1						1															1												
2	1			2	1		2	1	1		2	1	2	2	2		2	2	2	2	2	2	2	2		2		1	2	2	2		2	2		3			2	2	2
		2	2			2										2											1					2									
																2											1				2	2				3	2		2	2	2
1	1	1	1	1	1		1	1	1		1	1	1	1	1	1	1	1	1	1	1	1	1	1	1	1		1	1	1	1	1	1	1	1	2	1		1	1	1
1	1	1	1	1		1					1	1	1	1	1	1	1	1							1	1		1	1	1	1		1	1	1	2		1		1	1
	●	●	●	●	●	●	●	●	●	●	●	●	●	●	●	●	●	●	●	●	●	●	●	●	●	●	●	●	●	●	●	●	●	●	●	●	●	●	●	●	●
●	●	●	●	●		●	●	●	●	●	●	●	●		●	●	●	●							●	●	●	●	●	●	●	●	●	●	●	●	●	●	●	●	●
	●	●	●	●		●	●			●	●	●	●		●	●	●	●							●	●			●	●	●	●	●	●	●	●	●	●	●		

2
Compound Broths
Hearty and Nourishing

Compensating for variable cooking times
Pistou: a garlic and basil-flavoured soup
Browning to intensify flavour
Exploiting leftover meats
How to prepare tripe for cooking
A peppery sauce for fish soups

The first soup ever cooked was almost certainly a compound broth—a soup made with chopped ingredients that are eaten with the broth they flavour. Most compound broths include a large number of different ingredients, each of which retains its characteristic flavour and texture. In Mediterranean mixed vegetable soups (*page 42*), for example, up to a dozen soft, crisp and starchy vegetables are cooked together; in Scotch broth (*page 44*), mutton and turnips are set off by nutty grains of barley and sweet-tasting peas and a whole range of leftover meats can be combined with fresh vegetables to make a rustic broth (*opposite page and page 46*).

In fact, many compound broths are bulky, nourishing dishes that resemble main-course stews in their chief ingredients, in the herbs and aromatic vegetables that flavour them and in the poaching method by which they are cooked. But for compound broths the ingredients are cut up—usually at the start of cooking, sometimes at the end—into pieces small enough to be spooned up. And compound broths contain a higher proportion of liquid than stews. Water is the customary starting point, since it will gain plenty of flavour from the solid ingredients. For a highly flavoured soup, however, you can substitute a clear broth (*page 8*) or a velouté sauce—a broth cooked with a flour and butter roux. A velouté sauce finished with egg yolks and cream makes a smooth, rich liquid for the mussel soup demonstrated on page 52.

There are many classic compound broths that call for ingredients in more or less fixed proportions and combinations. In chowders, for example, fish or shellfish are combined with the sailor's rations of bacon, potatoes and onions; chicken broth and leeks are constant elements in cockie-leekie (*recipes, page 116*) and prunes are frequently added. Compound broths also offer an opportunity to experiment with different flavourings. Any cuisine you draw upon will give you fresh ideas for embellishing basic ingredients. In Mexico, for instance, tripe is garnished with red and green chili peppers to make *menudo* (*page 48*); in Philadelphia, whole peppercorns turn tripe soup into pepperpot; and in Italy, tripe soup is often finished with garlic and *prosciutto* fat (*recipe, page 124*).

Shredded cabbage is tipped into a casserole containing a chicken carcass and giblets, sliced aromatic vegetables, a bouquet garni and water for a leftover meat soup (*page 46*). After simmering, the bones and bouquet garni will be discarded; the vegetables and meat will be served in the broth.

Soups from Two Vegetables or from Many

When you make a soup from a mixture of vegetables, you must take into account the different cooking times they may need to reach the desired degree of doneness at the same moment. One way of controlling the result is by reducing the size of the vegetable pieces: the finer the vegetables are cut up, the faster the pieces cook, and the less significant any difference in cooking times becomes.

In the leek and potato soup shown here, for example, (*recipe, page 105*), both vegetables are sliced very thinly and tumbled into simmering salted water together. In just 15 minutes the slow-cooking potatoes and the faster-cooking leeks will both be tender, with the leeks still slightly resistant. If you prefer the leeks very soft, but the potatoes still intact, cut both vegetables into larger pieces and simmer them for about 30 minutes.

An alternative approach is to add the vegetables to the soup in stages, beginning with those that take the longest to cook. This method is especially useful for dealing with a large number of different types of vegetables, whose cooking times may differ widely.

In the soup shown opposite (*recipe, page 112*), sliced onion, leeks, carrots and potatoes are added first. They are accompanied by winter squash and fresh haricot beans. The fast-cooking squash chunks are deliberately added at this early stage so that they will partially disintegrate, contributing body to the broth. If you can only obtain dried beans, soak them overnight and pre-cook them before adding them to the broth at the start of cooking.

After 30 minutes of simmering, add the quick-cooking ingredients that you want to be tender but still slightly firm to the bite—here, sliced French beans, sliced courgettes and macaroni.

This soup can be served with freshly grated Parmesan cheese; or, for a silken finish, ladle on *pistou* (*box, opposite page; recipe, page 112*), a Provençal sauce fragrant with garlic, basil and olive oil.

Cutting finely for Even Cooking

1 **Preparing the vegetables.** Wash the leeks well and trim off the base of the roots and the tough, dark green parts of the leaves. Peel the potatoes and cut them lengthwise into quarters. Cut both the leeks and the potatoes into slices the thickness of a coin. Add them to a pan of boiling, salted water (*above*).

2 **Removing the scum.** Spoon off the frothy scum that will gather on the surface of the liquid (*above*) as the soup returns to the boil. Adjust the heat to keep the liquid at a light boil and cover the pan.

3 **Serving the soup.** After about 15 to 20 minutes cooking, both the leeks and the potatoes should be tender but still intact. Ladle the soup into warmed plates (*above*) and add a chunk of butter to each serving. Season with freshly ground black pepper and garnish with a sprinkling of chopped parsley or chives.□

A Medley of Vegetables with Pasta

1 **Starting the slow-cooking vegetables.** Shell the fresh haricot beans; cut up the trimmed carrots, potatoes, leeks, onions and squash. Bring salted water to the boil in a large pan and add the vegetables and a bouquet garni. Spoon off any scum that forms on the surface of the liquid as it returns to the boil, then lower the heat, cover the pan and simmer for 30 minutes.

2 **Adding quick-cooking vegetables.** Add sliced courgettes (*above, left*), French beans cut into 1 cm (½ inch) lengths and elbow macaroni (*above, right*). Stir well and simmer, uncovered, for a further 15 minutes or until the macaroni is soft but still slightly chewy and the vegetables are tender.

Making a Pistou

Pounding the sauce. In a mortar, pound some peeled garlic cloves and fresh basil leaves with salt and pepper. Add grated Parmesan and stir the mixture to make a stiff paste. Pound continuously, gradually adding skinned, seeded and chopped tomatoes, more cheese and olive oil, until the mixture reaches the consistency of a fluid paste. Slowly add more oil until the sauce is thick and creamy. Since *pistou* sauce separates if left to stand, stir it well before serving.

3 **Serving and garnishing the soup.** To serve, transfer the soup to a heated tureen or large earthenware vessel. Ladle the soup into warmed individual bowls and let the guests help themselves to garnishes, such as grated Parmesan cheese or, as demonstrated here, freshly made *pistou* sauce (*box, left*).□

A Substantial Blend of Mutton and Barley

Nourishing broths made with inexpensive meats and vegetables are a cherished tradition wherever good cooking is accompanied by thrifty housekeeping. The French, for example, poach gelatinous cuts of beef with aromatic vegetables to make pot au feu; the Scots fortify themselves with a combination of mutton, barley and vegetables known as Scotch broth (*recipe, page 115*).

Mutton is not widely available nowadays, but yearling lamb makes a good substitute in Scotch broth. Choose an inexpensive, bony cut, such as neck—used here—or shoulder. If you wish, add a veal knuckle for extra gelatine. The bones do not appear in the soup: during the latter stages of preparation, the cooked meat is removed from the bone, cut into small pieces and returned to the broth.

Start the meat in cold water. Heat it gently and spoon off the scum of albumin that forms as the liquid comes to the boil. Lamb or mutton is fatty, so skim off the liquid fat at intervals. Better still, make the soup a day in advance, leave it to cool, then spoon off the layer of fat that has congealed on the surface.

After the initial skimming, add the aromatic enrichments. Traditionally, the classic bouquet garni (*page 8*) is supplemented with fresh or dried petals of marigold, which carry a faint aroma of hay. Barley, softened by soaking overnight in cold water, is an invariable addition, and the range of suitable vegetables includes onions, carrots, leeks, turnips or swedes, and soaked dried peas.

During the two hours of cooking, the barley will swell and much of its starch will be dispersed through the liquid, thickening the broth. The long cooking will exhaust the flavour of the bouquet garni and the aromatic vegetables; discard them except for the onions and turnips or swedes. These can be puréed and returned to the broth to give it more body. Fresh garnish vegetables—carrots, peas, tomatoes, kale or cabbage—may be added towards the end of cooking.

1 **Cleansing the broth.** Cut the lamb—here, scrag end of neck—into even-sized pieces and trim away the fat. Put the lamb—with a veal knuckle, if you like—into a large pan. Cover with cold water and bring it slowly to the boil. Skim (*above*), add a cup of cold water and skim again as the water returns to the boil. Repeat until no more scum forms.

2 **Making a bouquet garni.** Prepare the flavouring herbs—here, parsley, thyme, celery leaves and dried marigold petals. To prevent the herbs from being dispersed through the liquid, place them on a square of muslin, gather the edges together to make a bag and secure with string. Quarter some onions and slice several carrots and leeks.

5 **Puréeing the reserved vegetables.** Add freshly shelled peas to the soup and bring it back to the boil. Sieve the reserved vegetables into the soup (*above*) to give the broth additional body. Return the meat to the soup, simmer for another 5 to 10 minutes until the peas are tender, then transfer the soup to a tureen.

3 **Adding vegetables and barley.** Add the prepared vegetables and the bouquet garni to the liquid. Strain the barley from the water in which it has been soaking and add it to the soup. If you are using dried peas, drain and add them, too. Bring the soup back to a simmer, remove any scum from its surface, and cook for 1¼ hours or until the meat is nearly tender. Spoon off the fat occasionally.

4 **Separating meat from bones.** Add quartered turnips or swedes and simmer the soup for about 30 minutes more. When the meat and barley are tender, remove all the solid ingredients except the barley, using a slotted spoon and tongs. Cut the meat away from the bones (*above*) and chop it into small pieces. Discard the bones, the bouquet garni and the exhausted carrots and leeks. Reserve the meat, onions and turnips or swedes.

6 **Garnishing.** Cut fresh carrots and turnips into *julienne* strips (*page 20*). Pour a ladleful of the broth into a small saucepan and simmer the *julienne* in it for 5 to 6 minutes until tender. Add them to the soup in the tureen. And, if you like, add a little lemon juice or a few capers preserved in vinegar to counteract the blandness of the barley. Serve the broth in warmed soup plates (*left*).□

Two More Ways to Use Meat

When making a meat-based soup, either choice or circumstance may lead you to vary the customary process of poaching only raw ingredients. To intensify the flavour and colour, for example, you can give the meat and aromatic vegetables an intitial browning in an oven, as demonstrated here with oxtail soup (*right; recipe, page 117*). Or you can improvise an original, quickly made soup with leftover cooked meats. Both of these variations can be applied to almost any cut of meat or any kind of poultry or game. However, do not use any liver; it would turn dry and bitter with long cooking.

The first step, when producing any browned-meat soup, is to roast the meat with the aromatics for about 30 minutes in a hot oven. The surface juices of the meat will coagulate and form a glaze, and the natural sugar in the vegetables will caramelize their cut surfaces. When the meat and vegetables are transferred to a soup pot for poaching—a 4-hour process in the case of fibrous but flavour-rich oxtail—the glaze and caramel will dissolve into the broth, surrendering extra flavour to the liquid and turning it a rich, brown colour. Both effects are intensified by adding chopped tomatoes for the last few minutes of cooking. After cooking, the oxtail meat is removed from the bones, cut into bite-size pieces, and returned to the broth. The bones themselves are discarded, as are the exhausted and tasteless aromatics.

When making a soup from already cooked meats, the cook has a free hand to use leftovers singly or in practically any combination available. The cooked meats—including any bones and juices—are put to simmer in water with raw aromatic and leaf vegetables. By the time the vegetables are cooked, the meat will be melting into the soup. Tender garnish vegetables—such as peas, beans or courgettes—can be added near the end of cooking. If leftover cooked vegetables are to be included, they should be reheated in the soup for only a brief time.

Browning Oxtails for a Rich, Dark Broth

1 **Preparation for the oven.** Choose a vessel that can be used both in the oven and on top of the stove. Line it with chopped vegetables—here, carrots, onions and celery. Trim and halve 1 or 2 oxtails and lay them on the vegetables. For extra body, add a veal knuckle. Put the pan, uncovered, in an oven preheated to 240°C (475°F or Mark 9).

2 **Starting the broth.** After 30 minutes, when the meat and vegetables are well browned, take the pan out of the oven. Transfer the meat to a large saucepan (*above*); cover the meat with water and bring it very slowly to the boil. Spoon off the copious scum that rises. Add a little cold water and continue heating and scumming until the liquid is clear.

Extracting Fresh Goodness from Leftover Meat

1 **Assembling the meats.** Collect all the suitable leftovers you have. The basic ingredients for the soup shown here are roast beef, a roast goose carcass, their roasting juices, raw goose giblets and cooked pork-chop bones. Cut the meats into small chunks and slice the giblets. Half fill a large cooking pot with water or leftover vegetable cooking water.

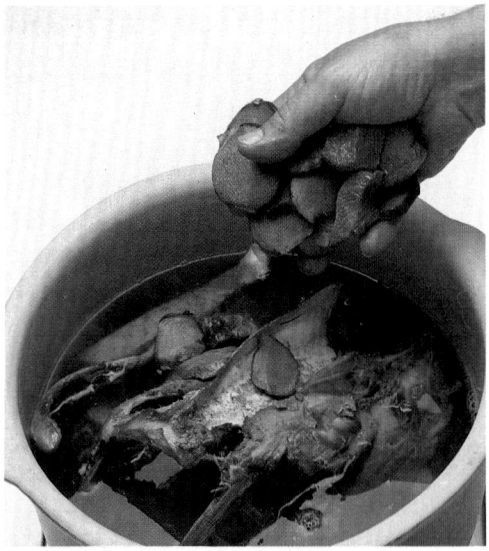

2 **Filling the soup pot.** Prepare the fresh aromatic and leaf vegetables—here, onions, carrots, a turnip, cabbage, lettuce and sorrel. Thickly slice the aromatics. Trim the ribs from the cabbage, then cut all the leaves into a *chiffonade* (*page 14*). Put the bones, meats and vegetables into the pot (*above*); add salt and a bouquet garni.

3 **Deglazing the roasting pan.** Leave the vegetables in the pan in which they were browned, add a cup of cold water and bring it to the boil. With a wooden spatula, scrape the bottom of the pan until all the coagulated juices have dissolved. Add the vegetables and liquid to the oxtails. Bring the soup back to the boil, spooning off any scum or fat.

4 **Removing the bones.** Simmer the soup for 4 hours, or until the meat is tender. Add chopped tomatoes 15 minutes before the end of the cooking time. Lift out the veal and the oxtails. When cool enough to handle, remove the meat from the bones (*above*), trim away the ligaments and cut up the meat. Strain the broth and discard the vegetables.

5 **Thickening the broth.** Skim any fat from the broth. In a small pan simmer a carrot and turnip *brunoise* (*page 14*) in a little broth for 5 minutes. Return the remaining broth to the saucepan; if you like, thicken it slightly with a little rice flour or semolina. Add the meat and simmer the soup for 1 minute. Combine soup and *brunoise* in a warmed tureen, and serve.□

3 **Adding garnish vegetables.** Bring the liquid to the boil and remove any scum that rises; there will not be much, since most of the meats have already been cooked. Simmer for about 45 minutes to extract the flavours, then add garnish vegetables—here peas and cut-up French beans. Simmer for 15 minutes, or until all the ingredients are tender.

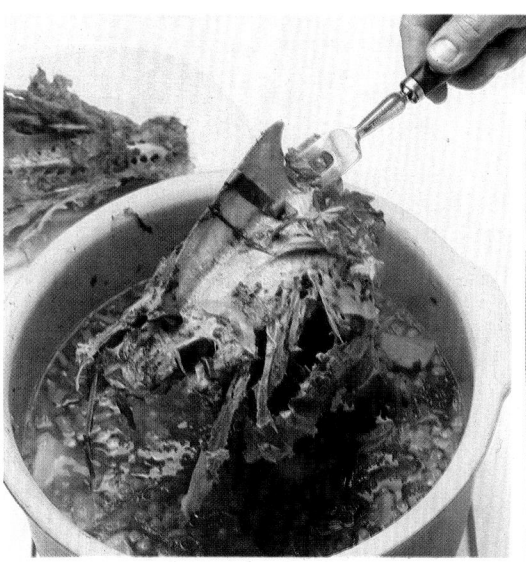

4 **Serving the soup.** With a fork, carefully remove and discard all the poultry and meat bones and the bouquet garni (*above*). Put a slice of dry bread in the bottom of each warmed bowl and ladle out the finished soup (*right*).□

A Tripe Soup Thickened with Natural Gelatine

The appeal of tripe lies as much in its slightly chewy texture as in its delicate flavour. In *menudo*, the Mexican tripe soup demonstrated here (*recipe, page 125*) the texture of the meat is complemented by a velvety broth, enriched by the gelatine from veal cuts. The mellow flavour of the tripe is drawn into the broth, serving as a background for more assertive seasonings and garnishes.

There are three kinds of beef tripe sold, each of which comes from a different chamber of the ruminant's stomach. Although their flavours are similar, each of the three—blanket, thick-seam and honeycomb tripe—has a different texture and calls for slightly different preparation (*Step 1, right*). When available, all types should be used in combination.

Tripe is parboiled as part of the cleansing and bleaching procedure before it is offered for sale. The extent of the preliminary boiling varies, however, so ask your butcher how much extra cooking his tripe will need. The answer may be as little as 2 hours or as much as 4 hours.

Many tripe soups, including *menudo*, are cooked in two stages. First, the parboiled tripe is simmered for $1\frac{1}{2}$ hours to $3\frac{1}{2}$ hours in water enriched with aromatic vegetables, a veal knuckle and for extra gelatine, some calf's feet. The long cooking tenderizes the tripe, releases the flavour of the vegetables and draws gelatine from the bones. Next, the spent vegetables and bones are discarded and new flavourings are set to simmer in the broth. Throughout, the cooking should proceed at a leisurely simmer: boiling would render the tripe stringy and dry.

Authentic *menudo* includes the processed dried maize kernels known as hominy. Instead of hominy, you can use chick peas. Dried hominy or chick peas should be soaked overnight and cooked with the tripe from the start; tinned, precooked chick peas or hominy only need to be heated and can be added during the last half hour of cooking.

With the *menudo*, offer bowls of chopped raw onion, dried oregano or chopped coriander leaves, pounded, dried red chili peppers and chopped, fresh, green ones. These head-clearing accompaniments have earned the soup a reputation as a sure-fire cure for hangovers.

1 **Cutting up the tripe.** The three kinds of tripe available (*above, left*) are clockwise from the top, honeycomb, thick-seam and blanket. To make the helmet-shaped honeycomb tripe lie flat, halve it symmetrically and make short nicks around the halves' edges. To prepare thick-seam tripe, cut right through the soft centre connecting the outer layers. Scrape away the fat and the lymph nodes on the layers' inner surfaces, as shown here. Cut all the tripe into rectangles (*above, right*).

5 **Introducing fresh flavourings.** Pour a ladleful of the broth into a sauté pan and cook a finely chopped onion, some chopped fresh coriander leaves and dried oregano for 5 to 6 minutes. Transfer these seasonings, the chopped meats and the strained broth to the rinsed-out saucepan.

6 **Adding hominy.** If you are using canned cooked hominy—as here—or canned chick peas, add them at this stage, drained of their liquid. Simmer the soup for about 30 minutes longer.

2 **Jointing the veal.** Cut through the joints of 2 or 3 calf's feet. Prise out the marrow from the veal knuckle with a knife and reserve for another dish. Put the tripe, knuckle and calf's feet in a large pan, cover with water and add a little salt.

3 **Adding vegetables.** Bring the water slowly to the boil; spoon off the scum. Add a cupful of cold water and skim the liquid again as it returns to the boil. Continue to skim until the liquid is clear. Add a bouquet garni and vegetables—here, unpeeled garlic cloves, sliced onions, carrots, celery and leeks.

4 **Straining the broth.** Cover the pan, leaving the lid slightly ajar. Simmer for at least 1½ hours, or until the tripe is just tender. Strain the liquid into a bowl. Take the veal meat off the bones. Cut the veal and tripe into bite-sized pieces (*above*); discard the bones, herbs and vegetables. Rinse the saucepan.

7 **Garnishing and serving.** With a pestle and mortar, pound whole, dried red chili peppers to coarse flakes. Wear rubber gloves, since chilies release volatile substances that can irritate the skin. Taking the same precautions, dice fresh green chili peppers, discarding their seeds. Offer the chilies, finely chopped onions and dried oregano—as here—or chopped coriander leaves, for guests to sprinkle on their soup (*left*).□

Fish Soup with a Mediterranean Flavour

Because fish have only a small endowment of connective tissue, fast boiling easily breaks up their flesh. Such fragility is a great asset in soup-making: in the *soupe de poisson* shown here (*recipe, page 128*), just a few minutes' vigorous cooking melts the fish flesh into the liquid, to give a broth rich in body and flavour.

The fish—together with aromatic vegetables, tomatoes and seasonings—is initially boiled vigorously, to strip the flesh off the bones, then simmered more gently lest any solids stick to the pan. After about 30 minutes, the soup is strained to produce a shimmering fish essence—thinner than a purée, but with a density lent by the minuscule particles of fish that pass freely through the sieve. The aromatic vegetables and the remains of the fish are discarded.

Many versions of *soupe de poisson* are found in Mediterranean lands. The version demonstrated here is distinguished as a Provençal speciality by the addition of garlic, saffron, stalks of fresh or dried fennel and the dried peel of Seville oranges. Locally, the soup is made with a mixture of small rockfish: mullets, wrasses and gurnards, for example. If these are not available, you can substitute a mixture of any lean fish—such as sea bass, whiting, plaice, halibut, haddock or cod. As an economy, supplement portions of large fish with a few fish carcasses and trimmings.

Noodles, boiled separately then added to the soup for the last minute of cooking, give more body to the broth. In Provence, *soupe de poisson* is traditionally garnished with either noodles or croûtons and served with *rouille* (*box, far right*; *recipe, page 166*), a mixture of olive oil, garlic, sweet red pepper and hot chili peppers blended into a thick, lustrous sauce.

1 **Stewing the vegetables.** Cover the bottom of a large saucepan with olive oil. Over a medium heat, stew sliced leeks and onions; whole, unpeeled garlic cloves and chopped tomatoes. Season with salt, a bay leaf, savory, dried Seville orange peel and fennel. Reinforce the fennel's flavour, if you like, with a splash of pastis—anise-flavoured spirit.

2 **Adding the fish.** Clean the fish and cut them up. After about 10 minutes, when the tomatoes have softened, add the fish—here, whiting, sea bass and two sole carcasses. Increase the heat, then add boiling water to cover the fish. Boil vigorously for a few minutes, stirring and prodding with a wooden spoon to break up the fish and extract the flavours.

4 **Cooking the pasta.** Home-made noodles (*page 17*)—here, flavoured with saffron—must first be parboiled in water so that any loose flour left clinging to them will not cloud the soup. Bring the pan of water to a rolling boil and add salt and a spoonful of olive oil to prevent the pasta ribbons from sticking together. Drop in the noodles (*above, left*), boil for 1 to 2 minutes, then drain them in a colander. Slide the pasta into the soup (*above, right*).

3 **Straining the broth.** Simmer the broth for 30 minutes, stirring occasionally. Ladle some of the broth into a fine sieve resting over a bowl (*above, left*). Press hard with a pestle to squeeze out all the fish juices (*above, right*), but do not grind the solids through the sieve. Discard the solids before ladling more broth into the sieve. After straining all the broth, return it to the rinsed-out pan, and bring to the boil. Stir in saffron grains dissolved in a little water to taste.

A Fiery Sauce for Fish Soups

Pounding and stirring the rouille. In a mortar, pound the dry ingredients—coarse salt, dried red chili peppers and peppercorns—to a powder. Add basil leaves and garlic cloves, and continue pounding. Next, incorporate crustless bread that has been soaked in warm water and squeezed dry. Add grilled, peeled, seeded and sliced red peppers (*page 14*). When the pounded paste is homogeneous, add olive oil drop by drop, stirring constantly, until the sauce reaches the consistency of a thick mayonnaise. To control the flow, dribble the oil through a narrow V-shaped groove cut in the cork stopper of a bottle.

5 **Stirring the sauce.** Bring the soup to the boil. Taste to see if the pasta is done: if not, simmer for a minute more until it is tender. Ladle the soup and noodles into plates. Offer *rouille* (*box, above*) for guests to stir into their soup (*left*).□

Serving Clams in Their Own Juice

The hinged shells of clams, mussels and other bivalves enclose tender, sweet flesh and a salty liquor. If the shellfish are cooked briefly in a little water or wine, their shells open and release enough liquor to serve as the basis of a soup. On the right, the liquor from clams is combined with milk, potatoes, onions, bacon—and the clams themselves—to make a chowder (*recipe, page 131*). Below, mussels and their cooking liquor are incorporated into a creamy velouté.

Bivalves should be inspected and any that have open or damaged shells must be discarded. The rest can be kept alive for up to 24 hours in a plastic bag in the refrigerator. Several hours before cooking, unwrap and place them in cold, salted water to flush out their grit.

The steaming that opens bivalves is usually sufficient to cook their flesh; longer cooking would merely toughen it. Only the rubbery necks of some clam species need extra cooking to tenderize them. The softer meat is simmered in the soup just long enough to reheat it.

1 **Cleaning the clams.** Soak the clams in cold, salted water for several hours. Change the water at intervals; it will become cloudy from grit expelled by the clams. Scrub the shells clean (*above*) and rinse the clams under the tap.

2 **Steaming the clams.** Put the clams in a large pan with about 2 cups of water. Cover with a tight-fitting lid and bring the water to a vigorous boil. Shake the pan occasionally to redistribute the clams so that they cook evenly. Remove them from the heat when they have opened—after about 10 minutes. Discard any clams that remain closed.

Using Mussel Liquor in a Velouté

The simplest mussel soup is made by steaming the bivalves with wine, herbs and aromatic vegetables. The liquor released by the mussels merges with these flavourings to become a fragrant broth. This dish, in which the unshelled mussels are served in the broth, is known as *moules à la marinière.*

For a richer soup, demonstrated here, the mussel broth is combined with a velouté sauce and thickened with egg yolks and cream to make a classic velouté soup (*page 28; recipe, page 132*). The shelled mussels are added to the soup at the last moment.

1 **Steaming the mussels.** Soak and scrub the mussels as for clams (*Step 1, top*), pull free their beards, then steam them until they open—about 5 minutes. Drain the broth (*above*) and strain it through muslin (*Step 3, top*). Shell the mussels.

2 **Preparing the soup.** Add the liquid to a roux-thickened fish broth cooked over a low heat. Bring slowly to the boil and skim. Add a little saffron, dissolved in hot water. Whisk egg yolks with cream; dilute them with a little warm soup.

3 **Adding the mussels.** Remove the soup from the heat and stir in the egg and cream mixture. Return the soup to a low heat and add the shelled mussels. Cook the soup for a minute longer, but do not let it simmer, lest the egg yolks curdle.

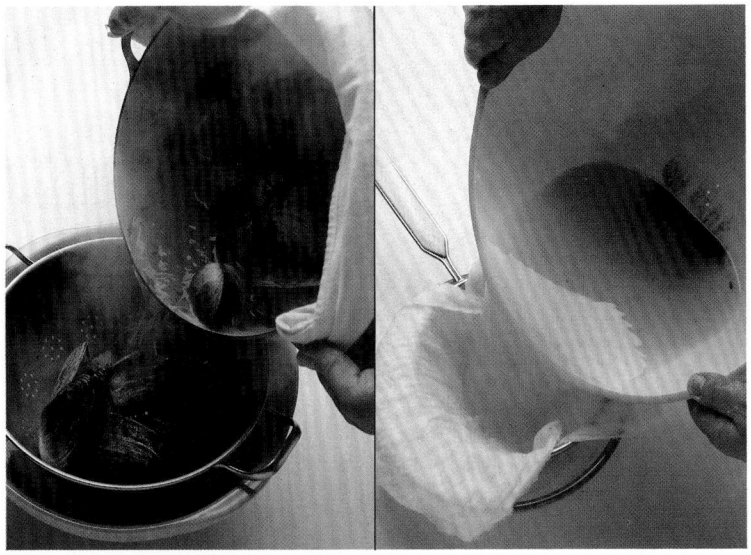

3 **Straining the broth.** Pour the contents of the pan into a colander resting in a bowl (*above, left*). Pull the clams from their shells and rinse them in the broth to flush out any remaining grit. Decant the broth through a fine sieve that you have first lined with a double layer of dampened muslin (*above, right*). The heavy particles of grit should stay behind in the first bowl, and the finer particles suspended in the broth will be held back by the muslin.

4 **Preparing the clam meat.** If you are using long-necked clams, as above, pull off and discard the black skin that covers the neck (*above, left*). Cut off the neck (*above, right*) and chop the tough meat finely. Chop the body meat coarsely, cover it with a clean, damp cloth to keep it moist and put it aside until required.

5 **Cooking the other ingredients.** Cut a thick slab of green bacon into 1 cm ($\frac{1}{2}$ inch) cubes. Heat a little oil in a casserole and fry the cubes lightly. Add thinly sliced onions and cook gently until they soften. Stir in sliced potatoes and cook for 2 to 3 minutes. Add the neck meat (*above*) and the strained broth, and simmer for 30 minutes.

6 **Completing the soup.** In a separate pan, heat some milk just to the boil. Add the scalded milk to the soup and spoon off any scum that rises to the surface. Add the remaining clam meat (*above*), with some butter and plenty of parsley and thyme. Season to taste with black pepper and cayenne pepper. Ladle the chowder into serving bowls (*right*).□

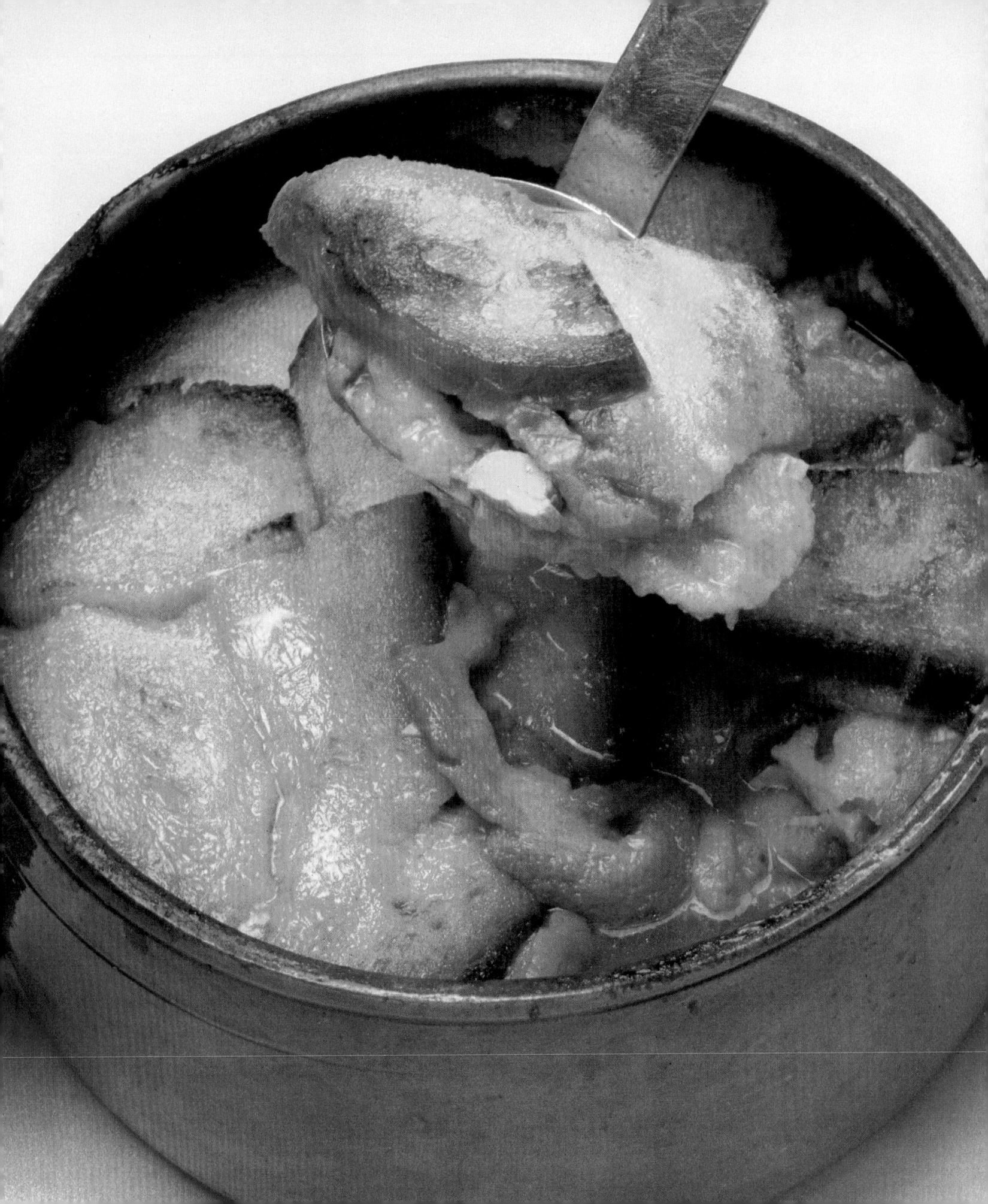

3

Bread Soups

Time-Honoured Staples

Cooking a simple *panade*
Assembling a layered bread soup
How to caramelize onions
A tureen shaped from a winter squash

Every diner has succumbed to the urge to soak up the last drops of soup with a scrap of bread. Indeed, bread and soup seem made to accompany each other. How logical it is, then, to combine them and make the bread an integral part of the soup. This alliance is celebrated in the cooking traditions of many countries (*recipes, pages 134-141*). In Portugal, for example, bread chunks are drenched in a garlic-flavoured broth, then combined with seafood, poultry or pork to make *açordas.* A popular German interpretation is *schwarzbrotsuppe*—black bread soup—made by simmering black bread in broth with soured cream or sliced bratwurst. In south-western France, slices of coarse country bread are moistened with saffron-flavoured chicken broth to make *mourtaïrol* (*opposite*).

Many ingredients can be incorporated into a bread soup, but the finished dish derives much of its texture and taste from the bread itself. Most commercial breads are too soft-textured or sweet for the purpose. A firm loaf made with flour, leavening, water and a little salt (*recipe, page 165*) is the ideal base for most bread soups; you can vary it, if you like, by experimenting with different kinds or combinations of flours. For soup-making, the loaf should be left for several days so that it develops a pronounced flavour and a heavy crumb that will soak up liquid readily. If only fresh bread is available, slice it fairly thin and dry the slices in an oven heated to its lowest setting.

Probably the most radically simple bread soup is a *panade,* a French dish that is made by steeping bread—traditionally, sourdough bread—in freshly boiled water, whisking the mixture to a purée and then enriching it with egg yolks and butter (*page 56*). You can substitute broth, milk or cream for all or part of the water, and you can include bits of cooked meat and vegetables in the soup.

More elaborate and substantial soups can be made in a casserole by layering the bread with other ingredients—cooked beef or lamb, for example—and baking the assembly in the oven. Other variations on the following pages range from an aromatic mixture of bread and richly caramelized onions to a melange of bread slices and puréed winter squash gratinéed and served in the squash's hollowed-out shell.

Slices of rough-textured bread turned golden by a saffron broth, are ladled intact from a *mourtaïrol.* Pieces of cooked chicken meat and sliced carrot have been layered with the bread in a casserole, moistened with broth, then baked for an hour to mingle their flavours.

Variations on the Simplest Bread Soup

The fundamental bread and broth mixture of a *panade*, excellent in itself, can be the departure point for a host of variations. The two bread soups shown here—a simple *panade* and its close cousin, a layered *mourtaïrol*—suggest how the addition of commonly available ingredients can give the basic mixture a different flavour and texture.

The white parts of leeks cooked in butter (*demonstration, right*; *recipe, page 140*) lend a sweet, oniony aroma to a basic *panade*. Sautéed garlic, sorrel or spinach could replace the leeks, as could parboiled celery or root vegetables.

A layered bread soup baked in a casserole offers even wider scope for improvisation. Here, the poached chicken and sliced carrots remaining from a *poule au pot* (*page 76*) are layered with bread and bathed with broth to make a substantial soup that can be served as a main course. Bread and saffron broth are the staple ingredients of a *mourtaïrol*: you can substitute cooked lamb or rabbit for the chicken and other cooked root or aromatic vegetables for the carrots.

Introducing Flavours with Vegetables

1 **Cooking the leeks.** Set an earthenware casserole on a fireproof mat over a low heat, melt some butter in it and add thin slices of leeks, white parts only. Cook until they soften but do not colour—about 10 minutes. Half fill the vessel with hot liquid—here, chicken broth.

2 **Adding the bread.** Remove the pot from the heat. Break a generous quantity of almost stale bread, crust included, into rough chunks. Add them to the broth (*above*) until the bread comes up to the surface of the liquid. Cover, and leave in a warm place for at least 10 minutes to allow the bread to soak up the broth.

Bread Layered with Chicken and Carrots

1 **Layering the ingredients.** Cut dry bread into thin slices, halving them if the slices are large. In a deep casserole, arrange a layer of cooked meat and sliced vegetables—here, pieces of poached chicken and carrots. Top with a layer of bread. Continue to alternate layers, ending with a layer of the bread.

2 **Infusing the saffron.** Place a little powdered saffron in a large serving spoon, and add to it several teaspoons of hot chicken broth (*above, left*). If you use saffron threads, dry them first in a cool oven, then pulverize them. When the mixture in the spoon is a deep red-orange, stir it into the broth (*above, right*).

3 **Puréeing the bread.** Whisk the mixture to break the bread into smaller pieces (*above*). Return the casserole to the mat over a medium heat and bring to the boil, then reduce the heat to maintain a steady simmer. Cook, uncovered, for 30 minutes, whisking once or twice (*above*) to break up the bread further.

4 **Finishing the soup.** At the end of the cooking time whisk briskly to disperse the bread evenly through the soup. Remove the casserole from the heat. Add a chunk of butter and 4 to 6 egg yolks, depending on their size, then whisk again to amalgamate them (*above*). Serve the soup in warmed bowls (*right*).□

3 **Moistening the soup.** Preheat the oven to 200°C (400°F or Mark 6). Ladle the saffron-flavoured chicken broth over the layered ingredients in the casserole (*above*). When the topmost layer of bread slices begins to float, add another cup or so of the liquid. Then put the uncovered casserole in the oven.

4 **Cooking and serving.** Let the casserole bake for about an hour: much of the liquid will be absorbed by the bread and a light gratin will form on the soup's surface. Serve the *mourtaïrol* heaped on to shallow soup plates (*above*).□

Two Classic Onion Soups

Onions, which carry an important supporting role in many dishes, can be used in quantity to make soups that are fragrant and warming. Properly cooked, an onion soup has none of the harshness that many people associate with the raw vegetable.

The sturdy soup shown on the opposite page, above, (*recipe, page 139*) may well be the ancestor of all onion soups. Its basic ingredients are slices of coarse, dry bread, sliced onions that are cooked to a golden-brown and shredded cheese. The bread slices are coated with cooked onions and cheese, layered in a broad casserole and moistened with water. The casserole is first simmered on top of the stove, then baked in the oven until a richly coloured crust forms on the surface of the soup.

The same ingredients used in different proportions appear in the onion soup so often featured on the menus of French bistros—in France and around the world. For this soup (*demonstration, opposite page, below; recipe, page 138*), the cooked and browned onions are simmered briefly in the soup liquid—beef broth, as here, or plain water. Then the broth is divided among individual casseroles and each portion is crowned with a single bread slice and a handful of cheese. Before serving, the cheese is passed under a grill until it has melted and is bubbling. Strictly speaking, the bread and cheese are merely a garnish, but they are such an invariable accompaniment that the dish would be unrecognizable without them.

The onions used in either soup should be tender and sweet; large, white summer onions, violet Bermudas or large Spanish onions are suitable. They are cooked for about 1 hour, in two stages—a long, slow simmer followed by a thorough browning over a slightly higher heat (*box, below*)—and any traces of rawness are eliminated. Cooked this way, raw sliced onions will reduce to about one third of their original volume by the time they are ready to be added to the liquid.

Freshly grated Gruyère and the sharper Parmesan—used singly or together—are the traditional cheeses for onion soup. If you substitute a Cheddar, Romano or other sharp cheese, pick one that is mature and relatively dry so that it shreds or grates easily. Any rough-textured bread is appropriate for the layered onion soup. Dried-out slices of *baguette*—the long, narrow French loaf—are the traditional choice for onion soup bistro-style.

The Gentle Process of Caramelizing Onions

Colouring without burning. In a sauté pan, melt butter over a very low heat. Fill the pan with thinly sliced onion. Add salt, then cover (*above, left*) and cook, stirring occasionally, until the onions are very soft but not coloured—about 40 minutes. Uncover the pan, raise the heat slightly and stir regularly (*above, centre*), until the onions turn a rich caramel (*above, right*)—about 30 minutes; if they are browning too quickly, reduce the heat.

An Onion Soup Gratinéed

1 **Layering the ingredients.** Spread dry bread slices with caramelized onions. Put a layer of the bread in a casserole and sprinkle with cheese. Repeat until two-thirds full, ending with cheese. Insert a funnel down the side of the pot and pour in boiling water (*inset*) until the bread floats a little above its original level.

2 **Cooking the soup.** Simmer the soup, uncovered, for 30 minutes. Meanwhile, preheat the oven to 170°C (325°F or Mark 3). Top up the soup, if necessary, with boiling water, then sprinkle on more cheese and thin shavings of butter. Bake, uncovered, for about 1 hour and serve in shallow soup plates.□

Onion Soup Bistro-Style

1 **Preparing the onion broth.** Pour boiling liquid—here, beef broth—into a pan containing caramelized onions. Bring the mixture to the boil, then lower the heat to maintain a simmer.

2 **Ladling into bowls.** Simmer the broth for 10 minutes to allow the onions' flavour to permeate the liquid. Skim off any butter that rises to the surface. Ladle the broth and the onions into individual, heat-proof bowls.

3 **Finishing the soup.** Top each bowl with a slice of dry French bread, and cover with shredded cheese. Put the bowls under a hot grill until the cheese begins to bubble, then serve immediately.□

A Pumpkin Soup Served in Its Shell

The golden flesh of a pumpkin or winter squash makes a rich base for a bread soup (*recipe, page 135*). Pumpkin or squash *panade* can also be given a special fillip: when the vegetable flesh is removed for cooking, the empty shell can be reserved for a natural—though inedible—container to hold the finished soup.

When choosing a pumpkin or winter squash to serve as a tureen, several factors should be kept in mind. The first is size: the pumpkin or squash must fit into your oven and you must be able to lift it out comfortably and safely after it is filled with hot soup. The 3.5 kg (8 lb) winter squash pictured here is about 30 cm (12 inches) in diameter; it holds an ample quantity of soup for eight people. In addition, the pumpkin or squash must have a flat base so that it stands upright firmly, and of course, it must be free of cracks and blemishes that could cause leaks.

Squash flesh is resistant, so choose a stout, sharp knife for carving open the vegetable. Cut around the top to create a broad enough opening to enable you to clean the squash easily and ladle out the soup comfortably. Scrape all seeds and the fibres from the inner surfaces of the squash shell, then carve away the flesh from the top and bottom. Because the skin must not be punctured, use implements you can control easily: a melon-ball scoop is effective for removing flesh from the base of the squash; a sharp spoon or small knife—one with a curved blade, if you have it—works well on the sides. Finally, shape the edge of the shell into a neat rim.

The squash flesh may first be stewed briefly in butter with onion, then simmered in a moderate amount of water (the squash will release a good deal of moisture during cooking). While the squash flesh simmers, put the shell in the oven to warm. Fill the preheated shell with successive layers of soup, bread and cheese and return it to the oven. After about 25 minutes, the grated cheese topping will be richly coloured, and the *panade* is ready for the table.

1 **Preparing the squash.** With the knife angled slightly downwards for easier control, cut away the top quarter or so of the squash (*below*). De-seed the squash and remove the fibres, then carefully scoop out the flesh (*right*). Leave at least 1 cm (½ inch) of flesh to prevent the squash shell from leaking; coarsely chop the scooped-out flesh.

2 **Combining the flesh with onions.** In a large saucepan, soften finely chopped onion in butter over a low heat, then add the squash pieces (*above*). Stir and toss the squash to keep it from sticking to the bottom of the pan.

3 **Cooking the soup.** When the squash begins to exude moisture, add hot water nearly to cover. For a thicker soup, add sliced potatoes. Season with salt and nutmeg, then bring to a light boil. Stir occasionally (*above*); after 40 minutes, the mixture should be purée soft.

4 **Enriching with cream.** Warm the empty squash shell in an oven preheated to 180°C (350°F or Mark 4) for 15 minutes while you finish the soup. Stir cream into the squash purée (*above*) and adjust the seasoning if necessary.

5 **Serving the soup.** Ladle some soup into the shell, then add a layer of dried bread slices and grated cheese—here, Gruyère. Continue the layers (*above*), ending with cheese. If you have included potatoes, substitute a topping of croûtons for the bread slices. Place on an ovenproof dish in a hot oven, 220°C (425°F or Mark 7), until the cheese forms a golden gratin, then serve (*right*).□

4

Cold Soups

Creations for Summer

Making and setting a jellied consommé
The technique of clarification
A sharp note of flavour from fermented bread
Blending your own spices
A choice of fruits

When hot weather parches throats and dulls appetites, cold soups make a reviving start to a meal. Many of them have a refreshing appearance—from the creamy pink of cherry soup (*opposite*) to the topaz reflections of a lightly gelled consommé bedded in cracked ice. And their ingredients—summer fruits, crisp vegetables and acidic liquids—are calculated to act as a tonic for the palate.

Raw ingredients are the special province of cold soups. The Spanish gazpacho (*page 66*), for example, is an invigorating mixture of uncooked peppers, cucumbers, onions and garlic floating in icy tomato juice. Soft fruits, such as berries and pears, are sometimes left raw in soups (*recipes, page 146*) so that their fresh flavours are unaltered.

The liquids used in cold soups frequently contrast with, rather than echo, the flavours of the soup's main ingredients. In a Senegalese (*page 70*), for example, the mild, milky liquid extracted from coconuts balances the pungency of hot curry spices. In cherry soup (*page 72*), dry white wine and soured cream provide a foil for the sweetness of the fruit. And in the Russian *botvinya* (*page 68*), a pleasantly acidic ferment of rye bread sets off poached fish, cooked green leaves and crisp salad vegetables.

In addition to the soups that are specifically designed to be eaten cold, most soups that are usually eaten hot can also be served chilled—although they may require some changes in preparation. For example, a consommé should be reinforced with gelatinous cuts of meat to ensure that the cooled broth sets to a light jelly.

When making purées to serve cold, keep butter to a minimum or avoid it altogether, and make sure that you skim off every particle of fat after cooking, since any fat will set to an unappetizing scum when chilled. To enrich a chilled purée, use soured cream or cream—as in the famous vichyssoise (*recipe, page 105*), a modern version of the ancient leek and potato soup. Cream also acts to dilute purées—a useful function, since soups become thicker as they chill. Even if you have tasted the soup after cooking, take another spoonful and taste again before serving: chilling mutes flavour and extra seasoning may be necessary.

A chilled cherry soup, thickened with soured cream and garnished with halved cherries, is served from a glass bowl that reveals the soup's ravishing colour at table. The stoned cherries were briefly soaked in warm wine to soften them and release some of their juices.

Clarifying Broth for a Jellied Consommé

Attractively garnished, a basic meat or chicken broth is an excellent soup in its own right. The soup can be endowed with a greater sublety and complexity of flavour, however, by enriching the broth a second time with fresh meat and vegetables. The result is what the French call a consommé, or consummate broth.

If the consommé is to be served cold and jellied, one of the enriching ingredients must be high in natural gelatine. In the demonstration here, a *consommé à la Madrilène* based on chicken broth (*recipe, page 143*) receives its secondary infusion from lean beef, chicken parts, aromatic vegetables and tomatoes, which add a rosy colour as well as flavour. The chicken parts, particularly the feet, provide enough gelatine to set the broth—when chilled—to a light jelly that turns to liquid in the warmth of the mouth.

The mark of a successful consommé, whether jellied or not, is perfect clarity. Prepare the basic broth by the slow-cooking method demonstrated on page 10, making sure that you skim and strain it meticulously. Chill it, then remove every speck of fat that solidifies on the surface.

Combine the cold broth with the enriching ingredients and simmer them gently for about 1 hour. During the cooking, very small particles of food, particularly from the tomato pulp in the case of a *consommé à la Madrilène,* are released into the soup. Some of these are too fine to be strained out, but they can be trapped by a protein molecule called albumin, some of which is contributed by the beef. Extra albumin is supplied by egg whites.

While the soup is heating, the albumin will coagulate and gather up the particles. But the cooking must by very gentle or the albumin will solidify before it has done its job. The cooked albumin, along with the trapped particles, is filtered out when the consommé is strained.

To display the clarity and jewel-like colour of a hot consommé, serve it from a warmed white tureen. A jellied consommé merits a more elaborate presentation: put it in a clear glass bowl nested in a larger vessel and surrounded with crushed ice. This will keep the consommé chilled and enhance the shimmering appearance of the jelly.

1 **Preparing the ingredients.** Trim off all the fat from a piece of lean beef—here, chuck—and chop it finely. Trim and clean the carrots and leeks, then chop them finely. Coarsely cut up unskinned tomatoes. Chop the chicken parts into chunky pieces (*above*) to expose their gelatine-rich tissues.

2 **Enriching the broth.** Put the beef, chicken and vegetables into a heavy pan. Add 1 or 2 egg whites (*above, left*) and stir them well into the solids. Ladle in cold chicken broth (*above, right*) and stir to combine it with the other ingredients. Heat the cold broth very slowly and gently so that the albumin does not solidify too soon.

3 **Simmering the broth.** Stir occasionally as the liquid slowly comes to the boil. Skimming is not necessary, since the impurities will be removed later. Partially cover, adjust the heat and let the soup barely simmer for an hour to extract all the flavour from the solid ingredients.

4 **Straining out the solids.** Line a fine sieve with several layers of muslin wrung out in cold water. Pour the cooked broth into the lined sieve and let it drain through into a bowl. To keep the broth absolutely clear, do not press the solids to extract extra drops of liquid.

5 **Serving the consommé.** Chill the consommé until it sets to a light jelly. To serve, put the bowl of consommé inside a larger bowl containing crushed ice. Ladle the soup into chilled consommé cups (*left*). Garnish (*below*) with diced sweet red pepper that has been grilled and skinned (*page 14*).□

Soups that Need No Cooking

When soups are not cooked, special attention must be paid to every aspect of the raw ingredients used, including texture and appearance. The success of the uncooked avocado soup shown on the right (*recipe, page 141*) depends upon the creamy, blemish-free ripeness of the avocado flesh. Avocados bought ripe are often marred by bruises from handling; to avoid this, buy firm fruit and ripen it at home for a few days. Avocados are ready when they yield slightly to gentle pressure.

For gazpacho, a raw vegetable soup from Spain (*below; recipes, pages 143-144*), the key is to preserve the fresh crunchiness of the chopped peppers, celery and onions. The tomato juice and water should be icy cold so that the vegetables soften as little as possible in the liquid.

Gazpacho looks particularly inviting when it is presented with a block of ice floating in the serving bowl. To make an ice block, simply freeze a small bowl of water; or fill a bowl with ice cubes, top it up with cold water and freeze until solid.

A Cool Blend of Avocado and Cream

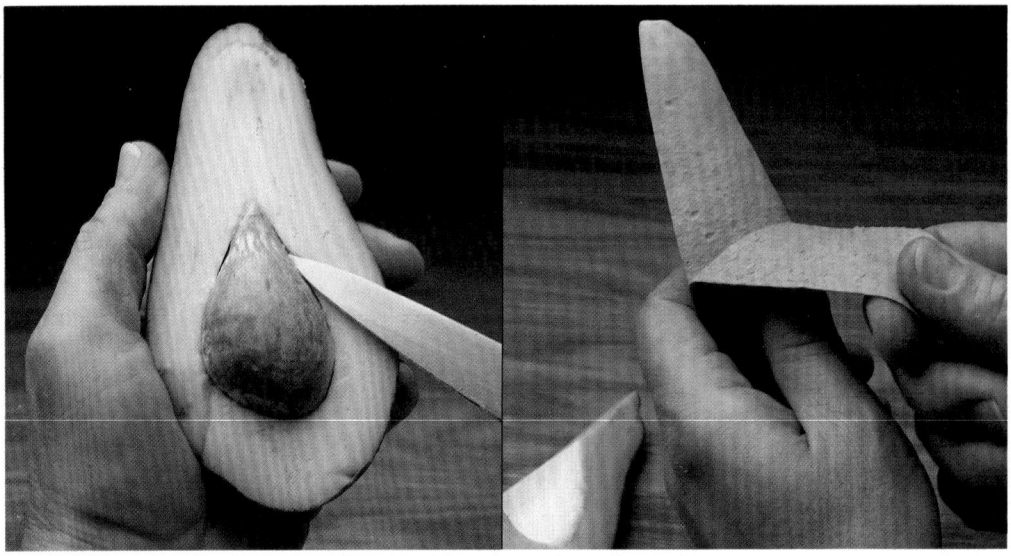

1 **Peeling an avocado.** Starting from the broader end, cut through the flesh to the stone. Rotate the knife around the stone to halve the avocado lengthwise. Pull the halves apart and prise out the stone with the knife tip (*above, left*). Slice each half in two and, starting at the stem end, peel the skin from each piece (*above, right*). For added colour, scrape off the dark green flesh that clings to the inside of the skin. Drench all the avocado flesh with lemon juice to prevent discoloration and to add a slight tartness.

Raw Vegetables for Crisp Textures

1 **Making a bread paste.** Put a few unpeeled cloves of garlic in a mortar; tap them a few times with a pestle to loosen their skins, then peel off the skins and discard. Begin pounding the cloves while you add, successively, fresh breadcrumbs, a few cumin seeds, red wine vinegar and olive oil. Work all the ingredients into a smooth paste.

2 **Preparing the fresh tomatoes.** With a small, sharp knife, cut out the stem end of each tomato in a conical section. Cut a small cross at the base of each tomato, and immerse the fruit in boiling water for 10 seconds to loosen its skin. Pinch the skin where it was slit at the base and peel off the skin in strips (*above, left*). Halve each tomato horizontally; gently squeeze each half to force out the seeds. With a large knife, chop the halves into a coarse purée. Put the purée into a mixing bowl with the bread paste (*above, right*).

2 **Puréeing.** Put the avocado flesh in a large bowl, and mash it with a fork to make a rough purée. If you want a smooth-textured soup, pass this purée through a food mill or press it through a fine sieve. For a varied texture, try mixing a very smooth purée with some flesh that has only been roughly mashed.

3 **Combining ingredients.** Stir into the purée enough cold liquid to make it easy to pour: both white wine or, as here, chicken broth are suitable. Add salt, white pepper and cayenne pepper; enrich the soup with sweet or soured cream. Pour the soup into a tureen, cover and chill in the refrigerator.

4 **Serving the soup.** Sprinkle finely chopped, fresh chives over the chilled avocado soup just before serving. Chopped fresh dill may be substituted for the slightly sweet contrast of flavour it contributes. Ladle the garnished soup into well-chilled soup plates.□

3 **Adding chopped vegetables.** Chop up the other raw gazpacho vegetables—in this case, sweet Spanish onions, stoned black olives and seeded red and green sweet peppers. Add them to the mixing bowl, together with a sprinkling of chopped, fresh marjoram and mint.

4 **Stirring in liquids and seasonings.** Pour chilled, thick tomato juice into the bowl. Stir to combine the juice with the other ingredients. Add iced water (*above*) to dilute the gazpacho to the desired consistency. In a mortar, pound black pepper, coarse salt and dried chili peppers. Stir them into the soup. Cover and refrigerate for 1 to 2 hours.

5 **Presenting the soup.** Put the gazpacho in a glass serving bowl with a large chunk of ice. Sprinkle on some chopped spring onions. Accompany the soup with bowls of small croûtons (*page 14*) and chopped fresh vegetables—here celery, peeled and seeded cucumbers, sweet peppers and onion. Let guests garnish the soup according to their taste.□

Fish and Vegetables Assembled in a Refreshing Liquor

Most soups are a fusion of flavours, the result of all ingredients being cooked together. But in *botvinya*, the Russian fish soup demonstrated here (*recipe, page 145*), the components are prepared separately and assembled just before serving so that each retains its own flavour.

Suitable fish for *botvinya* include salmon, trout, mackerel or any other firm-fleshed, full-flavoured species. The soup takes its name from *botva*, the Russian word for the root-vegetable leaves that are traditionally served with the fish; but it owes its special character to the inclusion of *kvas* (*box, below*), a refreshing, slightly bitter, beer-like liquid made by fermenting rye bread in water.

Kvas should ferment for at least three days. If you lack time, use white wine or dry cider. Cook the other ingredients a few hours before serving and chill well.

1 **Poaching the fish.** Choose an oval vessel large enough to accommodate the fish—here, a tail section of salmon. Line the vessel with a long strip of aluminium foil; the foil will keep the fish from sticking and simplify lifting it out. Put the fish in water with flavourings—sliced onion, fennel, thyme and a bay leaf—and poach until the flesh parts easily from the bone when probed with a knife. Grasp each end of the foil and lift out the fish.

Kvas: A Russian Home Brew

To make *kvas*, pour boiling water over pieces of stale, dark rye bread placed in a large pot (*above; recipe, page 145*). When the mixture is tepid, add molasses, and fresh or dried yeast dissolved in a spoonful of the liquid. Mix well, cover, and leave in a warm place overnight. Strain through muslin. Using a funnel, pour the liquid into clean bottles, each containing 2 or 3 raisins. Cork securely and store in a cool, dark place for 3 to 4 days before use.

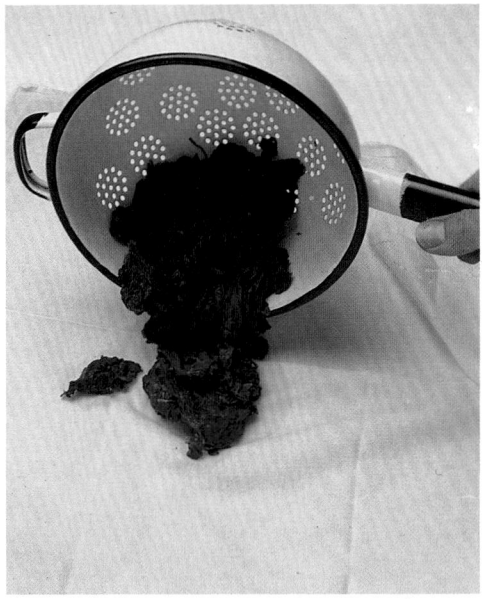

4 **Cooking the leaf vegetables.** Trim the ribs from spinach—used here—or young beet leaves. Boil the leaves for 1 minute in plenty of salted water, drain, empty on to a cloth (*above*), squeeze them dry, and chop coarsely. Parboil sorrel for a few seconds, then purée it using a fine-meshed nylon sieve (*page 28*).

5 **Cutting up the raw ingredients.** Peel a cucumber and slice it lengthwise into 4 or 5 sections. Cutting lengthwise again, divide each section into long strips, then cut the strips crosswise into small dice (*above*). Trim off the roots and tips of spring onions and chop them finely. Mince some parsley and fresh dill.

2 **Skinning and carving.** While the fish is still warm, slit the skin down the length of the back and peel it off in strips. Cut along the middle of the fish's flank to the tail, then cut back from the vent to the tail and ease the two flank sections off the bone (*above, left*). Prise out the backbone (*above, right*). Divide the remaining fish lengthwise into two fillets and cut each fillet into 3 or 4 pieces.

3 **Preparing the prawns.** Simmer the prawns in water for 5 minutes. Break off the heads and peel away the shells, but leave the tail fins for decoration. Put the heads and shells in a mortar with a little *kvas*. Pound the shells to fragments; strain and reserve the liquor.

6 **Combining the kvas and the vegetables.** Put the spinach and sorrel in a chilled tureen and pour in the *kvas* (*above*). Add the chopped raw vegetables, the minced herbs and the liquor flavoured with the prawns' heads and shells. To balance the sourness of the *kvas*, add 1 to 2 teaspoonfuls molasses or brown sugar. Stir the mixture well. Taste the soup and season it with salt.

7 **Presenting the garnishes.** Trim the ends from a horseradish, peel it with a sharp knife and grate it. Put it in a serving dish and sprinkle on lemon juice to prevent discolouring. On a separate plate, arrange radishes round a mound of coarse salt. Add the salmon pieces and the prawns to the soup then serve over ice with the horseradish and radish accompaniments (*above*).□

Hot Spices Blended in a Bland Liquid

Seasonings—which are generally added discreetly to hot soups—can be used more liberally in cold soups, since chilling mutes all flavours. Chilled soups need plenty of salt, and often benefit from the pungency of pepper and cayenne pepper. Senegalese, the soup demonstrated here (*recipe, page 144*) draws much if its piquancy from a liberal lacing of curry spices. You can use a commercial curry powder or blend your own from individual spices—coriander, cumin, fenugreek, black mustard seeds, turmeric root, dried chilies—in proportion to suit your taste (*box, opposite page, below*).

Senegalese is based on a velouté (*page 28*) in which the butter is first used to cook the spices, instead of being combined directly with the flour to produce a roux. You can choose chicken, meat or vegetable stock to finish the velouté.

Like many highly seasoned cold soups, Senegalese needs tempering. Double cream and milky coconut liquid, added to the finished soup, will offset the pungency of the spices. Finely grated coconut makes a suitably bland garnish.

1 **Preparing the spices and aromatics.** In a mortar, coarsely crush about a tablespoon each of coriander, cumin, fenugreek and black mustard seeds. Melt a little butter in a sauté pan and stew the spices over a low heat for a minute or so. Add sliced garlic cloves, chopped onions and celery (*above, left*), and cook them over a low heat, uncovered, until the onions are translucent. Add flour (*above, centre*), warmed broth—here, chicken broth—a bay leaf and some yellow turmeric root pounded to powder (*above, right*).

Tapping a Coconut's Sweetness

The milky liquid contained in a coconut can be used to flavour cold soups (*Step 3, right*) and its flesh can be used as a garnish (*Step 5, opposite page*). To tap the liquid, use a skewer to puncture two of the dark "eyes" at the nut's pointed end and pour out the fluid. Break the shell with a mallet and ease chunks of flesh from the husk with a knife. Grate the flesh finely; discard the brown skin.

2 **Simmering the soup.** Bring the broth rapidly to the boil. Lower the heat to a simmer, and skim off the film of butter and solids that collects on the surface. Skim until the soup is clear of impurities, then cover the pan and continue to simmer gently for at least 40 minutes.

3 **Straining the liquid.** Add coconut liquid (*box, left*) and a few dried chilies, roughly crushed. The coconut liquid is added at this late stage because longer cooking diminishes its flavour. The chilies would impart too much of their fieriness to the soup if cooked in it for long. Bring the soup back to a simmer, then strain it through a fine sieve into a bowl (*above*).

4 **Enriching with cream.** Cover the strained soup and chill it. Before serving, stir in double cream to thicken the liquid and mellow its flavour. The combination of cream and the turmeric powder will give the soup a striking yellow hue.

5 **Garnishing and serving.** Serve the soup in chilled soup plates (*right*). To balance the pungency of the spices, offer a dish of freshly grated coconut (*box, opposite page, left*) for guests to sprinkle on their soup.□

The Advantages of Blending Your Own Spices

The spices that flavour the Senegalese are common constituents of commercially blended curry powders. Many Western cooks could profit from the African and Asian practice of storing each spice separately and making a special blend for each dish that calls for curry powder. Blending your own spice mixtures enables you to adjust the proportions to your taste, and prevents a tired sameness of flavour in different dishes.

The pungent Senegalese is a good choice to begin experimenting with. So is mulligatawny (*recipe, page 119*), a thick meat broth that borrows from both Indian and British cooking traditions.

You can vary the basic curry spices in many ways. Among the milder spices that you can add in liberal amounts are coriander, cardamom, cinnamon and turmeric. Saffron, cumin and cloves should be used sparingly. Use mustard seeds and fenugreek with restraint, too; an excess of fenugreek is responsible for the bitterness that occurs in some commercial curry powders. For a heady sting, add peppercorns, red peppers or chilies and fresh or dried ginger root, peeled and grated just before use. But leave out these ingredients—especially chilies—if you do not like their fiery taste. White peppercorns are stronger, but less aromatic, than black.

Buy spices in their whole form when possible. Not only will they retain their flavour longer than powdered spices, but you can grind or crush them into fragments large enough to be strained off at the end of cooking. Use a pestle and mortar to crush spices coarsely, an electric food processor to reduce them to a fine powder. An electric blender will disperse spices finely if you blend them with a little liquid: use oil if you intend to fry the spices, otherwise water.

Heat brings out the flavour of many spices, including cumin, saffron, coriander, fenugreek, cinnamon and cloves. You can either fry the spices (*Step 1, opposite page*) or—if you like a stronger aroma—toast them in a dry, heavy pan over medium heat until they darken slightly and start to smell pungent. Cinnamon and cloves benefit from 5 to 7 minutes of toasting; most of the other spices need a little less. Cumin, however, should be heated only for a minute, otherwise it will become too strong. Turmeric burns easily, and should not be fried or toasted.

Many spices can be added either early or late to the soup, but turmeric is one that profits from lengthy cooking to mellow its flavour. Peppercorns, on the other hand, should be cooked for only a few minutes or they will become bitter. Chilies can easily burn out all other flavours; they should therefore be added when the soup is nearly ready.

Fruit Soups: a Balance of Sweet and Savoury

Fruit marries well with savoury and sour ingredients to make refreshing and unusual cold soups. The sweetness of the fruit is not masked—it may even be augmented with sugar—but it is balanced by more acerbic flavours.

The two fruit soups demonstrated here show how the balance of sweet and sharp flavours can be achieved with different ingredients. For the purée below, ripe pears are combined with chicken broth, lemon juice and some peppery leaves of watercress (*recipe, page 146*). Cream harmonizes these contrasting flavours. Other soft-fleshed fruits—peaches, berries or melons—can be prepared similarly.

For the soup shown opposite (*recipe, page 146*) cherries, which are both more acid and firmer in texture than pears, call for sugar to reinforce their natural sweetness. But lemon juice, cinnamon, soured cream and salt provide a foil to the sweetness, and a slightly bitter flavour can be introduced by adding an infusion of the cherry stones and stalks. The soup liquid—a medium-sweet white wine—contributes both sweet and acid flavours. Other firm-fleshed fruits—apricots or plums—can be substituted for cherries.

Frequently, fruits are left uncooked to preserve their fresh taste. For the soups demonstrated here, the pears are raw and the cherries merely warmed to soften them slightly. Soften crisp fruits, such as apples and rhubarb, by stewing them briefly in the soup liquid; most soups made from cooked fruit can be served either hot or cold.

Puréeing some or all of the fruit thickens the soup naturally. If you leave the fruit whole or cut it into pieces, the soup can be thickened with cream or a starchy ingredient such as rice, breadcrumbs, or some arrowroot or cornflour dissolved in a little cold water.

A Pear Purée Sharpened with Watercress

1 **Puréeing the pears.** Peel, quarter and core the pears and cover immediately with fat-free chicken broth (*recipe, page 164*) to stop discoloration. Leave to soften in the broth for 20 minutes, then put the pears and the broth through a food mill.

2 **Adding the watercress.** In more chicken broth, simmer the pear skins and cores for 10 minutes. Strain the broth, return it to the pan, and add finely chopped watercress. Bring the broth to the boil, then pour it into the pear purée.

3 **Finishing and serving the soup.** Squeeze in lemon juice. Season with salt and white pepper, then cover and chill. Wilt a few sprigs of watercress by dipping them into boiling water; this brightens their colour and softens them so they will float on the surface of the soup. Before serving, stir double cream into the soup and garnish with the wilted leaves.□

Capturing the Flavour and Colour of Cherries

1 **Preparing the cherries.** Stone the cherries with a cherry stoner (*above, left*), or by halving them with a knife. Fold about half of the stones in a napkin and rap them sharply with a mallet to expose the kernels, which contain an agreeably bitter flavour. Put the crushed stones, whole stones and cherry stalks into an enamelled pan (*above, right*)—do not use aluminium or cast iron which would react with the acid fruit and discolour the soup.

2 **Flavouring the liquid.** Pour in wine, then add sugar, a piece of cinnamon stick and some grated lemon rind. Bring the mixture to the boil and simmer for 5 to 10 minutes to draw the flavours into the wine. Strain the liquid through a nylon sieve, then pour it back into the pan.

3 **Assembling.** Halve and reserve a few cherries for a garnish. Put the rest to soften in the wine, off the stove. Whisk soured cream until it is smooth, then stir in the cherry mixture. Add lemon juice and salt until the liquid is slightly more tart than the fruit. Cover and chill.

4 **Serving.** Transfer the soup to a chilled serving bowl and garnish with the cherry halves. Serve in chilled soup plates, with slices of toasted *brioche* (*right*), a semi-sweet bread, or biscuits.□

5

Whole Meal Soups

Two Courses from a Single Pot

Stuffed cabbage leaf garnish
Bacon and beans: a filling combination
Making a garlic-flavoured mayonnaise
Vegetables: a meal in themselves
Fermenting beetroot
How to use cold, leftover borscht

Many soups are substantial enough to qualify as light meals in themselves. A generous serving of Scotch broth, for example, will assuage all but the heartiest of appetites; a bowl of thick onion soup is a customary late-night meal for revellers in Paris. The soups demonstrated in this chapter are prepared on an even more ample scale, however, for all of them provide two courses from a single pot.

The first course is a rich broth; the second is the meat, poultry or fish that has been cooked with vegetables in the broth. When the broth has been drunk, soup spoons are exchanged for knives and forks, and the platter of carved meat and vegetable accompaniments is presented. This arrangement is flexible, however: if you prefer, you can serve both broth and meat at the same time.

Whole meal soups often include a varied selection of meats or fish that will give the broth a great depth of flavour and make a splendid array for the second course. The dish shown opposite, for example—an especially generous version of *poule au pot* (*page 76*)—features not only a whole, stuffed chicken, but also two cuts of beef. And it is garnished with stuffed cabbage leaves in addition to the usual aromatic vegetables. On a less lavish scale, the bean and bacon soup demonstrated on page 78 is supplemented with fresh pork sausage and a pig's ear; and *bourride* (*page 80*)—identified by its garlic-flavoured mayonnaise—is made from a selection of firm, white-fleshed fish.

In spite of their generous proportions, whole meat soups originated as thrifty peasant dishes that could be prepared with the minimum of fuel and cooking utensils. Many of them have since been elevated to the status of classic dishes worthy of the most discriminating table. The borschts of Eastern Europe, for example, can be simple soups made with beetroot and other vegetables. However, an elaborate Ukrainian version (*page 84*) also includes smoked and green bacon, and beef, and is garnished with small savoury pastries; and the borscht served at the court of Tsar Nicholas II includes a whole duck (*recipe, page 147*). Borscht is so ample that it is unlikely to be consumed at a single sitting, giving you plenty for another full hot meal. Or you can serve the strained liquid, iced and garnished, for a light luncheon the following day (*page 86*).

The amber broth from the gentle poaching of stuffed chicken, beef and aromatic vegetables for *poule au pot* is ladled into plates. A garnish of toasted bread stuffed with puréed vegetables augments the broth; and carved meats, vegetables and stuffed cabbage await service as the second course.

Stuffed Chicken and Beef Poached in a Pot

Preparing a soup and a meat course in a single pot has been a rustic tradition since the days when broth was kept simmering permanently on the hearth and occasionally supplemented with a cut of meat or a fowl. The everlasting pot of broth is a thing of the past, but in rural France a Sunday meal of soup and poached beef (pot au feu) or chicken (*poule au pot*) is still customary. In the bounteous holiday version of *poule au pot* demonstrated here (*recipe, page 148*), beef as well as a whole stuffed chicken are cooked with vegetables to make a fragrant broth and a substantial main course.

The most important difference between the preparation of this dish and a basic broth (*page 8*) is that the cooking times for the beef and chicken must be carefully gauged so that the meats enrich the poaching liquid without themselves becoming tasteless and stringy. For a perfectly balanced dish, choose a boiling fowl and two different cuts of beef—here, a piece of shin and sections of short rib. The robustly flavoured shin, like the fowl, contains gelatine that not only keeps the flesh succulent, but also gives body to the broth; the rib, which has a more subtle flavour, contains layers of fat that help keep its meat moist during cooking.

Since the beef requires longer cooking than the chicken, poach it on its own for about an hour. In the meantime stuff and truss the chicken. The moist bread stuffing used here is in keeping with the economical character of the dish, but you can use any stuffing suitable for a roast bird. If you like, make more stuffing than you need and wrap the surplus in parboiled cabbage leaves (*box, right*). Since the flavour of cabbage is enhanced by fat, cook the stuffed leaves in a mixture of broth and liquid chicken fat spooned from the surface of the soup.

The vegetables are added to the broth with the chicken. In the two or more hours required to cook the chicken to tenderness, the vegetables will become exhausted of flavour: replace them with fresh ones about 30 minutes before the meal is to be served. You can mash the spent vegetables with a fork and spread them on dried or toasted crusts of bread to make a garnish for the finished dish (*page 16*).

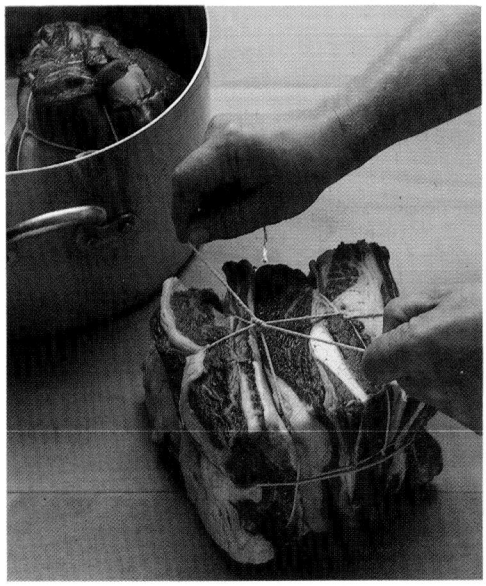

1 **Preparing the meat.** Using cotton string, tie the cuts of beef into compact bundles (*above*) that will cook evenly and carve easily at serving time. Put the trussed meat in a pot large enough to hold the chicken and vegetables as well. Cover the beef with cold water and set the pot on a low heat.

2 **Scumming the pot.** As the water comes to the boil, spoon off the thick, grey scum on the surface. To encourage the scum to form, add a cup of cold water when the liquid reaches the boil. Repeat until the scum is replaced by clear froth. Reduce the heat, place the lid slightly askew on the pot and barely simmer the beef; meanwhile, prepare the chicken.

Wrapping Bread Stuffing in Cabbage Leaves

1 **Stuffing the leaves.** Shave down stems of cabbage leaves if they are thick. Stack the leaves in a pan, pour in boiling water to cover and simmer for 5 minutes; drain well. Place stuffing at the base of each leaf, fold over the base, then the sides, and roll up the leaf.

2 **Cooking the leaves.** Place the rolled cabbage leaves, flap-side down, in a pan. Half submerge them with fatty broth, spooned from the surface of the soup, and simmer with the pan covered for about 30 minutes. Remove the rolled leaves with a slotted spoon.

3 **Stuffing and trussing the chicken.** To make the bird easier to carve, remove its wishbone: pull back the neck skin and locate the bone with your fingers; with a small knife, cut the bone free, then pull it out. Stuff the chicken loosely through the tail vent. Here, a bread stuffing with bacon, eggs, and chopped and sautéed chicken liver is used. Use a trussing needle and a length of string to sew up the tail vent. Truss the bird securely (*page 36*) or truss it so that it will retain its shape during cooking.

4 **Cooking the chicken and vegetables.** When the beef has cooked for about 1 hour, ladle out and reserve enough liquid to allow room for the chicken and vegetables. Add the bird, a peeled onion stuck with cloves, a head of garlic, carrots and a bouquet garni (*above*). Remove the scum given off by the chicken as the broth returns to the boil. Simmer for 2 hours, or until the chicken is tender, topping up as necessary with the reserved broth. Spoon off the fat that collects on the surface and reserve for cooking the stuffed cabbage leaves (*box, opposite page*).

5 **Presenting the dish.** About 30 minutes before serving, remove the vegetables: mash them and spread them on pieces of toasted bread. Add fresh vegetables and cook until tender. Carve the meat and fowl (*above*). Serve the broth with the bread first; then the meats, vegetables and the stuffed cabbage (*right*).□

Bacon and Beans: Warming Winter Staples

Soups in which salted or smoked pork take pride of place are generally large-scale, substantial dishes—reminiscent of the days when rural families had little winter meat other than the pig that they themselves had raised, killed and preserved. The *zuppa di fagioli* shown here combines smoked collar bacon with another winter staple, dried haricot beans (*recipe, page 151*). In fact, the earthy flavour of most dried pulses—kidney beans, peas and lentils, for example—would combine equally well with the strong-flavoured meat. You can make the soup meatier by including other inexpensive pork products: ham, pig's trotters and tails, for example, or—as here—a pig's ear and sausages.

The first step in preparing the soup is to soak the beans in cold water to restore their moisture and reduce their cooking time. Most beans—as well as chick peas—need either overnight soaking or the following quick-soaking treatment: cover the dry beans in cold water; bring it to the boil and cook for 2 minutes. Turn off the heat and let the beans soak for 1 hour. They can then go into the soup for further cooking. Split peas may require about 3 hours' soaking in cold water; lentils can be cooked without preliminary soaking.

The beans, bacon and pig's ear are simmered together for 1½ to 3 hours, depending on the tenderness of the beans; the sausages are added about 40 minutes before the end of cooking. If you are using split peas or lentils, cook them separately first and add them to the soup about 15 minutes before serving.

When the meats and pulses are tender, you can thicken the soup, if you like, by puréeing some of the beans. For a last-minute infusion of flavour and colour, add a *sofrito*—a reduction of sautéed onions, tomatoes and sometimes garlic that is often used in Mediterranean cookery.

Do not salt the soup until the end of cooking; the cured meats may provide all the necessary seasoning and salt added early on would also toughen the pulses' skins, hindering their absorption of moisture and slowing their cooking.

1 **Soaking the beans.** The night before you cook the soup, pick over the dried beans—here, white haricots—and remove any blemished specimens, stones or fibres. Put the beans in a large bowl and cover them with cold water (*above*). Leave the beans to let them soak overnight.

2 **Starting the soup.** In a large pot, put the meats that require long cooking—in this case, a piece of smoked collar bacon and a salted and rinsed pig's ear. Add aromatic vegetables and a bouquet garni including savory, which goes well with beans. Barely cover with cold water. Drain and add the beans.

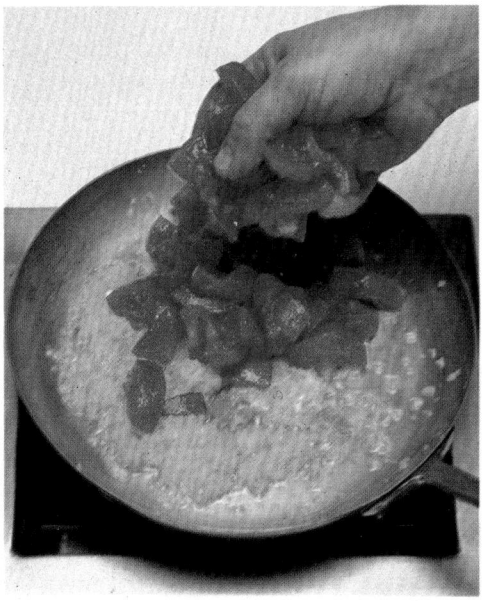

6 **Frying the sofrito.** In a sauté pan over a medium heat, cook chopped onions in olive oil until they begin to colour. Add peeled, seeded and coarsely chopped tomatoes (*above*) and cook, stirring occasionally with a wooden spoon, until most of the liquid has evaporated. Stir in some chopped, fresh parsley.

7 **Finishing the broth.** Increase the heat under the pot containing the broth and beans. As the liquid returns to a simmer, add the *sofrito* and stir the mixture well. Taste the soup for seasoning; reduce the heat and continue to cook for 2 to 3 minutes to amalgamate the flavours.

3 **Cleansing the soup.** Put the pot over a medium heat and bring the liquid to the boil, spooning off the surface scum. Adjust the heat to a simmer and partially cover the pot. Cook the soup for 1½ to 3 hours, or until the beans are tender.

4 **Adding quick-cooking meats.** Fresh or cured pork sausages require a shorter cooking time because the meat is minced up and therefore more easily penetrated by the heat. Prick the sausages to prevent their skins from splitting and add them to the pot 30 to 40 minutes before the end of cooking.

5 **Thickening the broth.** Lift out the cooked meats and keep in a warm place. Discard the aromatics. With a slotted spoon, scoop out some beans and put them in a wire sieve over the soup pot. Use a pestle to press the beans back into the pot, moistening them with some broth to facilitate sieving (*above*).

8 **Presenting the soup.** Slice up the bacon, pig's ear and sausages, and arrange them on a heated platter. Transfer the soup to a heated tureen and ladle it into warmed soup plates (*left*) and serve before, or with, the meats.□

A Fish Soup with a Lively Garlic Sauce

Because even a large section of fish will cook in under 30 minutes, you can prepare a fish soup—containing enough poached fish to make it a substantial meal—in a fraction of the time needed to make a meat soup. Often, potatoes are added to thicken and extend whole-meal fish soups (*recipes, pages 156 and 158*). The *bourride* shown here (*recipe, page 154*) is a traditional soup of Provence; it is thickened and enriched with *aïoli*, a pungent garlic-flavoured mayonnaise (*box, below*).

You can make *bourride* with any lean sea fish, such as brill, bass, cod, flounder or John Dory. The fish are cut into serving-sized pieces and poached for 15 minutes with aromatic vegetables and herbs in water or fish broth (*recipe, page 163*). The fish pieces are removed, the broth is strained, then mixed with *aïoli*. The fish portions may be served separately or, as here, immersed in the creamy yellow soup. More *aïoli* is offered as a garnish.

1 **Preparing the fish.** Cut up the fish into serving portions; here, tail of angler-fish and conger eel have been skinned and sliced crosswise into sections. Briefly soften chopped leeks, garlic cloves and chopped parsley in olive oil in a pan over a moderate heat. Arrange the fish pieces on the vegetables (*above*).

Blending an Aïoli

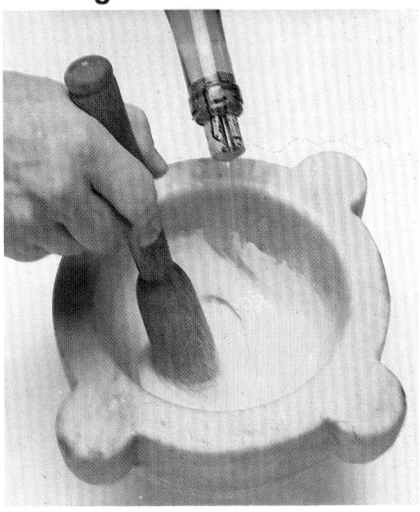

Making the emulsion. Let all ingredients warm to room temperature. In a mortar, pound peeled garlic and coarse salt to a smooth paste, add egg yolks and stir until the yolks lighten in colour. Stirring briskly, add oil, drop by drop from a bottle with a grooved cork (*page 51*). As the *aïoli* thickens, increase the flow of oil (*above*). When the sauce is stiff, dilute with lemon juice and add a little warm water to stabilize the emulsion. Dribble in the remaining oil, stirring continuously.

4 **Thickening the soup.** Put half the *aïoli* in a saucepan, reserving the rest as a garnish for the soup. Whisk in the broth, a ladleful at a time (*above*), over a very low heat. Cook, stirring, until the soup thickens just enough to coat the whisk. Do not let the soup boil, lest it curdle.

2 **Adding liquid.** Distribute more parsley, plus bay leaves, thyme sprigs and fennel leaves between and on top of the fish pieces; add some dried Seville orange peel. Pour in hot liquid—water or, as here, fish broth—to cover the fish. Bring the liquid to the boil; adjust the heat to the merest simmer and partly cover the pan.

3 **Straining the broth.** While the fish cooks, use the time to make the *aïoli* (*box, opposite page*). The fish is done when the flesh is opaque—about 15 minutes. Gently lift the cooked pieces from the broth with a slotted spoon. If you like, remove the bones from the fish. Place the fish in a heated tureen and keep it warm in the oven. Strain the broth through a fine sieve into a bowl (*above*).

5 **Serving the bourride.** Pour the soup over the cooked fish in the tureen (*above*). Garnish with finely cut chives. Serve pieces of fish and the thickened broth together, as here, or separately. Allow the diners to garnish their own portions with the reserved *aïoli* (*right*).□

The Solid Goodness of Vegetable Soup

There can never be a fixed formula for a peasant vegetable soup. What goes into the pot depends on the season and contents of the vegetable patch. The *garbure* of south-western France, for example, is made with cabbage, which is available the whole year round, and whatever other fresh vegetables are to hand (*recipe, page 159*); dried vegetables are sometimes included to extend the soup.

Some of these vegetables are served in the soup. The rest are extracted and served as a second course, accompanied by some preserved meat from the larder—sausage, a knuckle of ham or bacon that has simmered in the soup. In the Béarn region of France, a farmer's wife will probably include pieces of preserved goose, which will give the *garbure* a particularly pungent flavour.

Start the *garbure* by first sautéing and then simmering coarsely chopped aromatic and root vegetables. When they are nearly tender, add shredded cabbage. The tender, green-leafed variety used here is added raw; coarser varieties should be parboiled before being added to the soup.

When the cabbage goes into the pot, the meat is also added, along with tender vegetables—peas and French beans, for example—and dried pulses that have been soaked overnight and cooked separately. Whichever ingredients you choose, make generous use of them: according to tradition, *garbure* should be so thick that a wooden spoon thrust into the soup will stand upright.

1 **Preparing the vegetables.** Peel and coarsely chop the root and aromatic vegetables—here, potatoes, turnips, carrots, onions and leeks. For aromatic support, make a bouquet garni using parsley, thyme and bay leaf; add lovage, marjoram, savory and a dried red chili.

2 **Pre-cooking the vegetables.** Sauté the vegetables in goose fat—used here—or bacon fat for about 15 minutes. Half fill a pot with water and bring it to the boil. Add a whole, unpeeled garlic head, the bouquet garni and the softened vegetables (*above*) and simmer them.

5 **Presenting the garbure.** Cook the soup, covered, for a further 30 minutes, until the vegetables are tender and the flavour of the meat suffuses the soup. Scoop the bulk of the solids from the pot with a draining spoon and arrange them on a heated platter. Discard the bouquet garni and the garlic; carve the goose legs into serving portions. Put pieces of dried rye or wholemeal bread in a heated tureen and pour over the *garbure* broth (*above*).

3 **Preparing cabbage and broad beans.** Remove the leaves of a green cabbage and cut out the thick bases of the stems. Taking a few leaves at a time, stack them together, roll them into a tight bundle and slice them thinly to make a *chiffonade (above, left)*. Shell the broad beans; then, using your fingernails, pierce the skin of each bean and peel it off (*above, right*).

4 **Adding the final ingredients.** Add the cabbage, the broad beans and drained haricot beans—previously soaked, then cooked for about 2 hours—to the soup. Remove excess fat from the preserved meat—here, two goose legs—and add the meat to the pot.

6 **Serving and eating the soup.** Ladle the bread-thickened broth into bowls and top each serving with meat and vegetables (*left*). Serve the soup with a hearty red wine; traditionally, each guest empties his glass of wine into the last few spoonfuls of the *garbure* left at the bottom of his bowl (*below*).□

A Borscht on a Grand Scale

Soups made with beetroot are standbys in the kitchens of Russia, Poland and the Ukraine. These soups, known in the West by their Russian name, borscht (*recipes, pages 147-148*), vary from simple purées of beetroot with soured cream to the lavish Ukrainian speciality demonstrated here. This bountiful offering, which includes several different kinds of meat and shredded cabbage, is served with a medley of traditional garnishes.

The first step in making borscht as the Ukrainians do, takes place several days in advance of actual cooking, when a fermentation of beetroot is begun (*box, below, right*). The liquor produced by this fermentation is necessary to give the soup its characteristic sour tang and deep ruby colour. Passably tangy borscht can also be made by substituting *kvas* (*page 68*) for the beetroot ferment, or by using beetroots macerated in vinegar in place of fresh beetroots, and adding a little of the vinegar to the broth.

The cooking gets under way at least four hours before the soup is to be served. A selection of fresh and salted meats is set simmering to make a broth, and beetroots—left whole and unpeeled to preserve all their juices—are put in the oven to bake. After baking, the beetroots are cut up and simmered, along with shredded cabbage, in broth that has been mixed with beetroot ferment. The meats themselves are served separately.

The lengthy cooking process leaves adequate time to prepare a selection of the traditional borscht accompaniments. *Pirozhki* (*recipe, page 90*), little crescent-shaped pies, are served alongside the soup. Roasted buckwheat, or *kasha*, is baked with water and butter (*recipe, page 90*) and spooned into the individual soup plates before the broth.

Since a lot of time and effort go into making the soup, it is sensible to make a large quantity. Any leftover borscht will keep well in the refrigerator for up to a week, and can be served again; either reheated or chilled (*page 86*).

1 **Preparing the meats.** In a large pan, assemble an assortment of meats—here, beef shin and chuck, a smoked bacon hock and slab of salted bacon. Add several whole, peeled onions and two bay leaves. Pour in cold water to cover.

2 **Cooking the meats.** Bring the water to the boil, removing the scum. Cover partially and simmer the meats until tender—about 3 hours. Transfer the meats to a casserole, cover, and keep in a warm oven, 170°C (325°F or Mark 3). Strain and reserve the broth.

Making a Beet Liquor

Peel raw beetroots and grate them into a large pot (*above*). For 5 or 6 beetroots, add 2 litres (4 pints) of warm water and, to encourage fermentation, stale rye bread and a teaspoon of sugar. Cover with muslin and leave in a cool room for 3 to 4 days, then strain: the ferment is ready but will keep in a corked bottle in the refrigerator for several weeks.

5 **Assembling the borscht.** Bring the liquid to a simmer over a medium heat and cook the cabbage until it is just tender—about 10 minutes. Add the cooked beetroot strips (*above*), and reduce the heat to the barest simmer to warm the ingredients through.

3 **Baking the beetroots.** While the meats simmer, lightly scrub and then rinse the beetroots; do not peel or pierce them. Put the beetroots in a baking dish, cover it with aluminium foil and place it in a cool oven, preheated to 150°C (300°F or Mark 2). Bake for 3 to 3½ hours, depending on the beetroots' size. When they cool, peel them with a small, sharp knife (*above*), and cut into thick strips.

4 **Preparing the cabbage.** Pull off the leaves of a white cabbage. Cut out the tough ribs, then roll up and slice the leaves into narrow strips and put them in a large cooking pan. Cover the cabbage with the strained meat broth (*above, left*) and then about ½ litre (18 fl oz) of the strained beetroot ferment (*above, right*).

6 **Serving.** Take the meats from the casserole. Cut them into slices, removing any bones (*above*), and arrange the meats on a large, warmed platter. Serve the borscht from a warmed tureen, accompanied by the meats and other side dishes—here, *pirozhki* and *kasha*. Place a spoonful of *kasha* in each soup plate and ladle the borscht over it (*right*). Garnish the soup with a dollop of soured cream and a sprinkling of chopped dill or parsley.□

A Refreshing Way with Leftover Borscht

Strained, cleansed of any fat and chilled, a borscht (*page 84*) makes a refreshing dish for a summer luncheon. For a more elaborate presentation, you can pour the soup over a cluster of ice cubes, made by freezing a handful of individual cubes inside a plastic bag. Surround the ice with an array of mixed, chopped vegetables: raw sweet peppers, onions, spring onions, cucumber, celery, olives or freshly cooked, chilled beetroot. Scatter chopped fresh herbs, such as parsley, chives or dill, over each bowl of soup.

Soured cream is a traditional enrichment for borscht. For a marbled effect, gently stir a little cream into each person's bowl. If you prefer a uniform pink colour, whisk the cream and the soup together before serving (*Step 2, right*).

1 **Chilling the borscht.** Strain the borscht through a sieve into a large container and chill in a refrigerator. As the soup cools, it will gel slightly and develop a film of surface fat. Blot the surface with a paper towel to lift off the fat (*above*).

2 **Mixing in soured cream.** Spoon soured cream into a chilled tureen. Stir the cream well with a whisk to thin it slightly. Add the borscht, a ladleful at a time, stirring with the whisk as you pour to blend it thoroughly with the cream (*above*).

3 **Serving the borscht.** In the soup plates, arrange the vegetables—here, chopped red and green sweet peppers, spring onion and cucumber. At the centre of each plate, put a cluster of ice cubes, frozen together. Pour the borscht over the ice (*left*) and sprinkle each serving with chopped, fresh dill or other herbs.□

Anthology of Recipes

Drawing upon the cooking literature and culinary traditions of more than 20 different countries, the Editors and consultants for this volume have selected 215 published soup recipes for the Anthology that follows. The selections range from the simple to the sophisticated—from fresh vegetable soups to a luxurious crayfish bisque. The Anthology spans more than three centuries and includes recipes by 112 writers, many of them distinguished experts of the culinary art. Masters of the classic cuisine of France are included from La Varenne and Carême to today's noted chefs. Traditional household cookery is represented by recipes from such authors as Eliza Acton, Fannie Farmer and Madame St Ange. But there are also recipes by little-known authors of now rare and out-of-print books held in private collections. A number of the recipes have never been published in the English language before. Whatever the sources, the emphasis of the recipes is on authentic dishes meticulously prepared with fresh, natural ingredients.

Since many early recipe writers did not specify amounts of ingredients, the missing information has been judiciously included; and, where appropriate, introductory notes—printed in italics—have been added. Modern terms have been substituted for archaic language, but to preserve the character of the original recipes, and to create a true anthology, the authors' texts have been changed as little as possible. Some instructions have necessarily been expanded, but in any circumstance where cooking directions still seem somewhat abrupt, the reader need only to refer to the appropriate demonstration in the front of the book to find the technique explained. Cooking terms and ingredients that may be unfamiliar are explained in the combined Index and Glossary at the end of the book.

For ease of use, the Anthology is organized by type of soup, in the same way as the first half of the book. Recipes for standard preparations—basic broths, garnishes and sauces—appear at the end of the Anthology. The serving suggestions included in some of the recipes are, of course, optional.

In the ingredients list that begins each recipe, the main or title ingredients of each soup are listed first; the other ingredients are given in order of use. Metric and imperial weights for each ingredient are listed in separate columns. The two sets of figures are not exact equivalents, but are consistent for each recipe. Working from either metric or imperial weights and measures will produce equally good results, but the two systems should not be mixed. All spoon measures are level.

Simple Broths	88
Garnishes	90
Purées	93
Compound Broths	105
Bread Soups	134
Cold Soups	141
Whole Meal Soups	147
Standard Preparations	163

Simple Broths

There are more simple broths in the Standard Preparations section at the end of the anthology.

Consommé

To make about 4 litres (7 pints)

5 litres	water	9 pints
2.5 kg	beef (short ribs, plate, or shin) chicken carcasses and giblets (but not liver), as available	5lb
	salt	
300 g	carrots	10 oz
250 g	turnips	8 oz
1	parsnip	1
5	leeks	5
1	onion, stuck with a clove	1
1	stick celery	1
1	sprig parsley	1

Put the water, meat and salt into a marmite. Bring to the boil and skim, then add the vegetables and parsley. Cover, with the lid ajar, and cook over a low heat for 5 to 6 hours. When done, strain through a colander lined with damp muslin.

LEON ISNARD
LA CUISINE FRANÇAISE ET AFRICAINE

Swedish Beer Soup

Schwedische Biersuppe

To serve 4

¾ litre	beer	1½ pints
1	cinnamon stick	1
2 tbsp	flour	2 tbsp
4 tbsp	cold water	4 tbsp
3	egg yolks	3
3 tbsp	sugar	3 tbsp
¼ litre	milk, heated to boiling	8 fl oz

First bring the beer to the boil with the cinnamon. Mix the flour with the cold water and stir this into the beer. Bring the soup back to the boil. Meanwhile beat the egg yolks and sugar until light and frothy, and pour on the boiling milk, beating with a whisk. Remove the soup from the heat, remove the cinnamon stick, and add the egg mixture to the soup, beating vigorously. Serve immediately.

GRETE WILLINSKY
KOCHBUCH DER BÜCHERGILDE

Boiled Water

L'Aïgo Boulido

This Provençal infusion has extraordinary virtues. Nothing can resist it: hangover, illness, childbirth—there can be no convalescence without "boiled water". The proverb says: *Aïgo boulido sauova la vida.* Boiled water saves your life.

To serve 4

1 litre	water	2 pints
	salt	
12 to 15	garlic cloves	12 to 15
1 or 2	bay leaves	1 or 2
1 or 2	sprigs sage	1 or 2
4 tbsp	olive oil	4 tbsp
	slices dry bread	
	grated cheese (Gruyère or Parmesan)	

In a saucepan, salt the water, add the garlic, and bring to the boil. After 10 minutes, add the bay, sage and a dash of oil. Let cook a few minutes more, then take the pan off the heat, cover, and allow the soup to stand for about 10 minutes. Strain. Put the bread slices into a warmed soup tureen, cover with grated cheese, sprinkle with the remaining oil, and pour over the strained infusion.

JOSÉPHINE BESSON
LA MÈRE BESSON "MA CUISINE PROVENÇALE"

Japanese Soup Broth

Dashi

The so-called *dashi* broth is the basis of almost all Japanese soups, as well as of most casseroles, stews, sauces and so forth. Although its preparation is unfamiliar to Western housewives, *dashi* is easy and quick to make once the ingredients are purchased. They can be bought at any shop dealing in Japanese foodstuffs. You will probably be shown two types of bonito fillet (***katsuobushi***): one resembling a block of dried wood, the other ready shaved and packaged, called ***hanagatsuo.*** By all means use the packaged variety—shaving a dried bonito fillet is a lengthy job requiring a special tool.

To serve 6

1.5 litres	water	3 pints
15 g	kelp seaweed (*kombu*)	½ oz
15 g	dried bonito fillet (*katsuobushi*), shaved	½ oz

Bring the water to the boil and add the seaweed. Stir it around in the water for 3 to 4 minutes in order to release its flavour. Remove the seaweed and add the bonito shavings. Bring the water to the boil again, then immediately remove the pan from the fire. Allow the shavings to settle to the bottom; this takes only 2 or 3 minutes. Strain, and the broth is ready to use.

PETER AND JOAN MARTIN
JAPANESE COOKING

Brown Rabbit Soup

This clear broth was no doubt originally intended to be made with wild rabbits. By the end of the long cooking time, the flavour of the rabbits will have been completely extracted, and the meat should be discarded.

To serve 10 to 12

2	large (or 3 small) rabbits, skinned and cut into joints	2
100 g	butter	3½ oz
3	medium-sized onions, chopped	3
90 g	flour	3 oz
4 litres	water	7 pints
	salt	
1	bunch of parsley, tied together	1
4	small carrots	4
½ tsp	peppercorns	½ tsp
	croûtons	

Melt the butter in a large saucepan. Add the onions and fry them to a clear brown. Remove the onions from the pan. Toss the rabbit joints in the flour, and lightly fry them in the butter. Return the onions to the pan. Bring the water to the boil and gradually pour it into the pan, throw in the salt, and clear off all the scum with care as it rises. Then put into the soup the parsley, carrots and peppercorns. Cover and simmer very gently for 5 to 5½ hours. Add more salt if needed, strain off the soup and let it cool sufficiently for the fat to be skimmed clean from it. Heat it afresh, and serve with the croûtons.

ELIZA ACTON
MODERN COOKERY

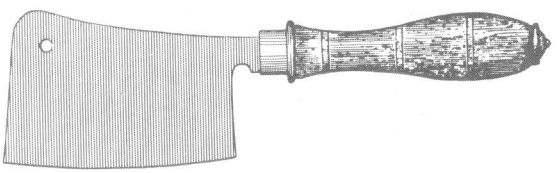

Rapid Broth

Bouillon d'une Heure

This is a good standby recipe for occasions when you need broth, but do not have time to make the classic version. The broth is coloured with caramel, which does not affect the taste or consistency. To make caramel, melt sugar slowly in a saucepan until it is amber-coloured. Pour in a glassful of water and let it boil for several minutes or until dissolved. The caramel can be kept in a small bottle, with a channel cut in the side of the cork so that it can be poured out drop by drop.

To serve 4

500 g	lean beef, fat and connective tissue removed, chopped	1 lb
1	carrot, chopped	1
1	leek, white part only, chopped	1
1	stick celery, chopped	1
	salt	
1 litre	water	2 pints
	caramel	

Put the meat, vegetables and seasoning in a saucepan, add the water, and bring to the boil, stirring continuously. Cover the pan, with the lid ajar, and leave to cook very slowly for 1 hour, over a fireproof mat if possible. Strain the broth through a fine sieve lined with damp muslin. Add a few drops of caramel to give the broth the colour of a pale gold coin.

ÉDOUARD NIGNON
LES PLAISIRS DE LA TABLE

Garnishes

Ravioli with Ricotta and Spinach

Ravioli con Ricotta e Spinaci

This stuffing, suitable for many kinds of stuffed pasta, may be varied almost endlessly. The spinach, for example, may be replaced by chard; or supplemented by leftover cooked meat, finely chopped; by sautéed chopped onion; by poached brains. More egg yolks or whole eggs may be used to moisten the meat. For stuffing and cooking the pasta, see the demonstration on page 17. The recipe for pasta dough is on page 165.

To serve 12

200 g	*ricotta*	½ lb
500 g	spinach, parboiled, drained, squeezed, and finely chopped	1 lb
30 g	butter	1 oz
3	egg yolks	3
	salt and pepper	
75 g	grated Parmesan cheese	3 oz

Pass the spinach through a sieve, then sauté it very briefly in the butter. Place the spinach in a mixing bowl and allow it to cool. Pass the *ricotta* through a sieve into the bowl. Add the egg yolks and cheese, and season with salt and a little pepper. Use the mixture to stuff small rounds of pasta dough.

ENRICA AND VERNON JARRATT
THE COMPLETE BOOK OF PASTA

Buckwheat

Kasha

This baked buckwheat is traditionally served with borscht, consommé, or cabbage soup.

To serve 6 to 8

500 g	buckwheat	1 lb
1 tsp	salt	1 tsp
30 g	butter	1 oz
About 1 litre	boiling water	About 2 pints

Put the buckwheat grains in a frying pan, without any fat or liquid, and roast over a medium heat, stirring, until the grains acquire a light golden colour. Put the buckwheat into a baking dish, season with salt, add the butter, and pour on just enough boiling water to cover. Bake, uncovered, in a slow oven preheated to 150°C (300°F or Mark 2) for 2½ to 3 hours, adding more water as necessary. The buckwheat should have a thin crust on top but the grains should fall apart easily.

NINA AND GEORGE FROUD
THE HOME BOOK OF RUSSIAN COOKING

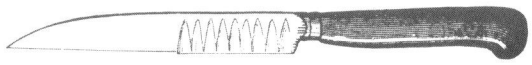

Little Russian Meat Pies

Pirozhki

Traditionally, *pirozhki* are served with soup in Russian cooking. They may have a meat filling, or a mixture of sautéed mushrooms, eggs, and onions, or one of browned onions and chopped cabbage. They can be made with any kind of dough, from puff paste to yeast dough.

To make 12 to 15 pies

Soured-cream dough

175 g	flour	6 oz
1 tsp	salt	1 tsp
60 g	butter	2 oz
4 to 6 tbsp	soured cream	4 to 6 tbsp
	beaten egg or milk	

Meat filling

15 g	onion, minced	½ oz
15 g	butter	½ oz
250 g	cooked meat or chicken, minced	8 oz
60 g	mushrooms, minced	2 oz
1	egg, hard-boiled and minced	1
¼ tsp	Worcestershire sauce	¼ tsp
1 tsp	chopped dill or parsley, or dill seed	1 tsp
	salt and pepper	
	broth (optional)	

For the filling, sauté the onion in the butter until soft. Add the remaining ingredients and cook for 5 to 10 minutes over low heat. If too dry, add 1 to 2 tablespoons broth. Cool before using.

For the pastry, sift the flour and salt together. Cut in the butter with a pastry cutter or two knives, leaving the mixture in coarse lumps. Add the soured cream, a little at a time, just enough to hold the dough together. Roll out the dough and fold it in three thicknesses. Chill for at least 1 hour.

Roll the dough out as thinly as possible. With a round cutter or the floured rim of a glass, cut out rounds 7.5 to 10 cm (3 to 4 inches) in diameter. Put 1 to 2 teaspoons of filling on each round. Fold over and pinch edges together carefully, so that the filling will not ooze out during baking. Paint with beaten egg or milk. Place on a greased baking sheet. Bake in an oven preheated to 220°C (425°F or Mark 7) for 15 to 20 minutes, or until golden-brown. Serve hot or cold.

NIKA STANDEN HAZELTON
THE CONTINENTAL FLAVOUR

Egg Balls

To serve 4

2	eggs, hard-boiled and rubbed through a sieve	2
1	egg yolk	1
1 tbsp	fresh breadcrumbs	1 tbsp
	salt and pepper	

Add the egg yolk to the sieved eggs, breadcrumbs and seasoning. With floured hands roll the mixture into tiny balls. Drop them into boiling soup, then simmer, covered, for 5 to 10 minutes. Alternatively, the egg balls can be cooked in boiling salted water, then added to soup just before serving.

FLORENCE GREENBERG
JEWISH COOKERY

Bread Balls

To serve 4

2	thick slices day-old bread, soaked in cold water	2
1 tbsp	finely chopped onion	1 tbsp
1 tbsp	rendered chicken fat	1 tbsp
2 tsp	finely chopped parsley	2 tsp
½	lemon, rind grated	½
	mixed herbs (optional)	
	salt and pepper	
1	egg, beaten	1
	fresh breadcrumbs	

Drain the soaked bread, squeeze it very dry and mash it in a bowl with a fork. Fry the onion in the fat until golden-brown, then add it to the soaked bread, together with the parsley, lemon rind and, if liked, a pinch of mixed herbs. Season with salt and pepper, add the beaten egg and sufficient breadcrumbs to absorb any excess moisture. Roll the mixture into tiny balls, drop them into boiling soup—any clear broth—and simmer, covered, for 15 to 20 minutes.

FLORENCE GREENBERG
JEWISH COOKERY

Brain Dumplings

To make 12 dumplings

100 g	brains, rubbed through a sieve	3½ oz
1	bread roll, soaked in 15 cl (¼ pint) milk and squeezed dry	1
50 g	breadcrumbs	2 oz
1	egg, beaten	1
1	egg yolk, beaten	1
1 tsp	salt	1 tsp
	pepper and marjoram	
2 tbsp	finely chopped parsley	2 tbsp

Mix the brains in a bowl until smooth, then add the soaked roll, breadcrumbs, egg and egg yolk, salt, pepper, marjoram and parsley. Mix well, form into balls and poach, covered, in salted water for 10 minutes; serve in clear meat soup.

JOZSEF VENESZ
HUNGARIAN CUISINE

Potato Dumplings

Burgonyagombóc

To make 20 to 25 dumplings

250 g	potatoes, cooked and mashed	8 oz
1 tbsp	semolina	1 tbsp
2 tsp	finely chopped onion	2 tsp
30 g	bacon dripping or butter	1 oz
1½ tsp	chopped parsley	1½ tsp
	salt and pepper	
½	beaten egg	½
1 to 2 tbsp	flour	1 to 2 tbsp

Mix the mashed potatoes with the semolina. Stew the onion for 5 to 10 minutes in the dripping or butter, and add to the potato mixture. Add the parsley and season with salt and pepper. Mix in the egg, and gradually add enough flour to make a soft, but cohesive, dough. Form small dumplings from the mixture and cook for 7 to 10 minutes in simmering salted water or broth.

FRED MACNICOL
HUNGARIAN COOKERY

Liver Dumplings

To make 12 dumplings

150 g	pig's or calf's liver, minced	5 oz
1	small onion, finely chopped	1
40 g	lard	1½ oz
1	bread roll, soaked in water and squeezed dry	1
	salt	
	freshly ground pepper	
1 tsp	finely chopped fresh marjoram	1 tsb
1	egg, lightly beaten	1
30 g	fine breadcrumbs	1 oz
40 g	flour	1½ oz
1	sprig parsley, finey chopped	1

Fry the onion in the lard until slightly browned. In a bowl, mix the liver, the bread roll, salt, pepper and marjoram. Add the fried onion, egg, breadcrumbs, flour and parsley and mix well. Roll this mixture into about 12 small balls, and simmer them, covered, in hot soup for 15 to 20 minutes.

JOZSEF VENESZ
HUNGARIAN CUISINE

Meat Dumplings

Frikadel'ki iz Govyadiny

Beef, veal or lamb may be used for these dumplings. The meat is chopped and pounded so it need not be a tender cut, but it should be lean, and every trace of fat and gristle should be trimmed off before the meat is chopped.

To serve 6

250 g	beef, veal, or lamb, finely chopped	8 oz
60 g	suet, finely chopped	2 oz
	salt and pepper	
	grated nutmeg	
2 tbsp	finely chopped onion	2 tbsp
60 g	bread, crusts removed, soaked in milk and squeezed	2 oz
2	eggs	2
2 tbsp	double cream	2 tbsp
3 to 4 tbsp	breadcrumbs, toasted	3 to 4 tbsp

In a bowl, mix the meat with the suet, seasonings, onion, bread, eggs and cream. When the ingredients are thoroughly blended, pound the mixture, a little at a time, in a mortar or process it in a liquidizer until perfectly smooth. Form the pounded dumpling mixture into walnut-sized balls, and roll them in the breadcrumbs. Add the dumplings to simmering soup or salted water, and cook for 10 to 15 minutes. If they are cooked in water, drain the dumplings in a slotted spoon and add to the soup just before serving.

ELENA MOLOKHOVETS
PODAROK MOLODÝM KHOZYAÎKAM

Pomeranian Dumpling Soup

Pommersche Kliebensuppe

It used to be a regular custom in Pomerania to eat this soup for breakfast.

To serve 4

1 litre	milk	2 pints
	grated lemon rind	

Dumplings

100 g	flour	3½ oz
2	eggs, beaten	2
2 tsp	sugar	2 tsp
	salt	

Bring the milk to the simmer with the lemon rind. Meanwhile make a thick batter with the flour, eggs, sugar and a pinch of salt, adding a little water if necessary. Pour the mixture through a slotted spoon into the simmering milk. Cook slowly, uncovered, for 5 to 10 minutes. As soon as the dumplings rise to the surface, the soup is ready. Serve hot.

FRITZ BECKER
DAS KOCHBUCH AUS MECKLENBURG, POMMERN UND OSTPREUSSEN

Consommé with Threads of Egg

Consommé aux Oeufs Filés

To serve 8

2 litres	consommé (*page 88*)	4 pints
3	eggs	3
1 tbsp	flour	1 tbsp
	salt and nutmeg	

Bring the consommé to the boil. Beat the eggs with the flour, and season with salt and nutmeg; turn the mixture into a cornet made of strong paper with the end cut off. Dribble the egg mixture into the boiling consommé. The egg will set immediately, and the soup should be served straight away.

LÉON ISNARD
LA CUISINE FRANÇAISE ET AFRICAINE

Marrow Dumpling Soup

Markklösschensuppe

For instructions on extracting beef marrow from a marrowbone, see page 18. If you do not have enough marrow to make the quantity of dumplings you wish, the marrow may be stretched by the addition of a little butter. The dumplings may be either cooked directly in the broth, or poached in salted water, drained, and added to the soup at serving time.

To serve 6

About 125 g	beef marrow	About 4 oz
	salt	
	grated nutmeg	
1	egg, lightly beaten in a warmed bowl	1
1 tbsp	chopped parsley	1 tbsp
2 to 3 tbsp	dry breadcrumbs	2 to 3 tbsp
1.5 litres	beef broth (*page 164*), simmering	3 pints

Chop the marrow finely, and sieve it, if necessary, to remove bone fragments. In a bowl, stir the marrow with salt and nutmeg until it is light and creamy. Stirring constantly, add the warmed egg, the parsley, and, gradually, enough breadcrumbs to make a firm dough that is neither dry nor sticky. Form small, round dumplings with the dough and drop them into the simmering broth. Cook for 10 to 12 minutes.

GRETE WILLINSKY
KOCHBUCH DER BÜCHERGILDE

Chicken Soup with Flakes of Egg and Cheese

Stracciatella

To serve 4 to 6

¾ litre	chicken broth (*page 164*)	1½ pints
2	eggs	2
20 g	Parmesan cheese, grated	¾ oz
15 g	parsley, finely chopped	½ oz
	grated nutmeg	
	salt	

In a small bowl, beat the eggs until they are just blended; then mix in the cheese, parsley, nutmeg and salt. Bring the chicken broth to a bubbling boil in a heavy saucepan over a high heat. Pour in the egg mixture, stirring gently and constantly with a whisk, and simmer, still stirring, for 2 to 3 minutes. The egg mixture will form tiny flakes in the broth. Taste for seasoning, then ladle the soup into a warmed tureen or individual soup bowls and serve at once.

THE EDITORS OF TIME-LIFE BOOKS
FOODS OF THE WORLD—THE COOKING OF ITALY

Purées

Raspberry Soup

Potage de Framboises

To serve 4

500 g	raspberries	1 lb
1 litre	milk	2 pints
	salt	

Select a few unblemished raspberries for garnish, and sieve the remainder, adding a little milk to make them pass easily through the sieve or vegetable mill. Bring the remaining milk to the boil, season it with salt, and add the raspberry purée. Stir well, garnish with the reserved raspberries, and serve.

LA VARENNE
LE VRAY CUISINIER FRANÇOIS

Apple Soup

To serve 12

750 g	cooking apples, peeled and cored	1½ lb
3 litres	mutton or beef broth (*page 164*)	5 pints
1 tsp	ground ginger	1 tsp
½ tsp	pepper	½ tsp

Clear the fat from the broth and strain it through a fine sieve into a large saucepan. Bring the broth to the boil, add the apples and stew them down very gently to a smooth pulp; press the whole through a strainer and add the ginger and pepper. Simmer the soup for a couple of minutes, skim, and serve it very hot, accompanied by a dish of boiled rice.

ELIZA ACTON
MODERN COOKERY

Carrot and Orange Soup

To serve 3

350 g	carrots, sliced	12 oz
2	large oranges, juice and 1 pared rind reserved	2
40 g	butter	1½ oz
2	medium-sized onions, sliced	2
¾ litre	stock or broth (*page 163*)	1½ pints
4 tbsp	double cream	4 tbsp
	salt and pepper	

Melt the butter in a saucepan over a low heat and stir in the carrots and onions. Cover the pan and let the vegetables sweat for 5 minutes. Pour in the stock, bring to the boil and simmer, covered, for 15 minutes. Allow to cool slightly and liquidize the vegetables and stock. Pour in the orange juice and blend for a few seconds more. Return the soup to the pan and stir in the cream. Season, and reheat gently without boiling.

Cut the orange rind into thin slivers. Simmer the slivers in water for 5 minutes, then drain them well. Float them on top of the soup just before serving.

GAIL DUFF
FRESH ALL THE YEAR

Carrot Soup

To serve 4

500 g	carrots, thinly sliced	1 lb
40 g	butter	1½ oz
2 tbsp	chopped onion	2 tbsp
1 litre	stock or water	2 pints
3 tbsp	rice, or 250 g (8 oz) stale white bread, crusts removed	3 tbsp
	salt	
1 tsp	sugar	1 tsp
	croûtons	

Gently cook the carrots, together with the onion, in half the butter. When they are tender, add the stock or water and the rice or bread. Season with a pinch of salt and the sugar. Simmer for 20 minutes, then pass the soup through a sieve, adding more stock or water if the purée is too stiff. Reheat with the rest of the butter and serve with golden croûtons.

TERENCE CONRAN AND MARIA KROLL
THE VEGETABLE BOOK

Pea Soup

Potage St. Germain

You will find the flavour and colour of this soup made of dried peas greatly improved if a cup of fresh green peas (or the pods of very young tender peas), which have been cooked until soft and then rubbed through a sieve, are added to the soup after it has beeen strained. We would have this soup the day before or after we had leek and potato soup because it uses up the green part of the leeks that are left.

To serve 6

350 g	split peas, soaked for 1 hour and drained	12 oz
1.5 litres	water, or 1 litre (2 pints) water and ½ litre (1 pint) stock	3 pints
1 tsp	salt	1 tsp
30 g	butter	1 oz
60 g	green streaky bacon, finely chopped	2 oz
1	medium-sized onion, chopped	1
1	medium-sized carrot, chopped	1
2	leeks, green parts only	2
60 g	spinach or lettuce leaves	2 oz
1	bay leaf	1
1	sprig thyme	1
	sugar (optional)	
	croûtons	

Put the peas in a saucepan with 1 litre (2 pints) of the water and the salt. Bring to the boil, skim, cover and cook slowly while preparing the following: melt half the butter in a saucepan, add the bacon and onion and cook until they soften and start to brown. Add the carrot, leeks, spinach or lettuce leaves, bay leaf and thyme and cook for a few minutes. Add this mixture to the peas. Continue cooking for about 1 hour or until the peas are soft. Rub through a sieve, add the remaining water or stock if the soup is very thick, and bring to the boil. Skim and correct the seasoning, adding a little sugar if desired. Add the remaining butter. Serve with croûtons.

LOUIS DIAT
FRENCH COOKING FOR AMERICANS

Fresh Pea Soup

If the peas are particularly young and fresh, water may be preferable to chicken stock as a cooking liquid. The heart of a small lettuce, finely sliced, may replace the onion for added freshness of flavour.

To serve 6

1 kg	fresh peas, shelled	2 to 2½ lb
3	leeks, finely chopped	3
1	onion, finely chopped	1
60 g	butter	2 oz
2 tbsp	flour	2 tbsp
1.5 litres	chicken stock or broth (*page 164*)	3 pints
1	sprig mint	1
	salt and freshly ground black pepper	
¼ litre	double or single cream	8 fl oz

Sauté the leeks and onion in the butter in a heavy saucepan until tender. Sprinkle with the flour and stir to mix.

Stir in the stock, bring to the boil and add the mint and peas. Cook, covered, until the peas are tender, about 15 minutes. Remove the mint.

Purée the mixture through a food mill or in batches in an electric blender. Return to the clean pan. Bring to the boil and add salt and pepper to taste and the cream. Reheat. If too thick, add a little milk. This soup is also delicious chilled.

JEAN HEWITT
THE NEW YORK TIMES NEW ENGLAND HERITAGE COOKBOOK

Broad Bean Soup

Potage aux Fèves de Marais

To serve 6

1.5 kg	broad beans, shelled and skinned	3 lb
2 litres	water	4 pints
2 tsp	salt	2 tsp
	sliced bread	
30 g	sorrel	1 oz
10 g	chervil	⅓ oz
50 g	butter	2 oz

In a saucepan, bring the water to the boil. Toss in the beans and salt, and boil for 10 minutes only. Place the bread in a warmed soup tureen; snip the sorrel and chervil into fine shreds over the bread; add the butter. Strain the liquid into the tureen through a sieve, and press the beans through with a wooden pestle. Check the seasoning and serve immediately.

MME. JEANNE SAVARIN (EDITOR)
LA CUISINE DES FAMILLES

Lettuce Purée

Soupe du Père Tranquille

To serve 2

1	lettuce, shredded	1
¾ litre	broth (*page 163*)	1½ pints
15 g	butter	½ oz
	very thinly sliced stale bread	

Over a low heat, simmer the lettuce in a little of the broth, adding more broth several times to replace the liquid that cooks away. When the lettuce is almost completely reduced to a purée, after 45 minutes to 1 hour, add enough broth to bring the soup to the desired consistency. Simmer the soup for 8 to 10 minutes more. Take out any bits of lettuce that are not completely melted, and add the butter. Put the bread into a warmed tureen, pour in the soup and cover. The soup will be ready to serve in 3 minutes.

B. RENAUDET
LES SECRETS DE LA BONNE TABLE

Jerusalem Artichoke Soup

Minestra di Carciofi di Giudea

To serve 4

6	large Jerusalem artichokes, peeled and sliced into a bowl of water with 1 tbsp lemon juice	6
60 g	butter	2 oz
1	onion, chopped	1
	salt and pepper	
1 litre	milk	2 pints
	single cream	
	chopped chervil	
	fried bread croûtons	

Melt the butter in a saucepan, put in the drained artichokes and the onion, and season lightly with salt and pepper. Cover and simmer gently for 10 minutes. Add the milk and bring to the boil. Simmer gently for a further 10 minutes and pass the soup through the fine disc of a vegetable mill. Return the soup to the saucepan, bring to the boil again and correct the seasoning. Before serving, add a little cream and chervil and the fried croûtons.

JANET ROSS AND MICHAEL WATERFIELD
LEAVES FROM OUR TUSCAN KITCHEN

Cream of Turnips

Crème à la Vierge

This soup is at its best made with new turnips in the spring.

To serve 6

12	turnips, peeled and thickly sliced	12
125 g	butter	4 oz
1.5 litres	milk	3 pints
	salt	
	mixed spice	
	white pepper	
	dry bread, sliced as thinly as possible	

Bring a large pot of water to the boil. Throw in the turnips, cover the pot, and remove from the heat; the water should not boil again. After 5 minutes, drain the turnips and plunge them into cold water, then drain them on a cloth.

Melt half the butter in a saucepan and sauté the turnips without letting them brown; add the milk, season with salt, spice and white pepper, and simmer over a low heat, covered,.

When the turnips are cooked, after about 20 minutes, pass the soup through a fine sieve, working the turnips through with a wooden pestle. If the purée is too thick, dilute it with a little additional boiling milk. Incorporate the remaining butter. From this moment, the soup should be kept very hot but not allowed to boil. Put the bread slices in the bottom of a warmed tureen, and pour in the soup.

B. RENAUDET
LES SECRETS DE LA BONNE TABLE

Mixed Vegetable Purée

Purée Léontine

To serve 6

1 kg	leeks, cut into chunks	2 to 2½ lb
60 g	spinach	2 oz
150 g	shelled green peas	5 oz
60 g	lettuce, shredded	2 oz
10 cl	olive oil	4 fl oz
	salt and pepper	
2 tbsp	lemon juice	2 tbsp
1 litre	water	2 pints
	milk (optional)	
1 tbsp each	chopped parsley, mint and celery	1 tbsp each

Into a thick marmite put the olive oil and when it is warm put in the leeks, seasoned with salt, pepper and the lemon juice. Simmer slowly for about 20 minutes. Now add the spinach, the peas, and the lettuce; stir for a minute or two, and add the water. Cook until all the vegetables are soft—about 10 minutes—then press the whole mixture through a sieve. If the purée is too thick, add a little milk, and before serving stir in the chopped parsley, mint and celery. This soup turns out an appetizing pale green.

ELIZABETH DAVID
A BOOK OF MEDITERRANEAN FOOD

Pumpkin Blossom Soup

Sopa de Flor de Calabaza

Epazote, *a herb native to Mexico, is sold dried in speciality shops under the name of* pazote.

To serve 6

40	large pumpkin flowers, stems and sepals removed, chopped	40
1 litre	well-seasoned chicken broth (*page 164*)	2 pints
2	tomatoes, grilled and skinned	2
½	small onion, chopped	½
45 g	butter	1½ oz
1	sprig *epazote*	1

Put the flowers in a saucepan with the broth and cook until tender, about 15 minutes. Transfer to a liquidizer and blend until smooth, then return to the pan. Put the tomatoes and the onion in the liquidizer and blend to a smooth purée. In a small frying pan, melt the butter and cook the tomato purée over a high heat for 5 minutes, stirring. Add it to the broth and cook over a medium heat for about 10 minutes. At the last moment, add a sprig of *epazote* to flavour the soup.

DIANA KENNEDY
THE CUISINES OF MEXICO

Chestnut Soup

To serve 8 to 10

1 kg	chestnuts, slit, parboiled, peeled, and skinned	2 to 2½ lb
3 litres	good stock or broth (*page 164*)	5½ pints
½ litre	double cream	1 pint
	salt	
	cayenne pepper	
4	lumps sugar	4

Put the chestnuts into a stew-pan, cover them with a little of the stock, and let them simmer slowly until quite soft, about 40 minutes. Then pound them smooth in a mortar, and press them through a fine sieve into the stew-pan; add to them very gradually, and stirring all the time, the remaining stock, the cream, a little salt and cayenne pepper, and the sugar. Boil the soup once, constantly stirring it, and serve it up very hot.

MARY JEWRY (EDITOR)
WARNE'S MODEL COOKERY AND HOUSEKEEPING BOOK

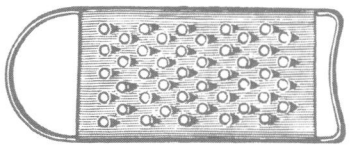

Black Bean Soup

This recipe is adapted from one used by the very fine Coach House restaurant in New York City.

To serve 10 to 12

500 g	dried black beans, washed, soaked in water overnight and drained	1 lb
2.5 litres	cold water	5 pints
1½	sticks celery, chopped	1½
1½	large onions, chopped	1½
60 g	butter or bacon fat	2 oz
1¼ tbsps	flour	1¼ tbsps
30 g	parsley, chopped	1 oz
	rind and bone of a smoked ham	
1½	leeks, trimmed and sliced	1½
1	bay leaf	1
2 tsp	salt	2 tsp
½ tsp	pepper	½ tsp
10 cl	Madeira	4 fl oz
2	eggs, hard-boiled and chopped	2
	lemon slices	

In a deep pot, combine the beans and water. Cook, covered, over a low heat for 1½ hours.

In a soup pot, sauté the celery and onion in the butter or bacon fat over a low heat until they are tender. Remove from the heat and blend in the flour and parsley. Return to a low heat for a few minutes, stirring constantly. Gradually stir in the beans and their liquid. Add the ham rind and bone, the leeks, bay leaf, salt and pepper. Simmer, covered, for 4 hours.

Discard the ham rind and bone and the bay leaf. Force the beans through a sieve, or purée them in a blender. Combine the puréed beans, their broth and the Madeira. Reheat the soup and remove from the stove. Stir in the chopped eggs, and add a thin slice of lemon to each serving.

PAULA PECK
PAULA PECK'S ART OF GOOD COOKING

Red Pottage

Lentils may be substituted for haricot beans in this recipe.

To serve 6

250 g	dried haricot beans, rinsed and soaked overnight in water	8 oz
30 g	butter	1 oz
1	medium-sized onion, sliced	1
1	stick celery or small parsnip, sliced	1
1	small cooked beetroot, thickly sliced	1
4	medium-sized tomatoes, sliced	4
2 litres	stock or water	4 pints
	salt and pepper	
1 tbsp	finely chopped mint	1 tbsp

Drain the beans well. Melt the butter in a large, heavy saucepan, add the beans and fresh vegetables and fry gently for 5 minutes, stirring occasionally. Add the stock or water, and season. Bring to the boil, skimming if necessary, and simmer gently for 3 hours or longer. Remove and discard the beetroot, and pass all the rest through a sieve. Reheat and serve the soup garnished with the chopped mint.

F. MARIAN McNEILL
THE SCOTS KITCHEN

Pumpkin Soup

Soupe des Maures

To serve 6 to 8

250 g	pumpkin, peeled, seeded and diced	8 oz
30 g	butter	1 oz
1	large onion, finely chopped	1
2 litres	beef or pot au feu broth, or haricot bean cooking liquid	4 pints
150 g	cooked white haricot beans	5 oz
100 g	thick vermicelli	3½ oz

Melt the butter in a large pan and lightly brown the onion. Pour in half the broth and add the pumpkin and the beans. Simmer, covered, for about 25 minutes or until the pumpkin is tender. Put the soup through a fine sieve, and thin down the resulting purée with the rest of the broth. Bring to the boil. Add the vermicelli and cook at a light boil for 12 minutes or until the pasta is *al dente*. Serve.

70 MÉDECINS DE FRANCE
LE TRÉSOR DE LA CUISINE DU BASSIN MÉDITERRANÉEN

Apricot and Vegetable Marrow Soup

To serve 4

500 g	apricots, stoned	1 lb
500 g	vegetable marrow, peeled and seeded	1 lb
1 tbsp	tapioca	1 tbsp
1 litre	water	2 pints
	sugar	
2 tbsp	lemon juice	2 tbsp
1 tbsp	brandy	1 tbsp

Put the apricots, marrow, tapioca and water in a saucepan and simmer, covered, for up to 30 minutes or until quite soft. Pass the soup through a sieve, and sweeten the resulting purée with sugar to taste. Flavour with lemon juice and brandy and serve hot.

MRS. C. F. LEYEL AND MISS OLGA HARTLEY
THE GENTLE ART OF COOKERY

Vegetable Broth

Bouillon de Légumes

To serve 8 to 10

250 g	carrots	8 oz
60 g	turnip or swede	2 oz
60 g	barley	2 oz
30 g	haricot beans, soaked overnight in water if dried	1 oz
	salt	
3	leeks	3
1	onion, stuck with a clove	1
1	bouquet garni	1
1	stick celery	1
100 g	potatoes	3½ oz
3.5 litres	water	6 pints
60 g	butter	2 oz

Put all the vegetables and seasonings together into the water, and simmer very slowly for several hours. At serving time, remove the bouquet garni from the broth, crush the vegetables through a sieve and add the butter.

SUZANNE ROBAGLIA
MARGARIDOU: JOURNAL ET RECETTES
D'UNE CUISINIÈRE AU PAYS D'AUVERGNE

Tomato Soup

Tomatensuppe

This soup can be served with toasted breadcrumbs and with eggs boiled for 5 to 6 minutes and shelled. If you choose this garnish, the rice should be omitted.

To serve 4 to 6

1 kg	ripe tomatoes, cut up	2 to 2½ lb
1	onion, sliced	1
30 g	butter or 2 tbsp oil	1 oz
1 litre	boiling water	2 pints
	salt and pepper	
½ tsp	thyme	½ tsp
3 tbsp	rice, washed	3 tbsp
30 g	butter (optional)	1 oz
	finely chopped parsley (optional)	

Cook the tomatoes and onion in the butter or oil until soft, pass them through a fine sieve into another saucepan and add the boiling water. Season with salt, pepper, and thyme, add the rice, and simmer for 20 minutes. The soup is improved by adding the extra butter and parsley just before serving.

GRETE WILLINSKY
KOCHBUCH DER BÜCHERGILDE

Cream of Tomato Soup

Crème de Tomate

To serve 4 to 6

750 g	tomatoes, roughly chopped	1½ lb
30 g	butter	1 oz
1	onion, chopped	1
1	carrot, chopped	1
3 tbsp	flour	3 tbsp
1 litre	chicken stock (*page 164*) or water	2 pints
1	small garlic clove	1
2	leeks, thinly sliced (optional)	2
4	white peppercorns	4
1 tsp	salt	1 tsp
1 tbsp	sugar	1 tbsp
	chicken carcass (optional)	
¼ litre	single cream	8 fl oz

Melt the butter in a deep saucepan, add the onion and carrot, and cook slowly until golden-brown. Add the flour and mix. Add the stock or water, the garlic, leeks (if available), white peppercorns, salt, sugar, tomatoes and chicken carcass (if using). Cover and cook over a low heat for 1 to 1½ hours, skimming as needed. Remove the chicken carcass, and rub the soup through a fine strainer. Combine the strained soup with the cream, and correct the seasoning. If the soup is too thick, add a little more stock or some milk to obtain the desired consistency. Serve with croûtons or with rice.

LOUIS DIAT
FRENCH COOKING FOR AMERICANS

White Soubise

This soothing onion soup comes from a booklet of 1912, sold in aid of the Marlow Cottage Hospital. Its ingredients are simple; but the bread thickening, which gives a slightly grainy texture, is unusual. This is almost a bread sauce soup.

It is an ideal soup to make if you have a solid-fuel or oil-fired stove that is on all the time. The pan can be moved to the edge of the stove for the long, slow cooking, then put on the hotter side that has been protected by the second lid.

To serve 3

500 g	onions, chopped	1 lb
60 g	butter	2 oz
30 cl	light stock or water	½ pint
30 cl	milk	½ pint
60 g	fresh white breadcrumbs	2 oz
	salt and pepper	
	croûtons	

Stew the onions in the butter in a covered pan, without browning them, for an hour. Keep the heat really low, or use a fireproof mat. The idea is that the onions should gently dissolve into a purée. Mix in the stock or water, the milk and the breadcrumbs. Raise the heat and bring just to boiling point. Sieve through the medium plate of a food mill (a liquidizer would make the purée too smooth). Season. Return to the heat to simmer for a further hour; again keep the mixture barely at simmering point. Check from time to time and give the soup a stir up. Add more water if the mixture becomes too thick. Serve with croûtons.

JANE GRIGSON
JANE GRIGSON'S VEGETABLE BOOK

Potato Purée

Potage Santé

To serve 4

250 g	floury potatoes, thickly sliced	8 oz
1	leek, white part only (or 2 small leeks), thinly sliced	1
30 g	butter	1 oz
	salt and pepper	
1 litre	boiling water	2 pints
60 g	sorrel, chopped	2 oz
2	egg yolks	2
15 cl	cream	¼ pint

Put the potatoes into a saucepan with the leek; add half the butter and season with salt and pepper. Cook gently for a few minutes, then add the boiling water. Boil quickly, uncovered, and when the vegetables are cooked—in about 15 minutes—put the soup through a sieve.

Meanwhile, heat the remaining butter and melt in it the sorrel. Add the melted sorrel to the soup, bring to the boil, reduce the heat and let the soup simmer for 5 to 6 minutes, then remove from the heat.

Mix the egg yolks with the cream and stir well into the soup. Serve at once.

X. MARCEL BOULESTIN
THE FINER COOKING

Cream of Mushroom Soup

To serve 4

250 g	mushrooms, chopped	8 oz
30 g	onion, chopped	1 oz
1 litre	stock or broth (*page 163*)	2 pints
60 g	butter	2 oz
30 g	flour	1 oz
¼ litre	single cream	8 fl oz
	salt and pepper	
6 tbsp	Sauternes	6 tbsp

Put the mushrooms and onion into the stock and simmer for 20 minutes; pass through a sieve. Put the purée back on the fire. Work the butter and flour together to make a paste, and whisk this into the soup to thicken it. Season with pepper and salt and stir in the cream. Add the wine at the last moment.

MRS. C. F. LEYEL AND MISS OLGA HARTLEY
THE GENTLE ART OF COOKERY

Spring Vegetable Soup

Potage Printannié en Maigre

Purslane is a wild salad green with a small, round leaf. It grows commonly in Europe and America.

To serve 4

500 g	new green peas, shelled	1 lb
60 g	chervil, chopped	2 oz
100 g	purslane, chopped	3½ oz
1	lettuce, halved, cored and shredded	1
250 g	sorrel, shredded	8 oz
3 or 4	onions, thinly sliced	3 or 4
1 tbsp	chopped parsley	1 tbsp
1 litre	water	2 pints
30 g	butter	1 oz
	salt	
	crusts of bread	
6	egg yolks	6

Put everything except the egg yolks and bread together in a pot and simmer, covered, over a medium heat until the vegetables are cooked, about 15 minutes. Press through a fine sieve into a bowl. Add the bread crusts to the cooking pot and pour three-quarters of the purée back over them. Simmer on a very low heat for another 10 minutes or so. Combine the remainder of the broth in a small pan with the egg yolks. Stir the yolk mixture over a low heat until thickened, being careful not to let it boil. At the last moment, stir the yolk mixture into the soup, check for salt, and serve.

MENON
LA CUISINIÈRE BOURGEOISE

Sorrel and Cream Soup

Potage Germiny

To serve 4

250 g	sorrel, stalks and centre ribs removed	8 oz
¼ litre	cream	8 fl oz
40 g	butter	1½ oz
About 1 litre	consommé (*page 88*)	About 2 pints
4	egg yolks	4
2 tbsp	chervil leaves	2 tbsp
	salt and pepper	

Melt the sorrel in 15 g (½ oz) of the butter, and add the consommé to it; bring to the boil and simmer for 8 to 10 minutes. Beat the egg yolks in a bowl with the cream. Two minutes before serving, add 2 tablespoonfuls of the hot soup, so as to warm the mixture. Then, off the heat, pour the mixture into the saucepan and put the soup over a very low heat: stir well with a ladle. It soon thickens, but be careful that it does not reach boiling point. Finish, away from the heat, by adding the remaining butter. Shake the pan gently till the butter has disappeared. Add the chervil. See that the soup is well seasoned, and serve with very small croûtons.

X. MARCEL BOULESTIN
RECIPES OF BOULESTIN

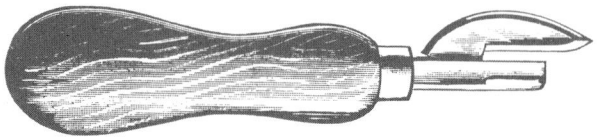

Thick Cream Soups

Potages Veloutés

This kind of soup can include a wide variety of additions. Vegetables such as carrots, celery, cauliflower, beans, pumpkin, mushrooms, or Jerusalem artichokes can be puréed and added, and the soup may be garnished with quenelles or with diced cooked chicken, game, or fish. Fantasy and improvisation can be given a free run. The cooking liquid from vegetables should always be saved for the soup pot, and, if possible, a few of the vegetables themselves should be kept for garnish.

To serve 6

60 g	butter	2 oz
60 g	flour	2 oz
1.5 litres	broth (*pages 163-164*), degreased and heated	3 pints
3	egg yolks	3
10 cl	cream	4 fl oz
	salt and pepper (optional)	

In a large saucepan, make a lightly coloured roux with the butter and flour. Remove it from the heat and dilute it with the warmed broth. Return to the heat and bring to the boil, stirring constantly. Then leave the soup to simmer over a low heat for at least 20 minutes, and preferably double that time, skimming occasionally.

At serving time, remove the soup from the heat. Beat the egg yolks with the cream and beat into the soup. The heat of the soup will cook the yolks. Check the seasoning and pour the soup through a sieve into a tureen. Serve with any garnish you wish, and, if you like, swirl in a bit of additional butter.

MADAME SAINT-ANGE
LA CUISINE DE MADAME SAINT-ANGE

Melon and Potato Soup

Sopa de Apatzingán

This soup is also good iced.

To serve 6

500 g	cantaloupe melon flesh (about ½ a large melon), diced	1 lb
500 g	potatoes, cooked, peeled and diced	1 lb
½ litre	milk	1 pint
60 g	butter	2 oz
	salt and white pepper	
4	egg yolks	4
	soured cream	

Put the melon and potatoes into a liquidizer with half the milk. Blend to a smooth purée.

Melt the butter, add the purée and cook gently for a few moments. Add the remaining milk, the salt and pepper and continue cooking for about 5 minutes over a low heat.

Beat the egg yolks together well until they are creamy and stir them gradually into the soup. Remove the saucepan from the heat as soon as the eggs have been added. After serving the soup, add a little soured cream to each bowl.

DIANA KENNEDY
THE CUISINES OF MEXICO

Spinach Soup

To serve 4 to 6

500 g	spinach, stemmed, washed and chopped	1 lb
30 g	butter	1 oz
1	small onion or shallot, finely chopped	1
1 litre	chicken stock or broth (*page 164*)	2 pints
3	egg yolks	3
2 tbsp	lemon juice	2 tbsp
	salt and pepper	
4 to 6	strips of lemon peel	4 to 6

Melt the butter in a large pan, add the onion and sweat very gently until it is tender, then add the spinach and let it sweat until it has wilted down. Bring the stock to the boil and pour it over the spinach. Allow to simmer for about 7 to 8 minutes until the spinach is completely tender but still green. Pass the mixture through the finest disc of a food mill, or liquidize.

Beat the egg yolks in a separate bowl with the lemon juice and gradually add ¼ litre (8 fl oz) of the hot purée, beating all the time. Return this liquid to the soup and heat very gently, stirring all the time until very slightly thickened. Do not let the soup boil after the eggs have been added. Season, and serve with a strip of lemon peel in each bowl. This soup is delicious chilled and served with a whirl of soured cream.

TERENCE CONRAN AND MARIA KROLL
THE VEGETABLE BOOK

Cream of Asparagus Soup

Crème d'Émeraude

For best results, the asparagus should be peeled and thinly sliced crosswise, then parboiled for no more than 2 to 3 minutes. The pistachios should be parboiled, drained, and rubbed in a towel to remove the skins.

To serve 4

500 g	green asparagus, parboiled and drained	1 lb
300 g	butter	10 oz
3 tbsp	flour	3 tbsp
1 litre	chicken broth (*page 164*)	2 pints
1	stick celery, chopped	1
1	sprig basil	1
	salt	
	cayenne pepper	
100 g	green pistachios, skinned and pounded in a mortar	4 oz
5	egg yolks	5
1 tbsp	lemon juice	1 tbsp

Melt 200 g (7 oz) of the butter in a pan, add the flour to make a roux, and whisk in the broth. Add the celery, basil, salt and cayenne pepper. Simmer slowly for 1 hour, skimming occasionally; a few minutes before the end of the cooking period, add the asparagus and the pistachios.

Purée the soup in a liquidizer, then pass it through a fine sieve into a clean pan. Beat a few tablespoons of the soup into the egg yolks, then stir the yolk mixture back into the soup. Reheat without allowing the soup to boil; off the heat, add the remaining butter and the lemon juice. Serve very hot.

LÉON ISNARD
LA CUISINE FRANÇAISE ET AFRICAINE

Crayfish Bisque

Bisque d'Écrevisses

Originally, a bisque was a purée of crayfish thickened with bread. Today, it is usually, with no improvement, thickened with rice or with flour and it may be fashioned from any crustacean. When cooking with bread, the quality of the bread is of the greatest importance—the best, for most purposes, is a rough, fairly heavy bread comparable to French or Italian peasant bread. It should not be fresh. The French say that it is *rassis*—settled down. In English, you have only the abominable word "stale" to describe the same thing and, for that reason, many cookery books call instead for "day-old bread". Only bad bread is *rassis* when it is 1 day old; good bread should be 1 week old.

To serve 8

30 to 40	live crayfish, washed	30 to 40
1	large onion, finely chopped	1
1	large carrot, finely chopped	1
1	stick celery, finely chopped	1
1	bay leaf, crumbled	1
1 tsp	thyme or mixed herbs (thyme, oregano, savory, marjoram)	1 tsp
4 tbsp	cognac	4 tbsp
40 cl	dry white wine	¾ pint
	salt	
	cayenne pepper	
1.25 litres	fish broth (*page 163*)	2 pints
100 g	crustless white bread, crumbled	3½ oz
15 cl	double cream	¼ pint

First make a *mirepoix*; cook the onion, carrot, celery, thyme and bay leaf in 30 g (1 oz) of the butter, over a low heat for about 15 minutes, stirring all the time, until softened but not coloured. Pour on the cognac and the wine. Increase the heat and add the live crayfish to the pan; the heat will kill them quickly. Season with salt and cayenne pepper. Reduce the heat, cover, and simmer for 8 to 10 minutes. Leave the mixture to cool. When the crayfish are cool enough to handle, remove them from the pan. Twist off the tails and shell them. Cut the tail meat into three pieces crosswise and reserve.

In a mortar, pound the carapaces and all the crayfish debris—heads, claws and tail shells—to a paste, a small portion at a time. Add this paste and the *mirepoix* with the crayfish cooking juices to a pan containing the fish broth. Bring the mixture to the boil and simmer for a few minutes. Then pass the soup through a food mill. Taste for salt—the soup may need to be heightened by a little more cayenne—and return to the saucepan. Add the bread, simmer for a further 10 minutes or so, and pass the soup through a very fine sieve. Stir in the double cream, return the soup to boiling point and serve, garnished with the crayfish tails.

PETITS PROPOS CULINAIRES

Cream of Prawns

Puré de Gambas

To serve 4

24	large uncooked prawns, washed	24
1.5 litres	water	3 pints
20 cl	white wine	7 fl oz
1	onion, very finely chopped	1
3	tomatoes, very finely chopped	3
2	carrots, very finely chopped	2
40 g	butter	1½ oz
3 tbsp	flour	3 tbsp
	fish stock or broth (*page 163*) or water	
	salt, pepper and powdered saffron	
2	egg yolks, beaten	2

Bring the water and wine to the boil, add the prawns and cook for 5 minutes. Take the prawns out of the water, and strain, reserving the liquid. Remove the tails of the prawns and keep. Crush the rest of the prawns—shells and all—in a large mortar into a smooth paste; or pass through a mincer. In a bowl, mix the vegetables with this prawn paste.

Melt the butter in a saucepan, sprinkle in the flour, and add the prawn and vegetable mixture. Fry until golden, then slowly add the water in which the prawns were boiled, stirring gently all the time. Cook for 1 hour, adding fish stock or water from time to time if necessary. Pass the soup through a fine sieve, rubbing the vegetable pulp through. Season to taste with salt, pepper and saffron and add the prawn tails. Beat some of the liquid with the egg yolks, then stir the mixture into the soup, and reheat without boiling.

MARINA PEREYRA DE AZNAR AND NINA FROUD
THE HOME BOOK OF SPANISH COOKERY

Scallop Soup

To serve 6

250 g	shelled scallops	8 oz
1 litre	water	2 pints
15 to 20 cl	dry white wine	6 fl oz
1	shallot, thinly sliced or 1 tbsp thinly sliced spring onion	1
⅛ tsp	powdered saffron	⅛ tsp
⅛ tsp	curry powder	⅛ tsp
¼ tsp	dry mustard	¼ tsp
1½ tsp	salt	1½ tsp
½ tsp	pepper	½ tsp
4 tbsp	double cream	4 tbsp
2 tsp	chopped chives or ½ tsp paprika	2 tsp

In a non-aluminium 2 litre (4 pint) pot put the water, wine, shallot or spring onion, saffron, curry powder, mustard, salt and pepper. Bring the liquid to the boil, cover and simmer for 15 minutes. Add the shelled scallops, cover and simmer for just 5 minutes more.

Purée the contents in a liquidizer, half at a time. The scallops do not purée completely, but remain in tiny pieces. Return the soup to the pot and add the cream; stir thoroughly. Reheat, but do not boil.

When ladling soup from the pot make sure you stir up the bottom to include pieces of scallop which will have collected there. Pour into individual soup bowls, and sprinkle with chives or paprika. Serve quite warm, but not hot.

CAROL CUTLER
THE SIX-MINUTE SOUFFLÉ AND OTHER CULINARY DELIGHTS

Cream of Pumpkin and Shrimp Soup

Potage Crème de Potiron aux Crevettes

To serve 6

1 kg	pumpkin, peeled, seeded and diced	2 to 2½ lb
125 g	peeled shrimps or prawns	4 oz
	salt and pepper	
1	stick celery, cut in pieces	1
¾ litre	boiled milk	1½ pints
½ litre	mild stock or water	1 pint
1 tsp	lemon juice	1 tsp
30 g	butter	1 oz

Season the pumpkin pieces with salt and pepper and put them into a thick saucepan with the celery. Cover them with the boiled milk and the stock or water, and simmer until the pumpkin is quite soft, about 30 minutes. Sieve the mixture; return the purée to a clean pan. Mash or pound in a mortar the shrimps or prawns, adding the lemon juice and diluting with a little of the pumpkin purée. Add this mixture to the soup, simmer gently for 10 minutes or so, and sieve again if the soup is not quite smooth. Taste for seasoning. When reheating, thin with a little more hot milk or stock if necessary. Immediately before serving stir in the butter. Pumpkin is a vegetable which tends to go sour very quickly, so this soup should be used up on the day, or day after, it is made.

ELIZABETH DAVID
FRENCH PROVINCIAL COOKING

Fennel and Almond Fish Soup

To serve 4 to 6

3	whiting, cleaned	3
24	almonds, blanched	24
½	bulb fennel, cut into small strips and blanched	½
2 tsps each	peppercorns and fennel seeds	2 tsps each
½ litre	water	1 pint
½ litre	white wine	1 pint
1	large Spanish onion	1
¼ litre	double cream	8 fl oz
3 to 4 tsp	pastis	3 to 4 tsp
	parsley, chives or dill	

Poach the whiting in the water and wine, with the onion and the peppercorns and fennel seeds. Strain the liquid into a pan and reduce by fast boiling to 90 cl (1½ pints). Put 250 g (8 oz) of the skinned and flaked cooked fish into a liquidizer with some of the stock and the blanched almonds. Blend to a cream, then pass through a fine sieve. Add this purée to the stock remaining in the pan and reheat. Just before serving, stir in the cream, pastis, and blanched fennel.

The soup is as white as snow, so sprinkle each bowl thickly with chopped parsley or chives before serving, or decorate with feathery dill leaves.

MARGARET COSTA
MARGARET COSTA'S FOUR SEASONS COOKERY BOOK

Purée of Chicken Soup

Potage Purée de Volaille à la Reine

This recipe has been extracted from a 16th-century recipe book. Soup *"à la reine"* used to be served every Thursday at the court of the Valois. Queen Marguerite de Valois, it is said, was very fond of it.

To serve 4 to 6

1	whole chicken breast, cut from a slightly under-roasted, still warm chicken, skin removed and meat sliced	1
30 g	bread, crusts removed	1 oz
½ litre	consommé (*page 88*)	1 pint
12	almonds, blanched	12
3	bitter almonds, blanched	3
6	hard-boiled egg yolks	6
30 cl	single cream	½ pint
	salt	

Add the bread to the consommé and bring to the boil a few times. Pound in a mortar the breast of chicken, almonds and egg yolks. When the mixture has been well pounded, add the consommé, with the bread and the cream. Rub the mixture through a sieve, season and keep hot in a bain-marie.

PROSPER MONTAGNÉ
LAROUSSE GASTRONOMIQUE

Puréed Chicken Soup

Potage à la Reine

Strips of lemon peel and hard-boiled egg yolks are often pounded with the chicken meat and almonds to add flavour and consistency. For a richer, thicker soup, stir up to 30 cl (½ pint) of double cream into the purée after it has been sieved.

To serve 4

1	large chicken	1
1 litre	chicken broth (*page 164*)	2 pints
6	almonds, skinned	6
30 g	white bread, crusts removed	1 oz
	croûtons	

Roast the chicken until slightly underdone, about 45 minutes, at 180°C (350°F or Mark 4). Strip the meat from the bones, removing all tendons, gristle, and bits of meat that are too hard or too browned. The skin and carcass of the chicken may be simmered in the broth to add flavour.

In a marble mortar, pound the chicken meat with the almonds until smooth. Soak the bread in the broth, then incorporate it into the pounded chicken. Moisten the pounded mixture with broth, and pass it through a fine sieve.

At serving time, reheat the purée over hot water in a double saucepan, and heat the remaining broth and stir it into the purée. The purée should never boil. Stir the croûtons into the soup just before serving.

JULES BRETEUIL
LE CUISINIER EUROPÉEN

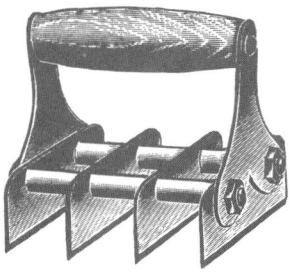

Game Soup

Potage Saint-Hubert

This recipe can be used for any game bird such as a young partridge, a quail, a woodcock, etc.

To serve 6 to 8

1	pheasant, singed and trussed	1
550 g	green lentils	1 lb 2 oz
1.5 litres	water	3 pints
1	onion	1
1	leek, white part only	1
1	sprig thyme	1
1	bay leaf	1
	salt and pepper	
60 g	butter, melted	2 oz
10 cl	double cream	4 fl oz

Rinse the lentils and put them into a saucepan with the water, onion, leek, thyme and bay leaf. Season with salt and cook for 1 hour or until the lentils are very soft.

Season the pheasant with salt and pepper, sprinkle with the melted butter, and roast at 180°C (350°F or Mark 4) for 30 minutes or until slightly underdone.

Cut the pheasant meat off the bones, saving the breast fillets to dice later. Pound the remaining meat in a mortar, strain the lentils, reserving their cooking liquid, and add them to the meat; pound again thoroughly until the mixture is perfectly smooth; rub it through a fine sieve into a saucepan; moisten it with the lentil stock. When quite hot, add the cream, taste to season, and pour the mixture into the tureen where you will have placed the diced pheasant.

J. BERJANE
FRENCH DISHES FOR ENGLISH TABLES

Compound Broths

Potato and Leek Soup

Potage aux Poireaux et Pommes de Terre

Prepared by the method described below, this soup is a compound broth. However, it may also be sieved when the vegetables are tender and served as a purée. Sieved, chilled and with the addition of double cream, the soup becomes a vichyssoise.

To serve 6

500 g	potatoes, quartered lengthwise and finely sliced	1 lb
500 g	leeks, tough green part removed, cleaned and finely sliced	1 lb
2 litres	boiling water	4 pints
	salt	
30 g	unsalted butter	1 oz

Add the vegetables to the salted, boiling water and cook, covered, at a light boil until the potatoes begin to come apart—or, until, when one is pressed against the side of the saucepan with a wooden spoon, it offers no resistance to crushing—about 15 to 20 minutes, depending on the potatoes. Add the butter at the moment of serving.

RICHARD OLNEY
SIMPLE FRENCH FOOD

Leek and Potato Soup

Crème Bonne Femme

To serve 8

4 or 5	leeks, white part only, sliced	4 or 5
1 kg	potatoes, sliced	2 to 2½ lb
50 g	sorrel	2 oz
30 g	butter	1 oz
2 litres	water, lightly salted	4 pints
100 g	very fine vermicelli	3½ oz
¼ litre	double cream	8 fl oz

Melt the butter in a large saucepan, add the sorrel, and cook gently until it melts into a purée. Add the leeks and potatoes and pour in the salted water. Bring to the boil and simmer, covered, for 15 minutes or until the vegetables are half cooked. Add the vermicelli and continue cooking, uncovered, until everything is done. Shortly before serving the soup, stir in the double cream.

CLARISSE OU LA VIEILLE CUISINIÈRE

Creamy Onion Soup

Tourin Bordelais

To serve 6

150 g	onions, finely sliced	5 oz
100 g	butter	3½ oz
3 tbsp	flour	3 tbsp
1.5 litres	milk, heated to simmering	3 pints
	salt and pepper	
3	egg yolks	3
15 cl	double cream	¼ pint
	small rounds French bread, dried in the oven	

In a saucepan, sauté the onions in half of the butter until they are golden but not browned, stirring constantly. Sprinkle on the flour and cook for several more minutes, stirring. Pour on the hot milk. Bring to the boil, season with salt and pepper, and let simmer very gently for 15 minutes. In a bowl, beat the egg yolks with the cream and a ladleful of the hot soup. Take the saucepan off the heat, allow to cool for 5 minutes, and stir in the egg yolk and cream *liaison*, stirring well. Add the remaining butter, put the dried rounds of French bread into a soup tureen, and pour over the soup.

JEAN E. PROGNEAUX
LES SPÉCIALITÉS ET RECETTES GASTRONOMIQUES BORDELAISES ET GIRONDINES

Grated Potato Soup

Sopa de Patata Rallada

To serve 4

500 g	potatoes, finely grated	1 lb
1.5 litres	stock or broth (*pages 163-164*)	3 pints
	salt and pepper	
1	egg, hard-boiled and chopped	1

Bring the stock to the boil, add the potatoes. Cook for 5 or 6 minutes, season to taste and serve with the chopped hard-boiled egg sprinkled on top.

MARINA PEREYRA DE AZNAR AND NINA FROUD
THE HOME BOOK OF SPANISH COOKERY

Green Herb Soup

Potage aux Herbes Maigres

If both sorrel and chervil are unobtainable, use instead spinach and parsley treated in the same fashion, but remember that spinach takes a little longer to cook than sorrel.

To serve 4

100 g	sorrel, stalks removed, finely chopped	3½ oz
2	lettuces, stalks removed, finely chopped	2
30 g	chervil, stalks removed, finely chopped	1 oz
30 g	butter	1 oz
1 litre	hot water	2 pints
	salt and pepper	
2	egg yolks, lightly beaten	2

Cook the sorrel, lettuce and chervil in butter till thoroughly soft and almost melted. Add the hot water, salt and pepper, bring to the boil, and let it simmer for half an hour or so. Just before serving, remove the soup from the heat and bind it by whisking in the egg yolks.

ELVIA AND MAURICE FIRUSKI (EDITORS)
THE BEST OF BOULESTIN

Soup of Green Herbs

Potage aux Herbes dit Hourtète

To serve 4

125 g	spinach, coarsely chopped	4 oz
60 g	celery leaves, chopped	2 oz
30 g	chervil, chopped	1 oz
100 g	sorrel, coarsely chopped	3½ oz
100 g	chard leaves, coarsely chopped	3½ oz
1 litre	water	2 pints
	salt	
1	garlic clove, finely sliced, or 1 small onion, finely sliced	1
	bread, thinly sliced	
	olive oil or butter	
3	egg yolks, lightly beaten	3
4	eggs (optional)	4

Bring the water to the boil and add the chopped green leaves. When the soup returns to the boil, season it with salt, add the garlic or onion, and leave to simmer until the vegetables are cooked—about 15 minutes.

Meanwhile, put the bread into a warmed soup tureen, and either sprinkle the bread with a little olive oil, or add a piece of butter to the soup.

Beat a little of the soup into the egg yolks and cook them a moment over a low heat, stirring with a wooden spoon. When this *liaison* begins to thicken, take it off the heat, stir in a little more broth and pour the *liaison* into the soup. Pour the soup over the bread in the tureen and serve.

Alternatively, when the soup is ready to be poured on to the bread, break 4 fresh eggs into the soup and allow them to poach. With a slotted spoon, transfer the eggs to the tureen and arrange them on the bread. Pour on the soup and serve.

CHARLES DURAND
LE CUISINIER DURAND

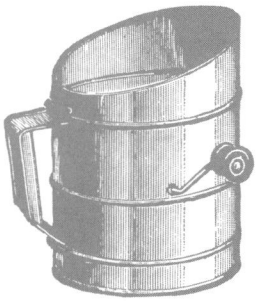

Green Soup with Fish Broth

Potage de Poisson aux Herbes

To serve 6

2	lettuce hearts, roughly chopped	2
15 g	chervil, chopped	½ oz
1	heart celery, finely sliced	1
100 g	sorrel, roughly chopped	3½ oz
1.5 litres	fish broth (*page 163*)	3 pints
3	egg yolks	3
	slices of dry bread	
	olive oil or butter	

Put the broth in a saucepan over high heat. When it comes to the boil, put in the lettuce, chervil, celery and sorrel, lower the heat and cook for about 15 minutes or until the vegetables are done. Put the egg yolks into a small pan and stir in 4 or 5 tablespoons of the hot broth. Cook over a very low heat, stirring with a wooden spoon for a few moments, or until the mixture starts to thicken. Take off the heat, stir in a little more broth, and pour the yolk mixture into the soup. Serve the soup ladled over slices of dry bread. Put a lump of butter in each serving, or sprinkle the bread with a good quality oil before ladling on the soup.

CHARLES DURAND
LE CUISINIER DURAND

Lettuce Soup

To serve 6

4	heads of lettuce, shredded	4
90 g	butter	3 oz
1	medium-sized onion, sliced	1
1	head of celery, finely chopped	1
1	bay leaf	1
6	medium-sized potatoes, sliced	6
1 litre	white stock	2 pints
2	egg yolks	2
2 tbsp	single cream	2 tbsp
	salt and pepper	

Melt 60 g (2 oz) of the butter in a large saucepan. Add the onion, celery, bay leaf and potatoes. Fry lightly for 5 minutes and then add the stock. Cook until the potatoes are just tender, about 15 minutes. Pass all through a fine sieve after removing the bay leaf. Meanwhile melt the rest of the butter in another saucepan, add the lettuce and cook gently for 8 minutes. Pour the strained soup over the lettuce, mixing well. Keep hot. Mix the egg yolks with the cream and strain into the soup, stirring well. Heat gently (without boiling) whilst stirring, for 5 minutes. Season to taste and serve.

IRISH RECIPES TRADITIONAL AND MODERN

Fresh Haricot Bean Soup

Potage de Petits Haricots Verts et Blancs

To serve 4

½ litre	small fresh white haricot beans, cooked in salted water, drained	1 pint
100 g	very small French beans, sliced diagonally, parboiled for 1 minute, drained on a towel	3½ oz
	croûtons, dried in the oven	
1 tsp	chopped chives	1 tsp
½ tsp	sugar	½ tsp
1 litre	boiling consommé (*page 88*)	2 pints

Put both kinds of beans into a warmed soup tureen with the croûtons, the chives and a pinch of sugar; pour the boiling consommé over them and serve immediately.

ANTONIN CARÊME
L'ART DE LA CUISINE FRANÇAISE AU DIX-NEUVIÈME SIÈCLE

Turnip Soup with Green Peas

Potage de Navets aux Petits Pois

To serve 4

6	turnips, peeled and diced	6
½ litre	shelled young peas, blanched until bright green (about 1 minute)	1 pint
30 g	butter	1 oz
1 litre	consommé (*page 88*)	2 pints
	sugar	
	croûtons	

Sweat the turnips in the butter for about 10 minutes or until they are yellowed, stirring constantly with a wooden spoon. Drain the turnips in a strainer. Bring the consommé to the simmer and add the turnips and a pinch of sugar. Continue to simmer, skimming frequently, until the turnips are cooked, about 10 minutes. Put the peas and croûtons into a warmed soup tureen. Pour in the turnips and consommé and serve.

ANTONIN CARÊME
L'ART DE LA CUISINE FRANÇAISE AU DIX-NEUVIÈME SIÈCLE

Cauliflower and Broccoli Soup with Parsley

Potage de Choux-Fleurs et de Brocolis au Persil

To serve 4

1	cauliflower, divided into florets	1
2	heads broccoli, stalks removed, divided into florets	2
1	bouquet of parsley, tied up	1
1 litre	consommé (*page 88*)	2 pints
	croûtons	

Blanch the cauliflower in boiling water for about 5 minutes, then plunge it into cold water and drain. Put it into a pan with a little of the consommé and the parsley, and simmer gently for 10 to 15 minutes, or until tender.

Meanwhile, blanch the broccoli in boiling water for 10 to 15 minutes, or until cooked; drain it and place it in a warmed soup tureen. When the cauliflower is done, remove the parsley and pour the cauliflower with its cooking liquid into the tureen. Bring the remaining consommé to the boil and add it to the tureen with the croûtons.

ANTONIN CARÊME
L'ART DE LA CUISINE FRANÇAISE AU DIX-NEUVIÈME SIÈCLE

Asparagus Soup

Potage aux Pointes de Grosses Asperges

To serve 4

1 kg	thick asparagus, tips only, cut into 2.5cm (1 inch) lengths	2 to 2½ lb
	small croûtons, fried in butter	
1 tbsp	chervil leaves	1 tbsp
¼ tsp	sugar	¼ tsp
	coarsely ground pepper	
1 litre	consommé (*page 88*), heated to boiling	2 pints

Blanch the asparagus in boiling water for 5 to 10 minutes, or until just tender, to give them a lovely spring-like freshness. Drain them on a cloth and put into a warmed soup tureen with the croûtons and the chervil. Add the sugar, grind in a pinch of pepper, then pour in the hot consommé and serve.

ANTONIN CARÊME
L'ART DE LA CUISINE FRANÇAISE AU DIX-NEUVIÈME SIÈCLE

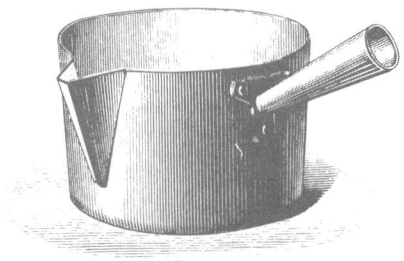

Ham and Winter Melon Soup

Sliced pork may be substituted for ham, but then ½ teaspoon of salt should be added. Old cucumbers can be substituted for winter melon, but take only 8 to 10 minutes to cook.

To serve 4 to 6

500 g	winter melon, peeled, seeded and cut into 1×5 cm (½×2 inch) slices	1 lb
125 g	cooked or uncooked cured ham, skin and any black surface removed, sliced	4 oz
½ litre	water	1 pint
½ litre	chicken broth (*page 164*)	1 pint
1	slice fresh ginger root	1

Cook the sliced melon with the water in a saucepan. Bring to the boil. Boil slowly over a low heat for 20 to 30 minutes until the melon is translucent and tender. Add the ham, chicken broth and ginger root. Cook for another 10 minutes. Remove the ginger root and serve hot.

JOYCE CHEN
JOYCE CHEN COOK BOOK

Spinach and Pork Soup

To serve 8

175 g	spinach, chopped into pieces about 2.5 cm (1 inch) square	6 oz
500 g	lean boneless pork, preferably fillet	1 lb
6 tbsp	light soy sauce	6 tbsp
2 litres	water	4 pints
1 tsp	salt	1 tsp
½ tsp	white pepper	½ tsp
1	2.5 cm (1 inch) piece fresh ginger root, grated, squeezed, juice reserved	1

Marinate the pork in the soy sauce for 1 hour. In a large saucepan, bring the water to the boil and add the pork and its marinade. Cover and simmer until the pork is done, about 40 minutes. Remove the piece of pork, putting it to cool. Add the salt and pepper, and the juice from the ginger root, to the stock in the saucepan. Taste for seasoning and correct if necessary.

Shred the pork by hand, pulling it apart into thin strips about 2.5 cm (1 inch) long. Add the pork to the stock and bring to the boil. Add the spinach and cook for a minute. Serve immediately. This soup may be garnished with a one-egg omelette, fried thin, rolled, and sliced across into strips.

PETER AND JOAN MARTIN
JAPANESE COOKING

Chicken and Cress Soup

Don Far Tong

To serve 6 to 8

1 litre	chicken stock or broth, rich and well seasoned (*page 164*)	2 pints
125 g	watercress leaves	4 oz
3	spring onions, white and tender green part, sliced	3
2	eggs	2
1 tsp	soy sauce	1 tsp

Cook the onions in the stock for 3 minutes. Beat the eggs slightly, just enough to mix, and add to them the soy sauce. Now bring the soup to a merry boil, pour in the egg mixture, and stir, not too vigorously, until the egg sets in long threads. Add the watercress and serve at once from a soup tureen.

HELEN EVANS BROWN
HELEN BROWN'S WEST COAST COOK BOOK

Wild Mushroom Soup

Pilz- oder Schwammerlsuppe

To serve 4

500 g	mixed wild mushrooms (of any edible sort, but including ceps and chanterelles), sliced	1 lb
4	potatoes, thinly sliced	4
1 litre	broth (*pages 163-164*)	2 pints
30 g	lard	1 oz
2	onions, finely chopped	2
	salt and pepper	
4 tbsp	cream	4 tbsp
1 tbsp	finely chopped *fines herbes*	1 tbsp

Boil the potatoes in the broth until soft, then pass the potatoes and broth through a sieve into another saucepan. Sauté the mushrooms in the lard with the onions for about 10 minutes until soft, season with salt and pepper and add the mixture to the purée. Cover the soup and allow it to steep over a very low heat for 10 to 15 minutes, keeping the soup well beneath the simmering point. Before serving, add cream and herbs.

GRETE WILLINSKY
KOCHBUCH DER BÜCHERGILDE

Cabbage Soup with Cream

Soupe aux Choux à la Crème

To serve 6

1	small white cabbage, outer leaves removed, quartered, cored and shredded	1
	soured cream	
60 g	butter	2 oz
250 g	fresh pork sausage	8 oz
1.5 litres	broth (*pages 163-164*) or water	3 pints
	salt	
500 g	potatoes, cut into pieces	1 lb

Plunge the cabbage into boiling water. Boil for 1 minute, then strain off the water. Put the cabbage in a stew-pan, add the butter, pork sausage, and the broth or water. Season with salt. Cover and cook for 1 hour. Add the potatoes and cook for a further 30 minutes. Remove the sausage, cut it into pieces and return it to the pan. The soup will be very thick. Serve the soured cream separately.

ÉDOUARD DE POMIANE
LE CARNET D'ANNA

Mushroom-Barley Soup

To serve 8

150 g	fresh mushrooms, thinly sliced	5 oz
200 g	barley	7 oz
500 g	beef bones, in small pieces if possible	1 lb
1	carrot, sliced	1
2	stalks celery, sliced	2
500 g	chicken backs and necks or wing tips	1 lb
3 litres	water	5½ pints
1 tbsp	salt	1 tbsp
½ tsp	freshly ground pepper	½ tsp
4 tbsp	lard or oil	4 tbsp
175 g	onion, finely chopped	6 oz
2 tbsp	chopped parsley	2 tbsp
2 to 3	dried mushrooms, broken up (optional)	2 to 3

Place the beef bones, carrot, celery, and chicken pieces in a soup pot. Add the water, salt and pepper. Bring to the boil, reduce heat, and simmer for 2 to 3 hours.

In 2 tablespoons of the lard, sauté half the barley until it starts to turn yellow and gives a crackling sound. Add the onion and continue cooking, stirring constantly, until the onion turns limp and glossy.

Melt the remaining lard in another pan and quickly sauté the fresh mushrooms with the parsley. Set aside. Strain the broth through a sieve. Discard the bones and vegetables.

Add to the stock the remaining, uncooked, barley. Add the dried mushrooms, if using, and cook for 30 minutes. Add the sautéed barley-onion mixture and cook for 30 minutes more. Add the mushroom-parsley mixture and simmer for 10 additional minutes. Let the soup stand, covered, for at least 30 minutes before reheating and serving. The sautéed barley will keep its shape; the rest will cook to a pulp, and this will give thickness to the soup.

LOUIS SZATHMARY
THE CHEF'S SECRET COOKBOOK

Sweet and Sour Cabbage Soup

To serve 6

1	small cabbage, cored and finely shredded	1
1.5 litres	stock or broth (*page 163*)	3 pints
15 cl	tomato juice or sieved tomatoes	¼ pint
3	apples, peeled and grated	3
1	onion, grated	1
	salt and pepper	
2 to 3 tbsp	lemon juice	2 to 3 tbsp
	sugar	

Put the stock and the tomato juice in a saucepan and bring to the boil; add the cabbage, apples and onion, cover and cook gently for 30 minutes. Season with salt and pepper, and before serving add the lemon juice and sugar to taste.

FLORENCE GREENBERG
JEWISH COOKERY

Fresh Mushroom and Cabbage Soup

Ch'ing Ts'ai Ma Ku T'ang

Mustard greens, watercress or lettuce may be used instead of Chinese cabbage, and soaked dried mushrooms may be used instead of fresh ones. For a substantial one-dish meal, add 10 to 20 pieces of fried wheat gluten to the soup and adjust the seasoning; or add 60 g (2 oz) of soaked cellophane noodles in addition to the fried wheat gluten, and this dish will become wheat gluten with cellophane noodle soup.

To serve 4

75 g	mushrooms, sliced	2½ oz
150 g	Chinese cabbage, cut into 2.5 cm (1 inch) chunks	5 oz
1 tbsp	groundnut or corn oil	1 tbsp
¾ litre	water	1½ pints
	salt	

Heat a cook-and-serve pot until hot. Add the oil and mushrooms and stir-fry until the mushrooms begin to soften. Add the cabbage and stir-fry for 2 more minutes. Add the water and bring to the boil. Cook, uncovered, for 2 to 3 minutes or until the cabbage is soft. Add salt to taste and serve hot.

FLORENCE LIN
FLORENCE LIN'S CHINESE VEGETARIAN COOKBOOK

Mushroom Vegetable Soup

Julienne aux Champignons

To serve 3 or 4

125 g	mushrooms, cut into *julienne* strips	4 oz
1 or 2	carrots, cut into *julienne* strips	1 or 2
2	turnips, cut into *julienne* strips	2
2	potatoes, cut into *julienne* strips	2
2	leeks, trimmed and cut into *julienne* strips	2
3 or 4	cabbage leaves, cut into *julienne* strips	3 or 4
60 g	butter	2 oz
1 litre	beef or pot au feu broth	2 pints
	croûtons	

Melt the butter in a saucepan over a medium heat; add the prepared vegetables (except the mushrooms) and cook until limp but not coloured. Add the broth, cover the pan, and simmer until the vegetables are thoroughly cooked, about 30 minutes. Ten minutes before serving, add the mushrooms. While the mushrooms are cooking, lightly fry some diced bread in butter; place these croûtons in the bottom of a warmed soup tureen. Pour in the soup and serve.

MME. JEANNE SAVARIN (EDITOR)
LA CUISINE DES FAMILLES

Italian Tomato Soup

Minestra di Pomidoro

To make *crostini*, saturate slices of bread with melted butter, spread them thickly with grated Parmesan and cook them in a moderate oven for 10 minutes. An anchovy fillet may be placed on each slice of bread.

To serve 4

750 g	tomatoes, skinned and chopped	1½ lb
6 tbsp	olive oil	6 tbsp
1	garlic clove, crushed	1
1 tbsp	chopped fresh parsley, basil or marjoram	1 tbsp
½ litre	meat or chicken stock or broth (*page 164*)	1 pint
	salt and pepper	
	sugar	
	crostini (optional)	

Melt the chopped tomatoes in the olive oil; add the garlic and parsley or basil or marjoram. Cook for 5 minutes, then add the stock, salt and pepper, and a pinch of sugar. Cook for 5 minutes more only. By this method the flavour of the tomatoes is retained, and the soup tastes very fresh. In the summer this soup can be eaten iced, accompanied by hot *crostini* of cheese and anchovy.

ELIZABETH DAVID
ITALIAN FOOD

Algerian Tomato Soup

Cherbah

To serve 4

4	tomatoes, skinned, seeded, and cut into large pieces	4
4	onions, cut into large pieces	4
30 g	butter	1 oz
1	large sprig mint, coarsely chopped	1
2 or 3	fresh chili peppers, seeded and finely chopped	2 or 3
	salt and pepper	
1 litre	hot water	2 pints
350 g	shoulder or neck of mutton or lamb	12 oz
125 g	dried apricots	4 oz
60 g	vermicelli	2 oz

In a large saucepan, fry the tomatoes and onions lightly in the butter with the mint and chili peppers. Season with salt and pepper. When slightly browned, add the water, the meat and the apricots; cook slowly, covered, for about 1½ hours. Take out the meat, bone it, cut it into tiny pieces, and return it to the soup. Add the vermicelli and simmer 10 more minutes or until the pasta is cooked; serve.

MRS C. F. LEYEL AND MISS OLGA HARTLEY
THE GENTLE ART OF COOKERY

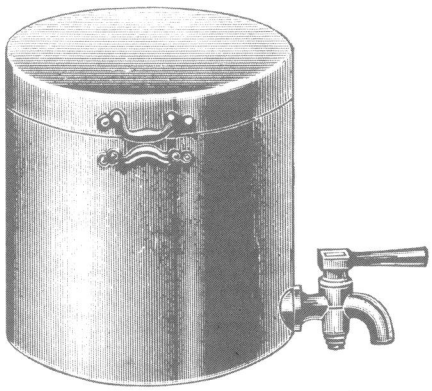

Mixed Vegetable Soup

Il Minestrone alla Milanese

In the summer, this soup may be served cold, topped with the slices of very lean bacon that have been cooked in the soup. Pork rinds may be substituted for the green bacon, and the soup may be enriched by the addition of some Parmesan cheese rinds, just before the end of the cooking time.

To serve 8

100 g	butter	3½ oz
2	small onions, chopped	2
1	leek, chopped	1
100 g	green bacon, blanched and cubed	3½ oz
1	bouquet garni of parsley, bay leaf and rosemary	1
200 g	tomatoes, skinned, seeded and coarsely chopped	7 oz
	salt and freshly ground pepper	
100 g each	potatoes, carrots and courgettes, diced	3½ oz each
100 g each	shelled broad beans and peas	3½ oz each
1	celery heart, finely chopped	1
200 g	fresh haricot beans, or 150 g (5 oz) dried beans, soaked and pre-cooked	7 oz
2 litres	veal or chicken broth (*page 164*)	4 pints
200 g	rice	7 oz
½	medium-sized green cabbage, cored, parboiled and shredded	½
6	basil leaves	6
6	sprigs parsley	6
6	garlic cloves	6
	freshly grated Parmesan cheese	

Melt 40 g (1½ oz) of the butter in a large saucepan and sweat the onions, leek, bacon and bouquet garni, covered, over a low heat for 15 to 20 minutes, without colouring. Discard the bouquet garni, add the chopped tomatoes and season with salt and pepper to taste. Put the remaining butter into another pan and sweat the diced vegetables, the broad beans, peas, celery and haricot beans in the butter for 8 minutes. Add these vegetables to the first saucepan, cook for a few minutes, and pour in the stock. Cover and simmer over a medium heat for 30 to 40 minutes, or until the haricot beans are tender and the vegetables are cooked but not mushy. Raise the heat and add first the rice, then the cabbage. Cook, uncovered, over a medium heat for 15 to 20 minutes. A few minutes before removing from the heat, finely chop the basil, parsley and garlic and add to the soup. Serve with the cheese.

GIANNI BRERA AND LUIGI VERONELLI
LA PACCIADA

Vegetable Soup with Basil and Garlic

Soupe au Pistou

To serve 4 to 6

2	medium-sized leeks, white and tender green parts only, finely sliced crosswise	2
175 g	onion, finely sliced	6 oz
175 g	carrots, quartered lengthwise, woody cores removed if necessary, thinly sliced	6 oz
350 g	potatoes, quartered lengthwise and sliced	12 oz
300 g	pumpkin-type squash, seeded, peeled and coarsely diced	10 oz
500 g	fresh white beans, shelled, or 175 g (6 oz) dried white beans, soaked and cooked	1 lb
1	bouquet garni, including stick celery	1
	salt	
2.5 litres	boiling water	5 pints
175 g	fresh green beans, tips snapped, cut crosswise (a handful at a time) into 1 cm (½ inch) lengths	6 oz
2 or 3	small, firm courgettes, cut into 5 mm (¼ inch) slices	2 or 3
90 g	short macaroni	3 oz

Pistou

4	large garlic cloves	4
60 g	basil leaves and flowers	2 oz
	salt and freshly ground pepper	
About 90 g	freshly grated Parmesan cheese	About 3 oz
1	medium-sized firm ripe tomato, skinned, seeded and cut into pieces	1
About 30 cl	olive oil	About ½ pint

Add the leeks, onion, carrots, potatoes, squash, white beans and bouquet garni to the salted boiling water and cook, covered, over a medium heat for 30 minutes; test the beans for doneness and, if necessary, cook them a bit longer, or until they may be crushed with little resistance while still remaining completely intact. Add the green beans, courgettes and macaroni and cook for about another 15 minutes, depending on the quality of the macaroni (it should be well cooked, but not falling apart) and on the tenderness of the green beans.

While the soup is cooking, prepare the *pistou*. Pound the garlic, basil, salt and pepper to a paste in a good-sized mortar—a 1 litre (2 pint) marble *aïoli* mortar is perfect, but use a wooden bowl if nothing else is available—using a wooden pestle and alternating between pounding and turning with a grinding motion. Work in some of the cheese until you have a very stiff paste, then add about one third of the tomato, pounding and grinding to a paste; more cheese and a bit of the olive oil; more tomato, and so forth, the final addition of cheese bringing the consistency to that of a barely fluid paste. Add the remainder of the olive oil slowly and continuously, turning the pestle all the while. The mixture will not become a genuine emulsion (and should not); *pistou* should be thoroughly mixed each time it is served out.

Serve the soup boiling hot, the mortar of *pistou* at the table. Each guest stirs a small ladleful (about 1 or 2 tablespoons, depending on taste) into his soup.

RICHARD OLNEY
SIMPLE FRENCH FOOD

Rich Country Broth

La Sobronade

To serve 6

750 g	dried white haricot beans, soaked overnight	1½ lb
250 g	ham, diced	8 oz
500 g	streaky pork, diced	1 lb
1	turnip, sliced	1
125 g	pork fat, chopped	4 oz
2 or 3	potatoes, sliced	2 or 3
3 or 4	carrots, sliced	3 or 4
1	stick celery, diced	1
1	large bouquet garni	1
1	onion, stuck with 2 cloves	1
2	garlic cloves, finely chopped	2
2 tbsp	chopped parsley	2 tbsp
	salt and pepper	
1.5 litres	hot water	3 pints
	thinly sliced bread	

Put the beans into a soup pot and cover with water. Add the ham and pork and bring to the boil. Sauté half the turnip in the pork fat until golden. Add to the beans with the remaining turnip, potatoes, carrots, celery, bouquet garni, onion, garlic

and parsley. Season with salt and pepper. Pour in the hot water and return to the boil. Simmer gently, covered, over a low heat for 2½ hours, then pour this thick, very much reduced soup into a tureen over the bread.

LA FRANCE À TABLE

Tuscan Minestrone Country-Style

Minestrone alla Contadina

Tuscan minestrone is usually made in a large quantity so there will be enough left over to make *ribollita* the next day. *Ribollita* means, literally, "reboiled". To make it, leave the minestrone overnight to allow it to thicken even further. Bring it to the boil and cook for about 1 minute. With a wooden spoon, mix well, breaking up the bread slices until the texture is almost homogeneous. Ladle into individual bowls, and pour 2 teaspoons of good olive oil over each serving.

To serve 6 to 8

250 g	dried cannellini beans, or any dried white beans, soaked in cold water overnight	8 oz
	salt	
2 to 3 litres	water, lightly salted	4 to 6 pints
90 g	raw cured ham, or 30 g (1 oz) green bacon and 60 g (2 oz) boiled ham	3 oz
6 tbsp	olive oil	6 tbsp
1	large red onion, coarsely chopped	1
1	stick celery, coarsely chopped	1
2	large garlic cloves, chopped	2
1	carrot, coarsely chopped	1
7 or 8	sprigs flat-leafed parsley, chopped	7 or 8
½	small Savoy cabbage, quartered cored and shredded	½
1 kg	kale, stripped from stems and shredded	2 to 2½ lb
1	potato, diced	1
250 g	tomatoes, skinned	8 oz
500 g	Swiss chard, stripped from stems and shredded	1 lb
	freshly ground pepper	
12	large, thick slices bread, several days old, or 9 to 12 tablespoons croûtons	12
6 to 8 tbsp	freshly grated Parmesan cheese	6 to 8 tbsp

Drain the beans and cook them in a large fireproof casserole with 2 litres (4 pints) of salted water, and the cured ham or the bacon and boiled ham. As the beans cook they will absorb water so more water must be added at frequent intervals; there should be 2 litres (4 pints) of liquid in the casserole at the end of the cooking time. When the beans are tender (after about 1 hour), remove them from the heat and let them stand in their liquid until needed.

Heat the olive oil in a stock-pot and sauté the onion, celery, garlic, carrot and parsley for 12 to 15 minutes. When they are light brown in colour, add the cabbage, kale, potato and tomatoes to the stock-pot. Cover and simmer the broth for 15 minutes, then add the Swiss chard.

Remove the cured ham (or bacon and boiled ham) from the bean casserole and discard. Purée two-thirds of the beans in a food mill and add them to the stock-pot. Simmer for 30 minutes, until the cabbage and kale are almost cooked.

Drain the remaining beans, reserving both them and the broth. Gradually add the bean broth to the stock-pot in which the vegetables are cooking until all is used.

When the cabbage and kale are ready, add the remaining beans to the stock-pot. Taste for salt and pepper, then cook for 5 minutes more.

If you are using bread, put a layer of bread slices on the bottom of a tureen and pour over two full ladles of soup. Add more layers of bread, each time pouring soup over them, until all the bread is used. Pour the remaining soup into the tureen, cover and let it stand for 20 minutes. Serve with a tablespoon of grated Parmesan cheese sprinkled over each portion.

If using croûtons instead of bread slices, allow the soup to stand for 20 minutes before serving, then place 1½ tablespoons croûtons in each individual soup bowl and pour over the soup. Sprinkle with Parmesan cheese and serve.

GIULIANO BUGIALLI
THE FINE ART OF ITALIAN COOKING

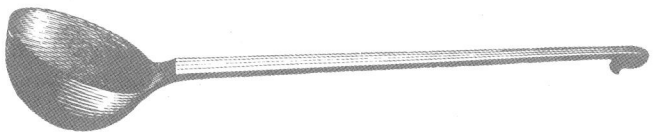

Chestnuts in Milk

Nouzillards

This used to be served as a wintertime supper in the country. The milk can be replaced by a young white wine, sugared.

To serve 4

1 kg	chestnuts	2 to 2½ lb
	salted water	
1 litre	milk	2 pints

Slash the chestnuts and boil them in salted water to cover until they are cooked, about 30 minutes. Drain, shell and skin them. Place them in warmed soup bowls, and pour on the milk, hot or cold. Eat with a spoon.

ROGER LALLEMAND
LA VRAIE CUISINE D'ANJOU ET DE LA TOURAINE

Chestnut and Rice Soup

Minestra di Castagne e Riso

Fontina *is a semi-soft cheese from the Val d'Aosta region of Italy. Gruyère is a suitable substitute.*

	To serve 8	
500 g	dried chestnuts, soaked overnight	1 lb
400 g	rice	14 oz
	salt	
2 litres	water	4 pints
50 g	butter	2 oz
100 g	*fontina* cheese, thinly sliced	3½ oz
	ground cinnamon	

Salt the water and heat it until it is lukewarm. Add the chestnuts and simmer, covered, until they are soft, about 1½ hours. Add the rice and cook until done, about 20 minutes. Add the butter and cheese, taste for salt, and sprinkle the soup with a little cinnamon. Stir well to allow the cheese to melt, then serve.

LAURA GRAS PORTINARI
CUCINA E VINI DEL PIEMONTE E DELLA VALLE D'AOSTA

Thrifty Housewife's Soups

Soupes de la Bonne Ménagère

	To serve 6	
2.5 litres	water	5 pints
	leftover bones from roast meat	
	raw or cooked chicken carcasses	
3	carrots	3
1	turnip	1
1	onion stuck with 2 or 3 cloves	1
	salt	
1	bouquet garni	1
1	cabbage, cored, coarsely shredded	1
2	hearts celery, cut into *julienne* strips	2
2	cabbage leaves, cut into *julienne* strips	2
3 or 4	leeks, cut into *julienne* strips	3 or 4
30 g	butter	1 oz
3 or 4	large waxy potatoes	3 or 4
	sliced bread	

Pour the water into a soup pot and add the bones, carcasses, carrots, turnip, onion, salt and bouquet garni. Cover and simmer very gently for 3 hours. One hour before serving, pour off half the broth and set it aside for the next day. Strain the remainder, add the shredded cabbage and continue simmering gently until it is cooked. Serve this as cabbage soup.

The next day, lightly fry the celery, cabbage and leeks in the butter over a medium heat. When the vegetables are half-cooked and golden, add the reserved broth and the whole potatoes. Simmer until the potatoes are cooked, about 40 minutes, then mash the potatoes into the soup with a wooden pestle or potato masher. Place the slices of bread in a soup tureen and pour in the soup. Serve.

L. E. AUDOT
LA CUISINIÈRE DE LA CAMPAGNE ET DE LA VILLE

Mother Onésime's Soup

Soupe de la Mère Onésime

As hearty as you care to make it, and excellent reheated, this is the traditional hunter's breakfast. It is improved by the addition of bones from roast meat, poultry carcasses, and the cooking juices from meat or vegetables. Lamb bones, pork, duck, and game are welcome. Everything you add must be perfectly fresh, and uncooked bones should be coloured in a hot oven before going into the soup pot.

	To serve 6 to 8	
1 tbsp	pork fat (or lard)	1 tbsp
100 g	carrot, thinly sliced	3½ oz
100 g	turnip, thinly sliced	3½ oz
50 g	leek, white part only, thinly sliced	2 oz
50 g	cabbage, thinly sliced	2 oz
1.5 litres	water or broth (*page 164*)	3 pints
	meat bones or poultry carcasses (optional)	
1	bouquet garni	1
1	sugar lump	1
90 g	fresh white haricot beans	3 oz
75 g	large green peas	2½ oz
50 g	green beans, cut up	2 oz
1 kg	fresh or dried pork sausage	2 to 2½ lb
	salt and pepper	

In a large heavy pot, melt the pork fat or lard, and gently stew the carrot, turnip, leek and cabbage for about 10 minutes, keeping the pan tightly covered. The vegetables should not colour. Add half the liquid, and leftover bones or carcasses if you have them. Bring to the boil over a high heat. Skim if necessary and add the bouquet garni and the sugar. Cover and simmer gently for 45 minutes.

If you have used small or splintery bones, sieve the soup at this point, puréeing the vegetables. Wipe out the pot and return the liquid and the purée to it. Whether or not you have sieved the soup, now add the remaining liquid and the haricot beans, peas, green beans and sausage. Return to the boil, lower the heat, and simmer, covered, for another 45 minutes.

To serve, remove the bouquet garni and the bones. Skim off the fat if you wish. Correct the seasoning. Slice the sausage, and put the slices in the tureen with the soup or serve them separately. Add a grind of fresh pepper to the tureen or to the individual bowls of soup.

MADAME SAINT-ANGE
LA CUISINE DE MADAME SAINT-ANGE

Scotch Broth

Vegetables for flavouring may be included for the first hour of cooking, then discarded and fresh vegetables added for the last 30 minutes, to be served with the soup. A bouquet garni may also be added to the broth; traditionally, this includes fresh or dried marigold petals.

To serve 8

750 g to 1kg	neck or shoulder of mutton or lamb, wiped and trimmed	1½ to 2 lb
2 litres	water	4 pints
60 g	barley, washed and soaked for 2 hours	2 oz
150 g	shelled peas or 60 g (2 oz) dried peas, washed and soaked overnight	5 oz
	salt	
150 g	turnip, diced	5 oz
150 g	carrot, diced	5 oz
1	small onion, chopped	1
1	leek, white part only, chopped	1
250 g	white cabbage, cored and finely shredded	8 oz
	pepper	
1 tbsp	chopped parsley	1 tbsp

Put the mutton into a large saucepan with the water and barley. If you are using dried peas, add them now. Add salt. Bring to the boil and skim. Cover and simmer the broth gently for about 1 hour, then add the remaining vegetables, except the cabbage. Allow to simmer, covered, for at least 2 hours longer. As soon as the mutton is cooked, lift it out of the broth, cut the meat off the bones, and return the meat to the broth. Ten minutes before serving, add the cabbage. Skim off the fat, season the broth to taste, and just before serving add the parsley. Serve very hot.

F. MARIAN MCNEILL
THE SCOTS KITCHEN

Fife Broth

This soup is traditionally served in Scotland with oatcakes.

To serve 6

12 or more	bare ribs of pork, saved from boned-out chops or roasts	12 or more
200 g	barley, soaked overnight	7 oz
	salt and pepper	
2 litres	water	4 pints
1	large onion, finely chopped	1
12	potatoes, sliced	12

Put the pork bones, barley, salt and pepper into a pan with the water. Cover and cook gently for about 2 hours, then add the onion and potatoes. Cook for another 30 minutes and, when ready, remove the bones and serve.

JANET MURRAY
WITH A FINE FEELING FOR FOOD

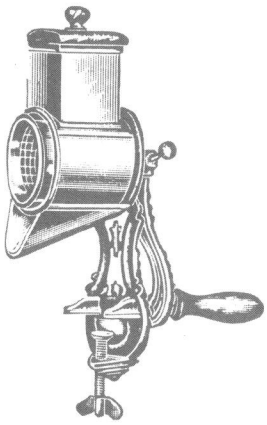

Turkey Soup

To serve 6

1	carcass of cold roast turkey, with any remaining stuffing and gravy	1
About 2 litres	water	About 4 pints
2 tsp	flour, mixed to a paste with water	2 tsp
	salt and pepper	

Place the turkey carcass, stuffing and gravy in a pot and cover with cold water. Simmer gently for 3 to 4 hours, then remove the pot from the heat and let it stand till the next day. Take off all the fat, and strain the liquid to remove the bones. Put the soup on to heat till it boils, then thicken slightly with flour wet up in water, and season to taste. Pick off all the bits of turkey from the bones, put them in the soup, boil up and serve.

OHIO USA HOUSEWIVES COMPANION, 1876

Cockie-Leekie

To serve 8 to 10

2 litres	chicken stock	4 pints
4 to 6	leeks, thinly sliced	4 to 6
30 g	oatmeal	1 oz
10 cl	water	4 fl oz
	salt and pepper	
¼ litre	cream	8 fl oz
2 tbsp	chopped parsley	2 tbsp

Bring the stock to the boil and add the leeks. Blend the oatmeal with the water and add to the stock. Season with salt and pepper, cover and cook until the leeks are tender. Skim if necessary. Put the cream and parsley into a warmed tureen and pour the boiling soup over them.

JANET MURRAY
WITH A FINE FEELING FOR FOOD

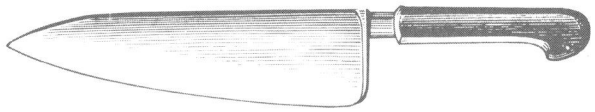

Cock-a-Leekie

Like most traditional soup recipes, this one admits of variations. The leeks added at the beginning, which have given up all their flavour to the broth, may be removed before the second batch is added. If the leeks used are old and tough, they should be blanched before being added to the soup. At the end of cooking, the chicken may be completely skinned and boned, and the meat returned to the pot.

To serve 8

1	boiling fowl, trussed	1
1 kg	leeks, trimmed, washed, and sliced	2 lb
2 litres	stock or broth (*page 164*) or water	4 pints
	bouquet garni of 1 clove, 1 blade mace, 1 sprig parsley, 6 peppercorns	
	salt	
	freshly ground allspice	
12	prunes	12

Place the fowl in a large pot with 3 or 4 of the leeks and the stock or water. If using water, add the bouquet garni, tied in a piece of muslin. Bring to the boil, skim, and cook gently for two hours or longer, until the fowl is tender, when it should be removed. Clear off all the grease with absorbent paper. Add the remainder of the leeks cut into small pieces, which may be split. Add salt if required, and allspice to taste. Simmer very gently until the leeks are tender. Half an hour before serving, add the prunes. A little minced fowl may also be added to the soup just before serving it.

F. MARIAN MCNEILL
THE SCOTS KITCHEN

Leek and Oatmeal Broth

Brotchan Roy

To serve 2

125 g	trimmed leeks, chopped	4 oz
30 g	oatmeal	1 oz
½ litre	liquid (water, milk, or meat or vegetable stock)	1 pint
15 g	butter	½ oz
	salt and pepper	
	powdered mace	
1 tsp	chopped parsley	1 tsp

Put the liquid and butter into a saucepan, bring to the boil and stir in the oatmeal. Keeping the liquid at the boil, add the leeks and season with salt, pepper, and a pinch of mace. Put on the lid and simmer for 45 minutes or until the oatmeal and leeks are cooked. Add the parsley. Boil for 3 minutes. Serve.

FLORENCE IRWIN
IRISH COUNTRY RECIPES

Grouse Soup

To serve 4 to 6

2	old grouse, slightly under-roasted	2
1 litre	stock	2 pints
	salt	
6	black peppercorns	6
2	white peppercorns	2
2	sticks celery (optional)	2
6 or 8	juniper berries, slightly crushed (optional)	6 or 8
75 g	butter	2½ oz
60 g	coarse oatmeal	2 oz
1 tbsp	red wine or port mixed with 1 tsp whisky, or 10 cl (4 fl oz) double cream	1 tbsp

Remove all the flesh from the grouse carcasses. Set aside two breasts, and pound the remaining flesh in a mortar. Put the bones into a pot with the stock. (Failing stock, use water with a marrow bone or 3 or 4 rashers of streaky bacon.) Bring to the boil and skim. Add salt, peppercorns, and the celery and juniper berries, if you are using them. Cover and simmer for 2 hours, and strain through a sieve.

Melt 60 g (2 oz) of the butter and fry the oatmeal to a warm brown. Add a little stock to make the mixture of the consistency of cream, then stir into the rest of the stock. Add the pounded flesh of the birds and simmer for 20 minutes longer. Dice the breast fillets, fry in the remaining butter, and add to the soup. Lastly add the wine and whisky mixture, or substitute some thick fresh cream.

F. MARIAN McNEILL
THE SCOTS KITCHEN

Pigeon Soup with Barley

Soupe de Pigeon à l'Orge

The water in this soup may be replaced by broth; at the end of the cooking time, the pigeon quarters may be skinned, boned, and diced, and the meat returned to the pot. The addition of green peas, when in season, gives an exquisite flavour to the soup.

To serve 6

2	large pigeons, cleaned, singed and quartered	2
6 to 8 tbsp	barley	6 to 8 tbsp
60 g	butter	2 oz
1	large onion, finely chopped	1
2	carrots, diced	2
1.5 litres	water	3 pints
2 tsp	salt	2 tsp
	pepper	
1	bay leaf	1
4 to 6 tbsp	shelled green peas (optional)	4 to 6 tbsp

Melt the butter in a large pan, add the onion, and cook for a few minutes over a low heat. Add the pigeons and cook for 8 to 10 minutes, then put in the carrots, barley, water, salt, pepper, and bay leaf. Cover and simmer over a low heat for about 1¼ hours, or until the pigeons are very tender. Ten minutes before the end of the cooking time, add the peas if you are using them. Correct the seasoning and serve.

A. ESCOFFIER
LE CARNET D'ÉPICURE

Oxtail Soup

An inexpensive and very nutritious soup may be made of oxtails, but it will be insipid in flavour without the addition of a little ham, knuckle of bacon, or other meat. To increase the savour of this soup when meat is not served in it, the onions, turnips and carrots may be gently fried until of a fine light brown, before they are added to it.

To serve 12

2 or 3	small oxtails, 1 to 2 kg (2 to 4 lb) in all, washed and soaked in water for 15 minutes	2 or 3
1	ham or bacon joint, about 750 g (1½lb)	1
4 litres	water or beef broth	7 pints
	salt	
4	medium-sized carrots	4
2 to 4	onions	2 to 4
1	bouquet garni	1
1	head celery	1
2	turnips	2
6 to 8	cloves	6 to 8
½ tsp	peppercorns	½ tsp
1 tbsp	arrowroot or rice flour	1 tbsp
	cayenne pepper	

Put the oxtails and the ham or bacon into a large pan and pour on the water or broth. Bring gradually to the boil, throw in 40 g (1½ oz) of salt, and clear off the scum carefully as soon as it forms upon the surface; when it ceases to rise, add the carrots, onions, bouquet garni, celery, turnips, cloves and peppercorns. Stew these gently from 3 to 3½ hours if the tails be very large; lift the tails out, strain the liquor, and skim off all the fat; divide the tails into joints, and put them into 2 litres (4 pints) or rather more of the stock; stir in, when these begin to boil, the arrowroot mixed with as much cayenne and salt as may be required to flavour the soup well, and serve it very hot.

If stewed down until the flesh falls away from the bones, the oxtails will make stock which will be quite a firm jelly when cold; and this, strained, thickened, and well flavoured with spices, catsup, or a little wine, would, to many tastes, be a superior soup to the above.

ELIZA ACTON
MODERN COOKERY

Mockturtle Soup

Soupe Fausse Tortue

An equivalent weight of calf's head, which is sold boned and rolled, may be substituted for the two calf's feet called for in this recipe. If water is substituted for broth, the quantity of beef should be doubled. The classic herbs used in turtle soup are basil, thyme, bay and marjoram, all fresh if possible; this recipe adds sage, savory and rosemary. By association, these herbs are intended to make calf's feet or head taste like turtle flesh: in fact, the only similarity is in the smooth firm gelatinous texture of the meat.

To serve 12 to 14

30 g	butter	1 oz
1	onion	1
2	carrots, sliced	2
500 g	veal knuckle	1 lb
1 kg	leg of beef, cut in small pieces	2 to 2½ lb
2	calf's feet, split, blanched and rinsed	2
4 tbsp	water	4 tbsp
4 litres	broth or water	7 pints
2	cloves	2
½ tsp	peppercorns	½ tsp
1	bay leaf	1
1 tbsp	flour	1 tbsp
4 tbsp	puréed tomato	4 tbsp
1	shallot, finely chopped	1
1 sprig each	thyme, sage, savory, rosemary, basil, marjoram	1 sprig each
10 cl	Madeira	4 fl oz
60 g	mushrooms, sliced, sautéed briefly in butter	2 oz
	cayenne pepper	
5 or 6	hard-boiled egg yolks, chopped	5 or 6

Melt half the butter in a large, thick-bottomed saucepan. Add the onion, carrot, veal knuckle, beef, and calf's feet. Add 4 tablespoons of water, cover, and cook over low heat until the water has completely evaporated and the meats are lightly coloured—in 30 to 40 minutes. Pour on the broth or water and add the cloves, peppercorns, and bay leaf. Bring to the boil, put the lid on slightly tilted, and cook the meats very slowly until they are tender, about 3 hours. Take out the calf's feet, bone them, and put the meat on a plate with a weight on top to press it as it cools. Strain and degrease the broth, discarding both the beef and the veal knuckle.

In a large saucepan, melt the remaining butter, stir in the flour, and add the broth and the puréed tomato. Simmer over a very low heat for about 30 minutes, removing the skin as it forms on the surface of the soup. Meanwhile, put the shallot and the herbs into a small pan with the Madeira. Simmer, covered, for 5 minutes. Cut the meat from the calf's feet into small dice and put into a saucepan. Strain in the Madeira and herb infusion, add the mushrooms, and keep warm.

Remove any remaining traces of fat and season the soup with the cayenne pepper. Pour the soup through a sieve into a warmed tureen, add the herb infusion with the diced meat and mushroom mixture, and serve garnished with the chopped hard-boiled egg yolks.

JEAN DE GOUY
LA CUISINE ET LA PATISSERIE BOURGEOISES

Green Borscht

Borchtch Vert

The bacon rind in this soup may be replaced by pork spare ribs or by oxtail; the latter requires a longer cooking time, and both require additional salt. At the end of the cooking, the meat should be boned, diced, and returned to the soup.

To serve 6 to 8

250 g	green bacon rind with some meat attached, soaked overnight and drained	8 oz
2 litres	water	4 pints
200 g	sorrel, stemmed	7 oz
150 g	spinach, stemmed (optional)	5 oz
50 g	butter	2 oz
3	onions, finely chopped and lightly sautéed in butter	3
1 tbsp	flour	1 tbsp
5 or 6	potatoes, cut up	5 or 6
	salt	
20 cl	double cream or soured cream	7 fl oz
3	eggs, hard-boiled and chopped	3

Put the bacon rind into the water and bring to the boil. In another saucepan, gently cook the sorrel—and the spinach, if using—in the butter until it becomes a purée, about 10 minutes. Stir in the onions and flour, then add this mixture to the soup and cook for 45 minutes to 1 hour. Thirty minutes before the end of the cooking time, add the potatoes. These will help to neutralise the acidity of the sorrel. When the potatoes are tender, cut the rind and meat into serving pieces and return to the soup. Taste for salt. Serve the cream and the chopped eggs in separate dishes.

H. WITWICKA AND S. SOSKINE
LA CUISINE RUSSE CLASSIQUE

Mulligatawny Soup

The word mulligatawny came into English in the 18th century, from the Tamil, *milakutanni* (meaning pepper-water).

	To serve 4 to 6	
2 kg	boiling fowl, jointed, or the equivalent weight of drumsticks, thigh joints, giblets and carcasses from roasting birds	4 lb
2	onions, sliced	2
90 g	butter	3 oz
175to250g	moist fresh white cheese or yogurt	6 to 8 oz
	salt	
1.5 litres	water	3 pints
4	cloves	4
3 tbsp	lemon juice	3 tbsp
	rice, boiled	

	Curry seasoning	
4 tsp	finely chopped onion	4 tsp
1 tsp	ground turmeric	1 tsp
1 tsp	chili powder	1 tsp
½ tsp	ground ginger	½ tsp
¼ tsp	finely chopped garlic	¼ tsp
½ tsp	ground, roasted coriander seed	½ tsp
¼ tsp	ground, roasted cumin seed	¼ tsp

To make the curry seasoning, pound together all the ingredients to a paste. Brown the onion in 60 g (2 oz) of the butter with the chicken pieces. Stir in the curry seasoning, the cheese or yogurt and some salt, and stew for a little while until the juices turn to a brownish crust on the bottom of the pan. They should not burn, so this needs watching. Pour in the water, and leave to cook. Melt the remaining butter in a little pan with the cloves; after a few minutes you will be able to crush the cloves down with a wooden spoon. Pour in the lemon juice, mix it all up well and tip it into the large pan of soup. Stew, covered, for an hour or more depending on the age and toughness of the chicken: the soup is ready when the meat parts easily from the bones, which can then be removed and thrown away. Correct the seasoning, pour the soup into a tureen and serve with a separate bowl of boiled rice. This mulligatawny soup, unlike some of the other recipes, contains no apple, but if you like you can always serve a dish of chopped apple sprinkled with lemon juice to be added to the soup with the rice by each diner.

JANE GRIGSON
ENGLISH FOOD

Aubergine or Marrow Soup

Sajur Terung atau Labu

Laos powder, which resembles ginger, and curry leaves are available in shops specialising in Asian foods.

	To serve 4	
2	small aubergines, marrows, chokos, large cucumbers or squash etc, sliced or diced	2
½ tsp	coriander seeds	½ tsp
⅛ tsp	cumin seeds	⅛ tsp
3	macadamia nuts or almonds	3
¼ tsp	turmeric	¼ tsp
7	red chilies, fresh or dried, or 2 tsp ground chili	7
2 tbsp	peanut oil	2 tbsp
1½	Spanish onions, chopped	1½
1	large garlic clove, chopped	1
1	thin slice fresh green ginger	1
2 tbsp	beef or chicken, chopped	2 tbsp
	salt	
¼ tsp	laos powder (optional)	¼ tsp
2	curry leaves	2
175 g	desiccated coconut, soaked in 40 cl (¾ pint) hot water for 20 minutes	6 oz
½	lime or lemon	½

Grind the coriander, cumin, nuts, turmeric and dried or ground chili in a blender or mortar. Heat the oil in a saucepan and fry the onions and garlic until they are just yellow. Add the ground spices, ginger, and sliced fresh chili if you are using it, and stir. Add the meat, salt to taste, cover with water and bring to the boil. Add laos powder, if using, and curry leaves and allow to simmer for about 15 minutes or until the meat is half cooked. Strain the soaked coconut, pressing out all the liquid, and add a little salt; discard the pulp. Add this coconut milk to the pan and simmer, uncovered, for about 10 minutes. Finally add the aubergines, or whichever vegetable you are using, and continue cooking without a lid until they are tender but not overcooked. Remove from the stove, add a squeeze of lime or lemon juice, stir and serve.

ROSEMARY BRISSENDEN
SOUTH EAST ASIAN FOOD

Red Kidney Bean Soup

Bruine Bonensoep

This soup can be served as a meal in itself or as a first course, depending on the size of the portions.

To serve 4 to 6

500 g	dried red kidney beans, soaked overnight and drained	1 lb
3.5 litres	water	6 pints
1	bouquet of 2 cloves, 1 small red chili pepper, 1 bay leaf, wrapped in muslin	1
250 g	potatoes, diced	8 oz
1	large onion, chopped	1
60 g	butter	2 oz
2 tsp	curry powder	2 tsp
	salt and pepper	
	Worcestershire sauce	
30 g	bacon, diced and fried (optional)	1 oz
8	small gherkins, sliced (optional)	8
4 tbsp	red wine or Madeira	4 tbsp

Put the beans in a soup kettle, cover them with the water and add the bouquet of cloves, chili pepper and bay leaf. Bring slowly to the boil, lower the heat and simmer for 1 hour. Add the potatoes and simmer for 30 minutes more.

Meanwhile, in a frying pan, fry the chopped onion in the butter to a golden-brown. Stir in the curry powder. Discard the bouquet from the soup kettle and coarsely mash the beans and potatoes in their cooking liquid using a potato masher. Add the fried onion and curry powder mixture and simmer for some 20 minutes more until the soup has thickened. Season to taste with salt, pepper and Worcestershire sauce.

If you like, add the diced fried bacon and sliced gherkins, and stir in some red wine or Madeira. Serve with croûtons.

C.A.H. HAITSMA MULIER-VAN BEUSEKOM (EDITOR)
CULINAIRE ENCYCLOPÉDIE

Indonesian Rice Soup

Nasi tim voor 2 zieken

This thick soup was traditionally cooked in a closed pot placed in another pan of boiling water, which was also closed—a sort of covered bain-marie.

To serve 2

200 g	raw, unwashed long-grain rice	7 oz
2	chicken drumsticks	2
¾ litre	chicken broth (*page 164*)	1½ pints

Meat balls

200 g	minced lean beef	7 oz
¼ tsp	powdered coriander seeds	¼ tsp
⅛ tsp	powdered cumin seeds	⅛ tsp
⅛ tsp	grated nutmeg	⅛ tsp
	salt	
1	egg yolk	1

Put half of the rice into a soup pot. Mix together all the meat ball ingredients, shape into small meat balls, and arrange on top of the rice. Cover with half the remaining rice. Put the chicken legs on top and cover with the rest of the rice. Pour on the broth, cover tightly, bring to the boil, and simmer very gently for 2 hours. Serve the soup very hot.

HUGH JANS
VRIJ NEDERLANDS KOOKBOEK

Meat-Rice Barrel Soup

Yuvarelakia Soupa Avgolemono

To serve 6

500 g	minced beef, veal or lamb	1 lb
1	onion, grated	1
2	garlic cloves, crushed (optional)	
6 tbsp	long-grain white rice	6 tbsp
3 tbsp	chopped parsley	3 tbsp
2 tbsp	chopped mint, basil, or dill	2 tbsp
1 tsp	dried oregano or thyme	1 tsp
	salt and freshly ground pepper	
3	eggs	3
1.25 litres	water, stock or broth (*page 164*)	2½ pints
1	onion, chopped	1
1	stick celery, chopped	1
½	carrot, chopped	½
3 to 5 tbsp	lemon juice	3 to 5 tbsp
2 tbsp	chopped parsley (optional)	2 tbsp

In a large bowl, combine the meat, grated onion, garlic, rice, herbs, salt and pepper, and one egg slightly beaten. Knead for a few minutes, then shape the mixture into walnut-sized barrel shapes and set aside.

In a soup pot, bring the water or stock to the boil with the chopped vegetables and salt and pepper to taste. Reduce the heat and add the meat and rice barrels. Simmer, covered, for 30 minutes, then remove from the heat. Beat the 2 remaining eggs for 2 minutes, then, continuing to beat, gradually add the lemon juice. Gradually beat in, by droplets, several ladlefuls of the hot soup. With a wooden spoon, stir the egg and lemon mixture back into the soup. Return to a low heat and stir until the soup has thickened lightly, being careful not to let it start to boil. Serve hot, garnished with additional chopped parsley if desired.

VILMA LIACOURAS CHANTILES
THE FOOD OF GREECE

Rice Soup

Soupa Rizi Avgholemono

To serve 4

100 g	rice	3½ oz
1.5 litres	beef or chicken stock	3 pints
	salt (optional)	
2	eggs	2
2 or 3 tbsp	lemon juice	2 or 3 tbsp

Bring to the boil the beef or chicken stock. Add the rice, cover and cook until tender, about 20 minutes. Add salt, if necessary. Beat the eggs and lemon juice in a bowl. Gradually add about 8 tablespoons of the stock, stirring constantly. Pour the egg and lemon mixture into the remaining stock in the saucepan. Heat the soup over a very low heat, stirring constantly. Take care that it does not boil. Serve at once.

CHRISSA PARADISSIS
THE BEST BOOK OF GREEK COOKERY

"Little Chickens" Soup Antonio

Pulcini Zuppa all'Antonio

Pulcini *are small pasta shapes, used in soups. If they are unavailable, any other small soup pasta may be substituted.*

To serve 4 to 6

90 g	*pulcini*	3 oz
40 g	butter	1½ oz
1	veal sweetbread, parboiled, cooled, fat and membrane removed, diced	1
1	carrot, chopped	1
½ tsp	salt	½ tsp
	freshly ground pepper	
2	artichoke bottoms, diced	2
2 litres	chicken broth (*page 164*)	4 pints
1 tbsp	chopped flat-leafed parsley	1 tbsp

Melt the butter, sprinkle the sweetbread and carrot with the salt and pepper and sauté the pieces until they are brown. Stir in the artichoke bottoms and simmer for 5 minutes. Cook the *pulcini* until *al dente* and drain them. In a separate pan, bring the chicken broth to a simmer, stir in the sweetbread and artichoke mixture and the pasta; simmer for 5 minutes. Serve in warm soup bowls, with parsley sprinkled on each serving.

JACK DENTON SCOTT
THE COMPLETE BOOK OF PASTA

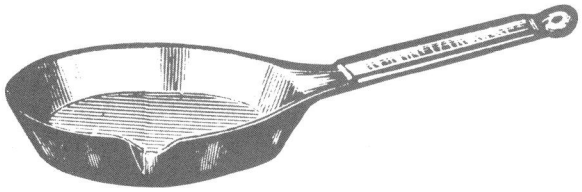

Catalan Soup

Sopa de Mandonghuilles a la Casolana

Picada *is a Spanish seasoning paste similar to Italian* pesto.

To serve 4

½	garlic clove, crushed	½
250 g	minced beef	8 oz
2 tbsp	chopped parsley	2 tbsp
	salt and black pepper	
40 g	flour	1½ oz
	oil or lard for frying	
1 litre	chicken broth (*page 164*)	2 pints
4	slices toast	4

Picada

¼ tsp	powdered saffron	¼ tsp
2	garlic cloves	2
⅛ tsp	salt	⅛ tsp
30g each	hazelnuts and almonds, peeled and toasted	1 oz each
½ tsp	ground cinnamon	½ tsp
2	sprigs parsley	2
1 tbsp	sherry	1 tbsp

To make the *picada*, pound all the dry *picada* ingredients together in a mortar, then add the sherry and enough water to make a fine paste. Mix the garlic with the minced beef, chopped parsley, salt and pepper. Make this into tiny balls and roll them in flour. Heat a little oil or lard in a frying pan and brown the meat balls lightly all over. In a separate pan, bring the chicken broth to the boil, add the toast and let it disintegrate, then add the meat balls and the *picada* and cook gently for 15 to 20 minutes.

ANNA MACMIADHACHÁIN
SPANISH REGIONAL COOKERY

Soup Made in the Gruzian Way

Harcho

To serve 6

500 g	boned breast of mutton or lamb, cut into small cubes	1 lb
1.5 litres	water	3 pints
1 tsp	salt	1 tsp
100 g	onion, finely chopped	3½ oz
60 g	butter	2oz
30 g	puréed tomato	1 oz
100 g	rice	3½ oz
1	garlic clove, crushed	1
60 g	celery leaves, finely chopped	2 oz
60 g	pickled plums	2 oz
2 tbsp	finely chopped dill	2 tbsp

Put the meat into the water and bring to the boil. Skim off the froth, add the salt and onions, and bring to the boil again. Cover and simmer for 1 hour.

In another pan, heat the butter, mix in the puréed tomato and add this to the soup. Then add the rice, garlic, celery leaves and plums. Let the soup simmer for about 20 minutes or until the rice is cooked. Sprinkle on the dill before serving.

JOZSEF VENESZ
HUNGARIAN CUISINE

Leek Soup with Dumplings

Potage de Poireaux aux Kliotzki

To serve 6

4 or 5	leeks	4 or 5
1.5 litres	salted water	3 pints
1 tbsp	finely chopped parsley	1 tbsp

Dumplings

30 g	butter	1 oz
2 tbsp	boiling water	2 tbsp
1	egg	1
1 tbsp	semolina	1 tbsp
	salt	
3 to 4 tbsp	flour	3 to 4 tbsp

To make the dumplings, place the butter in a bowl and pour on the boiling water. When the butter is melted, stir in the egg, semolina, salt, and enough flour to make a fairly stiff dough. Mix well, knead for a few minutes, and then allow the dough to rest for several hours.

Cook the leeks in the salted water for about 30 minutes. Remove the leeks and reserve them to eat at another meal with a vinaigrette sauce.

Bring the leek broth back to the boil. To shape each dumpling, dip a teaspoon in cold water and use to take a small spoonful of the dumpling dough and slide it off into the broth. Alternatively, the spoon may be dipped in oil and the dough dropped into the broth by tapping the spoon against the rim of the pan. Cook for 8 to 10 minutes over low heat, until all the dumplings rise to the surface. Serve the soup sprinkled with the chopped parsley.

H. WITWICKA AND S. SOSKINE
LA CUISINE RUSSE CLASSIQUE

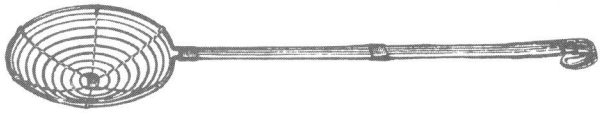

Pickled Cucumber and Kidney Soup

Razsolnik

To serve 8

5 or 6	pickled cucumbers, thinly sliced, with their juice	5 or 6
1	beef kidney, membrane and fat removed, rinsed	1
2 or 3	potatoes, cut into pieces	2 or 3
15 to 20 cl	double cream or soured cream	6 fl oz

Broth

1 kg	beef chuck, cut up, or goose giblets and trimmings	2 to 2½ lb
3 litres	water	5½ pints
1	Hamburg parsley root	1
1	leek	1
½	head celery	½
10 to 15	juniper berries	10 to 15
2 or 3	bay leaves	2 or 3
2 or 3	dried mushrooms	2 or 3

Put all the broth ingredients in a pot, bring to the boil, and simmer, lid half on, for 1½ hours. Strain the broth into a clean pot; add the cucumbers, kidney and potatoes. A little cucumber juice may be poured into the soup to give it a pleasant tang. Cook, covered, for 30 minutes. Before serving, complete the soup by adding the cream and bringing the soup back to the boil. Slice the kidney very finely, put it into a warmed tureen and pour the soup over it.

H. WITWICKA AND S. SOSKINE
LA CUISINE RUSSE CLASSIQUE

Soup of Lights

Soupe aux Poumons de Porc ou de Veau

In Germany, this soup is sometimes thickened with breadcrumbs or semolina instead of the flour used in this recipe.

To serve 4

500 g	pork or veal lights, soaked for 2 hours, drained, and beaten with a mallet to rid them of air	1 lb
1 litre	water or broth (*page 164*)	2 pints
40 g	butter	1½ oz
2 tbsp	flour	2 tbsp
1	large bouquet garni	1
	grated nutmeg	
1 tbsp	chopped dill and chives, or chopped parsley	1 tbsp

Put the lights in a pan with the water or broth and bring to the boil. Simmer 1½ hours, or until tender. Chop the lights very finely, and reserve the cooking stock. Make a roux with 30 g (1 oz) of the butter and the flour; cook until lightly browned, then stir in the stock. Add the bouquet garni and simmer for 30 minutes, then skim. Remove the bouquet garni. Sauté the chopped lights in the remaining butter for a few minutes, add a pinch of nutmeg, and put them into the soup. Finish with the chopped herbs, and serve.

JEAN DE GOUY
LA CUISINE ET LA PATISSERIE BOURGEOISES

Chicken Mousse in Broth

Budino di Pollo in Brodo

This is a very delicate and delicious soup, worth taking the trouble over for an occasional treat. It makes a light and excellent beginning to any meal. I am indebted for the recipe to the Pappagallo restaurant in Bologna, for good reason one of the most famous in all Italy.

To serve 6

175 g	uncooked white chicken meat, minced	6 oz
1.5 litres	very good, clear chicken broth (*page 164*)	3 pints
4	eggs	4
60 g	Parmesan cheese, grated	2 oz
	salt and pepper	
	nutmeg	

Pound the minced chicken meat in a mortar, adding from time to time a little of the broth, about 8 cl (3 fl oz) in all; it must now be put through a sieve, so that a fine cream is obtained. Beat the eggs, pour them through a strainer into the chicken mixture, and mix them thoroughly. Add the grated cheese, and season with salt, pepper and nutmeg.

Put the chicken cream, which should be very smooth, into 6 small buttered moulds or china ramekins, of the kind in which eggs are baked. Put the ramekins in a pan containing water, about half-way up the little pots; cover, and cook gently for 15 minutes, until the chicken mixture is firm. Turn each one out on to a soup plate and pour over the hot broth.

ELIZABETH DAVID
ITALIAN FOOD

Rice and Chicken Liver Soup

La Minestra di Riso e Fegatini

Chicken hearts and gizzards may be used in this recipe in addition to chicken livers; they should be thinly sliced and thoroughly cooked in stock before being added to the soup.

To serve 6 to 8

200 g	Piedmont rice, unwashed	7 oz
150 g	chicken livers, cut into small pieces	5 oz
2 litres	chicken stock or broth (*page 164*)	4 pints
40 g	butter (optional)	1½ oz
1 tbsp	chopped parsley	1 tbsp
	freshly grated Parmesan cheese	

Bring the stock to the boil, add the rice, and cook, covered, over a medium heat for 18 to 20 minutes or until the rice is tender.

Meanwhile, in another pan, cook the chicken livers in a few spoonfuls of the stock or, if preferred, sauté them in the butter for 5 minutes. When the rice is cooked, transfer the livers with their cooking juices to the rice pan. Add the parsley and serve very hot with the grated cheese.

GIANNI BRERA AND LUIGI VERONELLI
LA PACCIADA

Tripe Soup

Soppi Mondongo

If the tripe is bought from the butcher pre-cooked, it may be tender after about 1 hour's cooking. For the technique of preparing tripe, see page 48.

Cooks in Curaçao say this soup should be left to cool and stand for 3 hours or so after it is cooked, then reheated, as this improves the flavour. They often add a tablespoon of dry sherry or brandy to each soup plate.

To serve 10 to 12

1 kg	tripe, washed and drained	2 to 2½ lb
3 tbsp	lime juice	3 tbsp
2	pig's trotters, split and cleaned	2
2.5 litres	water, salted	5 pints
250 g	corned beef	8 oz
1	onion, coarsely chopped	1
3	shallots, chopped	3
1	stick celery, coarsely chopped	1
500 g	pumpkin, peeled, seeded, and cut into 2.5 cm (1 inch) cubes	1 lb
1	sweet potato, diced	1
3	potatoes, diced	3
6	green olives, stoned	6
1 tbsp	capers	1 tbsp
1 tbsp	seedless raisins	1 tbsp
1	sweet green pepper, seeded and coarsely chopped	1
1	green chili pepper, seeded and chopped	1
	freshly ground pepper	
¼ tsp each	grated nutmeg and ground cloves	¼ tsp each

In a bowl, pour the lime juice over the tripe and let it stand for 10 minutes. Transfer the tripe to a large saucepan. Add the pig's trotters and the salted water. Simmer, covered, until tender—about 2½ to 3 hours. Meanwhile, pour boiling water over the corned beef, and allow to stand for 45 minutes.

Drain, rinse and add the corned beef to the pan in which the tripe is cooking. When the meats are tender, allow them to cool. Cut the tripe into strips about 2 cm (¾ inch) wide, and the corned beef into 1 cm (½ inch) cubes. Remove the meat from the pig's trotters and discard the bones. Put all the vegetables into the stock, with the meats and remaining ingredients. Simmer gently for about 30 minutes until the vegetables are tender. Serve the soup with crusty French bread.

ELISABETH LAMBERT ORTIZ
CARIBBEAN COOKING

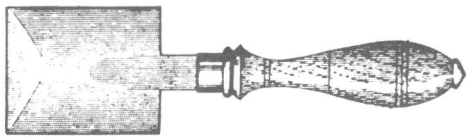

Milanese Tripe Soup

Minestra di Trippe alla Milanese

If the tripe you buy is pre-cooked, it will need only about 1 hour of cooking. For the technique of preparing tripe, see page 48.

To serve 12

2 kg	honeycomb tripe, cleaned, washed and cut into 10 cm (4 inch) squares	4 lb
4.5 litres	stock or lightly salted water	8 pints
1	onion, stuck with 2 cloves	1
2	sticks celery	2
200 g	dried white beans, soaked in water overnight and drained	7 oz
	salt	
1	medium-sized cabbage, trimmed and the leaves separated	1
50 g	butter	2 oz
200 g	rashers bacon, cut into 2.5 cm (1 inch) pieces and parboiled for 5 minutes	7 oz
1	medium-sized onion, thinly sliced	1
3	leeks, white part only, thinly sliced	3
1	heart celery, thinly sliced	1
4	small carrots, thinly sliced	4
2	tomatoes, skinned, seeded, squeezed and chopped	2
	freshly ground pepper	
3	medium-sized potatoes, cubed	3
4 tbsp	chopped *prosciutto* fat	4 tbsp
1	garlic clove, chopped	1
	grated Parmesan cheese	
	bread croûtons	

Put the tripe into a large, flameproof, earthenware or enamelled iron pot. Add the stock (or lightly salted water, if you wish, although the soup will not be so flavoursome), the onion stuck with cloves and the celery. Bring to the boil, reduce the heat to moderate, and cook, covered, for about 3 hours. Drain the tripe, slice it into thin strips, and put aside. Strain the stock through a very fine strainer and reserve.

Meanwhile, in another pot cook the beans in lightly salted water over a low heat for 1½ hours or until tender. Cook the cabbage in boiling water for 10 minutes, drain and cut into fine shreds. Melt the butter in a large, heavy pot over a medium heat, add the bacon, the onion and the leeks. As soon as they are lightly golden, add the celery, carrots and tomatoes and blend well. Cook gently, stirring occasionally, for 10 minutes. Add the sliced tripe, pour in 3.5 litres (6 pints) of the reserved tripe liquid, add salt and pepper if necessary, return to the boil, and reduce the heat. Add the potatoes and simmer, covered, over a moderate heat for 20 minutes. Then add the cooked beans and cabbage and simmer for about 5 minutes.

When ready to serve, sauté the chopped *prosciutto* fat and garlic in a frying pan for 5 minutes, and add the fat pieces and garlic to the soup. Pour into soup bowls and serve the Parmesan cheese and the croûtons separately.

LUIGI CARNACINA
GREAT ITALIAN COOKING

Mexican Tripe Soup

Menudo

For the technique of preparing tripe, see page 48.

Nixtamal hominy is the white fermented corn used in the authentic Mexican ***menudo***, a soup which is traditionally cooked over a hickory or mesquite fire.

To serve 10 to 12

2 kg	tripe, washed and cut into 2.5 cm (1 inch) cubes	4 lb
2	calves' feet or 1 veal knuckle, washed	2
6 litres	water	11 pints
600 g	*nixtamal* hominy, rinsed, or two 850 g (1¾ lb) cans hominy, drained	1¼ lb
2	onions, chopped	2
4	garlic cloves, finely chopped	4
1 tbsp	crushed dried oregano	1 tbsp
2 tbsp	chopped fresh coriander	2 tbsp
	salt and freshly ground pepper	

Bring the water to the boil in a stock-pot. If using calves' feet, add them to the pot; cover and simmer for 1 hour before adding the tripe and the rest of the ingredients. If veal knuckle is being used instead, add it to the pot with the tripe, the *nixtamal* hominy, onions, garlic, oregano, coriander, and salt and pepper to taste. (If you are using canned hominy, this is added during the last hour of cooking.) Bring to the boil, cover, reduce the heat and simmer for 3 to 4 hours, or until the tripe is tender. Serve, providing dishes of additional chopped onions, chopped coriander and chili peppers for each person to add according to his taste.

JANA ALLEN AND MARGARET GIN
INNARDS AND OTHER VARIETY MEATS

Philadelphia Pepper Pot

Peppery pot, piping hot! In colonial days, the pepper-pot vendor plodded Philadelphia's twisting streets and alleyways chanting the pepper-pot call:

All hot! All hot!
Pepper pot! Pepper pot!
Makes back strong,
Makes live long,
All hot! Pepper pot!

To serve 8 to 10

1 kg	honeycomb tripe, pre-cooked, cut into 1 cm (½ inch) squares	2 to 2½ lb
1	veal knuckle	1
3.5 litres	cold water	6 pints
1	bouquet garni or 2 bay leaves, 10 sprigs parsley, 2 sprigs celery leaves	1
1½ tsp	salt	1½ tsp
12	peppercorns, slightly bruised	12
2	onions, each stuck with a clove	2
4	potatoes, cubed	4

Suet dumplings

175 g	beef suet, chopped	7 oz
270 g	flour	9 oz
½ tsp	salt	½ tsp
	chopped parsley	

Put the tripe and veal knuckle into a kettle with the water, bring to the boil, and skim carefully. Add the bouquet garni and simmer gently for 3 hours, adding, after 2 hours, the salt and peppercorns. Remove the meat from the bones, and cut into small pieces. Strain the broth, return it to the kettle, then add the onions. Simmer for 1 hour, then add the potatoes, meat and tripe. Taste for seasoning, and let simmer gently while you make the dumplings.

For the dumplings, combine the suet, 250 g (8 oz) of the flour and salt. Add enough ice-cold water to make a workable dough, and form it into dumplings about the size of marbles. Roll them well in the remaining flour to prevent sticking, and drop them into the simmering soup. Cook about 8 to 10 minutes. Stir some chopped parsley into the soup and serve, in heated soup plates, accompanied by brown bread and butter.

LOUIS P. DE GOUY
THE SOUP BOOK

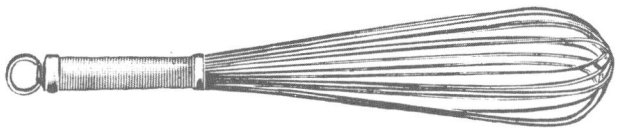

Jamaica Pepperpot Soup

The coco *used in this soup is a Jamaican variety of sweet potato. Ordinary sweet potato may be substituted for* coco. *Shrimp or prawns may replace the crayfish; whatever your choice, they should be parboiled for about 5 minutes in salted water. To make coconut milk, pour 10 cl (4 fl oz) of boiling water over 60 g (2 oz) of grated fresh coconut, allow to steep for a few minutes, and strain through a cloth, squeezing hard.*

To serve 12

750 g	soup meat such as boneless shin of beef, cubed	1½ lb
2	pig's tails	2
4 litres	water	7 pints
250 g	*coco*, coarsely chopped	8 oz
1 or 2	sprigs thyme	1 or 2
1 kg	spinach, finely chopped	2 to 2½ lb
12	okra, sliced into thin rounds	12
1	medium-sized onion, chopped	1
1	garlic clove, crushed	1
1	small aubergine, peeled and coarsely chopped	1
750 g	kale, finely chopped	1½ lb
3	large spring onions, finely chopped	3
	salt	
1	green chili pepper	1
500 g	crayfish, parboiled and shelled	1 lb
10 cl	coconut milk	4 fl oz

Place the soup meat and pig's tails in a large soup kettle with the water. Bring to the boil and simmer, covered, until the meat is nearly cooked, about 2 hours. Add the *coco*.

Place the thyme and all the vegetables except the chili pepper in a separate saucepan without adding water, and steam, covered, for about 10 minutes or until cooked. Rub the vegetables through a coarse strainer into the soup kettle.

Add the chili pepper and salt to taste. Add more boiling water, if needed. Simmer until the soup has thickened, then add the crayfish. Lastly add the coconut milk and cook for just 5 minutes more. Remove the chili pepper before serving.

LEILA BRANDON
A MERRY-GO-ROUND OF RECIPES FROM JAMAICA

Three-Helping Bean Soup

This recipe calls for fresh beans, or any of the varieties that are usually dried: haricot, cranberry, or pinto. If dried beans are substituted, soak them overnight, drain, and cook them in fresh water for 1½ to 2 hours or until they are almost tender.

To serve 6

125 g	fresh shelled beans	4 oz
2	smoked pig's feet	2
250 g	smoked pork ribs	8 oz
2.25 litres	water	4½ pints
1	celeriac, diced	1
1	medium-sized onion, chopped	1
15 g	lard	½ oz
1 tbsp	chopped flat-leafed parsley	1 tbsp
1 tbsp	flour	1 tbsp
½ tbsp	paprika	½ tbsp
1	garlic clove, crushed	1
250 g	smoked pork sausage, cut into 2.5 cm (1 inch) pieces	8 oz
	salt	
2 tbsp	soured cream	2 tbsp
	small dumplings (*page 18*)	

Put the pig's feet and pork ribs in 2 litres (4 pints) of the water, bring to the boil, and simmer for 2 hours or until the meat comes off the bones easily. Strain the broth into another pan. Cut the meat off the bones and reserve the meat.

Add the diced celeriac and shelled beans to the broth and cook over a medium heat until the beans are tender, approximately 30 to 40 minutes.

Meanwhile, fry the onion in the lard over a low heat. When the onion is soft, add the parsley and flour and, over the lowest heat possible, cook, stirring often, for about 10 minutes until a brown roux is made. Mix in the paprika and garlic and the remaining cold water. Whisk until smooth, then pour the mixure into the bean broth. Add the sausage, season with salt, and stir and simmer for 10 minutes more.

Cut the reserved cooked meats into small pieces and add them to the soup. Add the soured cream and serve with small dumplings, cooked separately in simmering water.

THE GREAT COOKS COOKBOOK

Pig's Ear Soup

Soupe aux Oreilles de Porc

To serve 8

2 or 3	pig's ears, singed	2 or 3
100 g	butter	3½ oz
100 g	carrot, finely sliced	3½ oz
100 g	onion, finely sliced	3½ oz
100 g	leek, finely sliced	3½ oz
100 g	celeriac, finely sliced	3½ oz
20 cl	white wine	7 fl oz
2.5 litres	pot au feu or chicken broth (*page 164*)	5 pints
	bouquet garni	
3 tbsp	flour	3 tbsp
60 g	raw cured ham	2 oz
6 tbsp	Madeira	6 tbsp
	cayenne pepper	

Boil the pig's ears in plenty of water for 20 minutes, drain and plunge into cold water. Melt half of the butter in a large pan, add the vegetables and cook until lightly browned. Add the wine and the broth; bring to the boil and add the bouquet garni and the pig's ears. Simmer, covered, for about 2 hours or until the ears are tender. Strain and degrease the broth, and cut the ears into small pieces.

Melt the remaining butter, stir in the flour to make a roux, and cook for a few minutes over a low heat without letting it colour. Pour in the cooking broth, and stir over a medium heat until it boils. Draw the pan half off the heat, add the ham, and cook gently for 45 minutes, skimming. Strain the soup and add the Madeira, a little cayenne pepper and the pig's ears. Cook for a little longer and serve. The soup is very good.

URBAIN DUBOIS
ÉCOLE DES CUISINIÈRES

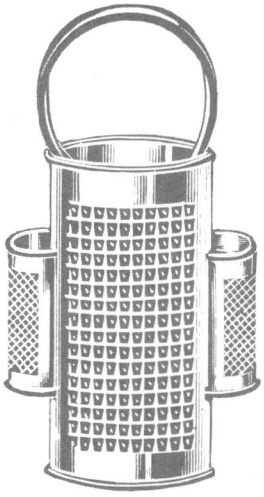

Mackerel Soup

To serve 6

2 or 3	mackerel with heads removed, cleaned and cut into 2.5 cm (1 inch) pieces	2 or 3
1.5 litres	water	3 pints
10	white peppercorns	10
2 tbsp	salt	2 tbsp
8	sprigs dill	8
4 tbsp	single cream	4 tbsp
2 to 3 tbsp	lemon juice	2 to 3 tbsp
2	egg yolks	2

Simmer the mackerel pieces in the water with the peppercorns, salt and most of the dill sprigs for 10 minutes, then remove the pieces of fish and set them aside to cool. Strain the stock into another saucepan, and add most of the cream and 2 tablespoons of the lemon juice. Simmer for a few minutes. Bone and skin the mackerel pieces carefully and add them to the soup. Remove the saucepan from the heat; mix together the egg yolks and the remaining cream, and gradually stir the mixture into the soup to thicken it. Finely chop the remaining dill and add it to the soup. Check the seasoning, adding more lemon juice if necessary, then serve.

BENGT PETERSEN
DELICIOUS FISH DISHES

Sole Soup

Potage aux Soles

To serve 6

500 g	sole, filleted, carcass reserved	1 lb
75 g	butter	2½ oz
2	carrots, diced	2
2	onions, diced	2
30 cl	cider	½ pint
1 litre	water	2 pints
	salt	
50 g	flour	2 oz
10 cl	double cream	4 fl oz
1	egg yolk	1

Chop the fish carcass into several pieces. Melt 15 g (½ oz) of the butter in a deep saucepan, and sauté the carrots and onions gently without letting them colour. Add the fish carcass, cover, and cook for several minutes. Add the cider and the water, bring to the boil, season with salt to taste, and cook, covered, for one hour.

Make a roux with the remaining butter and flour. Strain the cooking liquid, reserving 10 cl (4 fl oz), and whisk the remainder into the roux. Whisk until the mixture reaches the boil, and then simmer gently over a very low fire, skimming and skinning, without stirring, for at least ½ hour or until the skin ceases to form on the surface.

Cut the sole fillets crosswise into strips, and poach them gently in the reserved broth. Beat the cream and egg yolk together, beat in a few spoonfuls of the thickened broth, and return the cream mixture to the pan. Heat, stirring constantly, being careful not to let the soup boil. Add the cooked fish to the soup as a garnish, and serve immediately.

ROGER LALLEMAND
LA VRAIE CUISINE DE LA NORMANDIE

Angler-Fish Soup

Baudroie à l'Aigo Sau

This is a recipe of Roland Petrini, chef at the Hotel Jules-César, Arles. Angler-fish is always sold already beheaded, cleaned and skinned.

To serve 4

500 g	angler-fish, sliced	1 lb
3	potatoes, thinly sliced	3
2	garlic cloves, thinly sliced	2
10	button mushrooms	10
10	small onions	10
3	artichoke bottoms, quartered	3
1	bouquet garni of parsley, fennel and bay leaf	1
2	strips dried orange peel	2
20 cl	olive oil	7 fl oz
	salt and pepper	
1 or 2	tomatoes, skinned, seeded and chopped (optional)	1 or 2
	slices of stale bread, toasted, rubbed with garlic and sprinkled with olive oil	

Put the potatoes and garlic into a saucepan with the mushrooms, shallots, artichoke quarters, bouquet garni, orange peel, fish and half of the olive oil. Season with salt and pepper and add the tomatoes if you wish. Cover with water and bring rapidly to the boil. Cook for 12 to 15 minutes, skimming carefully. Remove the bouquet garni and the orange peel. Adjust the seasoning if necessary, pour the soup into a warmed earthenware tureen, and sprinkle over the remaining oil. Serve the croûtons separately.

LA CUISINE NATURELLE À L'HUILE D'OLIVE

Rock Fish Soup

Soupe de Poisson du Moulin de Mougins

This soup is traditionally made from fish fry or small fish, which are used uncleaned. The important thing is to have a selection of several varieties of fish. Small bream, fish heads and carcasses, and trimmings from conger eel or angler fish may also be used. For instructions on how to make rouille, ***the red pepper sauce accompaniment, see the demonstration on page 51 (recipe, page 166).***

To serve 6 to 8

1.5 to 2 kg	mixed fish	3 to 4lb
400 g	large yellow onions, chopped	14 oz
¼ litre	olive oil	8 fl oz
4	large very ripe tomatoes, sliced	4
½	head garlic, crushed	½
2	sprigs thyme	2
1	bay leaf	1
2	sprigs dried fennel	2
2 litres	water	4 pints
	salt	
½ tsp	powdered saffron	½ tsp
	freshly ground pepper	
	grated Parmesan cheese (optional)	
12	slices dried French bread, rubbed with garlic	12
	rouille (optional)	

Sweat the onions in the olive oil, without letting them colour, until they are soft and transparent. Turn up the heat and add the fish with the tomatoes, garlic and herbs. Mix vigorously with a wooden spatula while cooking for about 12 minutes, then pour in the water. Salt lightly and boil for 20 minutes.

Put the soup through a vegetable mill, then through a fine sieve, pressing hard to extract all the juices. Return the soup to the heat and bring to a gentle boil. Add the saffron and pepper (pepper added too early gives a disagreeable flavour), and season to taste with salt. Add the grated cheese if you wish. Serve the soup garnished with the bread croûtons, and with *rouille* if desired.

LES PRINCES DE LA GASTRONOMIE

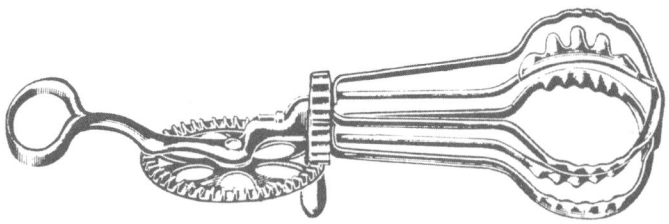

Fruit Soup with Cod

Sødsuppe

Danes enjoy soups that are made with fruit and sago, or tapioca, and served as a last course. In Vendsyssel, north of Limfjord, there is an exotic version of fruit soup that incorporates cod; it is thought suitable for celebrating weddings; but can be used as an everyday dish.

To serve 4

1 litre	fresh fruit juice, including redcurrant juice if possible	2 pints
250 g	boiled cod, skinned, boned and cut into small pieces	8 oz
40 g	sago, tapioca or oatmeal	1½ oz
2	strips lemon peel	2
½ tsp	ground cinnamon	½ tsp
30 g	raisins, soaked	1 oz
100 g	prunes, soaked and stoned	3½ oz

Bring the fruit juice to a gentle boil, stir in the sago, tapioca or oatmeal and cook for 30 minutes, uncovered. Add the strips of lemon peel, the cinnamon, the soaked raisins and prunes, and the small pieces of boiled cod. Bring back to boiling point, and when all is hot, serve it.

ALAN DAVIDSON
NORTH ATLANTIC SEAFOOD

Octopus Soup

Sopa de Pulpo

To clean octopus, remove the thin, purplish skin, empty the body sac, and cut off the hard beak.

This soup is equally delicious made with skate.

To serve 6

1 kg	octopus, cleaned and cut into small pieces	2 to 2½ lb
1	medium-sized onion, sliced	1
2 to 3	tomatoes, skinned and sliced	2 or 3
2 tbsp	olive oil	2 tbsp
2 tbsp	chopped parsley	2 tbsp
1.5 litres	water	3 pints
	salt and pepper	
	bread slices, fried in olive oil	

In a saucepan sauté the onion and tomatoes in the oil for 5 to 10 minutes. Add the octopus pieces and cook for 10 to 15 minutes more. Add the parsley and water and simmer, covered, for 2 hours. Season to taste. Allowing several slices per person, drop the bread slices into the soup, cook for another 15 minutes and serve immediately.

MARINA PEREYRA DE AZNAR AND NINA FROUD
THE HOME BOOK OF SPANISH COOKERY

Borscht with Squid

Borshch S Kal'Marami

To serve 4

500 g	squid, cleaned	1 lb
50 g	salted pork fat, diced	2 oz
3	medium-sized beetroots, cut into strips	3
1	carrot, cut into strips	1
1	Hamburg parsley root, cut into strips	1
	vinegar	
2 tbsp	tomato purée	2 tbsp
1 litre	water	1¾ pints
	salt	
200 g	cabbage, shredded	7 oz
2	potatoes, diced	2
	sugar	
1 or 2	garlic cloves, pounded with salt	1 or 2
2½ tbsp	soured cream	2½ tbsp
1 tbsp	finely chopped parsley	1 tbsp

Heat the pork fat in a thick frying pan and add the beetroot, carrot and parsley root with a little vinegar and the tomato purée. Cover and stew gently until soft.

Boil the squid in salted water for 3 to 5 minutes; then remove it and cut it into strips. Add the cabbage to the same boiling water and, 15 minutes later, the potato. When the potato is almost done, add the stewed vegetables and the squid; bring back to the boil and add sugar, garlic and vinegar to taste. Serve with a dollop of soured cream in each bowl and sprinkle the chopped parsley on top.

ALAN DAVIDSON
NORTH ATLANTIC SEAFOOD

Hamburg Eel Soup

Hamburger Aalsuppe

North Germans like things sweet and sour. They have excellent pork products; and in the early summer a fine array of fresh vegetables comes into season. So it has been their practice for centuries to make, especially at this time of year, what they call ***saure suppe***, which is a sort of sweet and sour soup. It is made from a smoked ham bone with scraps of ham still on it, fresh vegetables, dried fruit to provide a sweet counterpart to the salty ham, and dumplings for extra body.

Hamburg eel soup is achieved quite simply by adding pieces of eel, which have been cooked separately, to this ***saure suppe***. It is a relatively recent development, dating back to the 19th century, and it is an excellent one.

	To serve 6	
500 g	eel, skinned, cleaned and cut crosswise into 3 cm (1¼ inch) pieces	1 lb
1	smoked ham bone	1
1.5 litres	water	3 pints
1.5 kg	mixed vegetables (carrot, cauliflower, kohlrabi, celery, leek, string beans, peas—the more kinds the better) all diced	3 lb
250 g	dried fruit (prunes, apricots, apple rings), soaked in water for 1 hour	8 oz
1	bouquet garni, including 2 bay leaves and 2 sprigs of summer savory	1
1 tbsp	vinegar	1 tbsp
	sugar (optional)	
	salt (optional)	
	Dumplings	
250 g	flour	8 oz
	salt	
40 g	marrow, suet or butter	1½ oz
1	egg	1
About 15 cl	water	About ¼ pint

Prepare the dumplings by sifting the flour with a little salt; rub in the fat, then add the egg and enough water to make a springy dough; form into walnut-sized balls.

Set the ham bone to simmer in the water. After 20 minutes remove any scum and add the vegetables. Put in last those vegetables that require least cooking. Then add the fruit and continue to simmer until the vegetables are cooked.

Meanwhile, poach the pieces of eel separately for about 15 minutes in water flavoured with the bouquet garni and the vinegar. Poach the dumplings for 5 minutes or until done in a pan of simmering salted water.

Remove the ham bone from the vegetable broth. Take the scraps of meat off it, chop them and return them to the broth. Add the pieces of cooked eel and the dumplings. Correct the seasoning with a little sugar or salt, if necessary. Simmer for a few minutes, to let the flavours blend, then serve.

ALAN DAVIDSON
NORTH ATLANTIC SEAFOOD

Eel Soup

If salted eel is unavailable, rub a fresh eel with salt, leave overnight, and rinse in fresh water before using.

	To serve 4 or 5	
750 g	lightly salted eel, cut into 2.5 cm (1 inch) slices	1½ lb
1 litre	water	2 pints
3	white peppercorns	3
3	allspice berries	3
1	large carrot, finely chopped	1
2	leeks, finely chopped	2
1	parsnip, finely chopped	1
1	small celery stalk, finely chopped	1
5 or 6	potatoes, cut into 5 mm (¼ inch) cubes	5 or 6
⅛ tsp	white pepper	⅛ tsp
	salt	
1 tbsp	finely chopped dill	1 tbsp
1 tbsp	finely chopped parsley	1 tbsp

Cook the eel in the water for 10 minutes with the peppercorns and allspice. Add the carrot, leeks, parsnip and celery. Skim thoroughly. After a further 10 minutes, add the potatoes. Continue to cook the soup, covered, over a low heat until the potatoes are done, about 15 minutes. Season to taste with the pepper and salt. Finally, sprinkle the chopped dill and parsley over the soup before serving.

OSKAR JAKOBSSON
GOOD FOOD IN SWEDEN

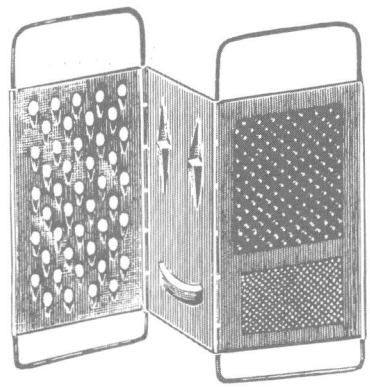

Smoked Fish Chowder

To serve 6

750 g	Finnan haddock, cut into 2 cm (1 inch) pieces	1½ lb
125 g	green bacon, diced	4 oz
1	large onion, sliced	1
4	medium-sized potatoes, sliced	4
	salt and freshly ground pepper	
1	bay leaf	1
1 litre	milk	2 pints

In a large saucepan, brown the bacon. Add the onion and sauté until soft. Add the potatoes and enough water to cover them. Add salt, pepper and the bay leaf. Cover and simmer until the potatoes are barely tender. Add the milk and fish and simmer for 15 to 20 minutes. Remove the bay leaf and serve.

MARJORIE PAGE BLANCHARD
TREASURED RECIPES FROM EARLY NEW ENGLAND KITCHENS

Manhattan Clam Chowder

To serve 10

1.5 litres	live clams	3 pints
2 litres	water	4 pints
350 g	green bacon, diced	12 oz
4	small onions, chopped	4
1 kg	tomatoes, skinned, seeded and chopped	2 to 2½ lb
300 g	celery, chopped	10 oz
200 g	carrots, chopped	7 oz
3 tbsp	finely chopped parsley	3 tbsp
½ tsp	thyme	½ tsp
1	large bay leaf	1
3	potatoes, cut into 1 cm (½ inch) cubes	3
	salt and freshly ground pepper	
4	cream crackers, crushed	4

Place the clams in a soup kettle, cover with water, and steam them open. Strain the liquid through a sieve lined with several thicknesses of cheesecloth and reserve. Remove the clams from the shells and mince very finely.

Render the bacon in a soup kettle. Remove the browned bits. Sauté the onions in the bacon fat until golden and transparent. Add the tomatoes to the onions in the soup kettle and simmer for several minutes, stirring constantly. Add the celery, carrots, parsley, thyme, bay leaf, clam liquid and remaining water. Simmer, covered, for about 1 hour. Add the potatoes to the soup and simmer for 15 minutes. Add the clams and simmer for 8 minutes more, or until the potatoes are tender. Adjust the seasonings. Put some crushed crackers in each soup bowl, and pour over the soup. Serve steaming hot.

YVONNE YOUNG TARR
THE NEW YORK TIMES BREAD AND SOUP COOKBOOK

New England Clam Chowder

To open the clams, scrub them and put them in a saucepan with the water. Cover the pan and cook over a high heat until all the clams are opened, 5 to 10 minutes. Remove the clams from their shells and strain the liquor through muslin.

To serve 4

1 litre	live clams, cooked in ½ litre (1 pint) water until open, shelled and the broth reserved	2 pints
90 g	green bacon, finely diced	3 oz
1	medium-sized onion, sliced	1
3	potatoes, diced	3
30 g	butter	1 oz
¼ litre	milk	8 fl oz
¼ litre	double cream	8 fl oz
	salt and pepper	
	cream crackers (optional)	

Mince the shelled clams. In a heavy saucepan, fry the bacon until lightly browned. Stir in the onion and cook until limp but not brown. Add the clam broth and potatoes and cook until the potatoes are tender, about 20 minutes. Stir in the butter, milk, cream and clams, and season to taste with salt and pepper. Heat but do not boil, and pour immediately into large, warmed soup bowls. Serve with crackers if desired.

THE EDITORS OF AMERICAN HERITAGE
THE AMERICAN HERITAGE COOKBOOK

Old-Fashioned Fish Chowder

To serve 8

2 kg	cod or haddock, skinned, filleted, and cut into 5 cm (2 inch pieces); the head, tail and bones broken into pieces	4 lb
½ litre	cold water	1 pint
60 g	fat salt pork, diced	2 oz
1	onion, thinly sliced	1
750 g	potatoes, thinly sliced	1½ lb
½ litre	boiling water	1 pint
1 litre	scalded milk or cream	2 pints
1 tbsp	salt	1 tbsp
	pepper	
40 g	butter	1½ oz

Put the pieces of head, tail and bones in a deep fish kettle. Add the cold water. Bring to the boil and simmer slowly for 10 minutes, drain and save the liquid. Put the diced salt pork in a small frying pan. Cook slowly for 5 minutes. Add the onion and cook until it is soft—about 5 minutes. Strain the fat into a deep pan and set aside the onion and pork. Add to the fat the potatoes and boiling water. Cook for 5 minutes. Add the fish and the reserved liquid; cover and simmer for 10 minutes. Add the onion and pork pieces, the scalded milk or cream, the salt, pepper to taste and butter. Heat, but do not boil.

FANNIE MERRITT FARMER
THE FANNIE FARMER COOKBOOK

Mussel Soup with Milk

Kraeklingasúpa úr Mjólk

To serve 4

25	live mussels, scrubbed and bearded	25
½ litre	milk, or a mixture of milk and cream	1 pint
30 cl	water	½ pint
150 g	green bacon, diced	5 oz
1	medium-sized onion, chopped	1
3 or 4	potatoes, diced	3 or 4
½	bay leaf	½
1	sprig thyme	1
	salt and pepper	
30 g	butter (optional)	1 oz

Bring the water to the boil and put in the mussels. Cover the pot and boil until the shells open, in 3 or 4 minutes. Remove the mussels, extract the meat from the shells, chop it up and leave it in a covered dish, so that it does not dry out. Strain the cooking broth through a sieve and reserve.

Fry the bacon in a large heavy saucepan until light brown. Remove the bacon pieces, and add the onion to the bacon fat left in the pan. Cook the onion gently, without letting it colour. Pour the strained broth into the pan and add the potatoes, bay leaf, thyme, and a light seasoning of salt and pepper. Simmer for 15 to 20 minutes, then add the milk, or milk and cream, and simmer for another 5 minutes.

Return the mussels to the soup together with the bacon and butter if used. Heat through and serve with crackers.

HELGA SIGURDADÓTTIR
MATUR OG DRYKKUR

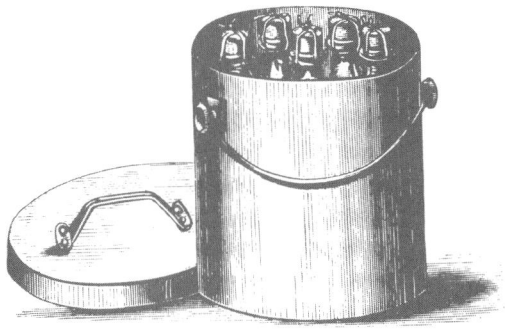

Velouté of Mussels

To colour and flavour the soup, a pinch of powdered saffron or saffron threads may be dissolved in a tablespoon of hot water, and stirred into the velouté before the final thickening with the egg yolks and the double cream.

To serve 4 to 6

2 litres	live mussels, scrubbed and bearded	4 pints
10 cl	white wine	4 fl oz
1	onion, thinly sliced	1
2	garlic cloves, crushed	2
1	bouquet garni	1
50 g	butter	2 oz
40 g	flour	1½ oz
¾ litre	fish broth (*page 163*)	1½ pints
	salt and pepper	
	saffron (optional)	
2	egg yolks	2
15 cl	double cream	¼ pint

Pack the cleaned mussels into a large saucepan with the wine, onion, garlic and bouquet garni. Cover tightly and steam over a high heat for 10 minutes or until all the mussels have opened. Remove the mussels from their shells and keep warm in a covered dish; strain the cooking liquor through a muslin-lined sieve into a bowl and reserve it.

Melt the butter in a saucepan over a low heat, and stir in the flour to make a roux. Whisk in the fish broth, and stir until the soup comes to the boil. Simmer slowly for at least 40 minutes, skimming the skin that forms on the surface. Season with salt and pepper to taste. Add the mussel cooking liquor and return the soup to the boil, skimming if necessary. If you are using it, dissolve the saffron in hot water and add it to the soup.

In a small bowl, whisk the egg yolks and cream together. Gradually whisk in a ladleful of the hot soup. Stir the egg mixture into the soup, and heat slowly, without boiling, until the soup thickens lightly. Add the shelled mussels to the soup, and pour into a warmed tureen to serve.

GEORGE LASSALLE
THE ADVENTUROUS FISH COOK

Mussel and Tomato Soup

To serve 4

1 kg	live mussels, scrubbed and bearded	2 to 2½ lb
2 tbsp	olive oil	2 tbsp
2	large garlic cloves, crushed	2
350 g	tomatoes, skinned, or drained canned tomatoes	12 oz
	salt and pepper	
	sugar	
	tomato purée (optional)	
	croûtons of bread fried in olive oil	

Put 6 mm (¼ inch) of water in a large pan, add the mussels, and cook, covered, over a high heat until they open. Remove them from their shells (which should be thrown away). Strain the mussel liquor into a measuring jug, and add sufficient water to bring it up to 1 litre (2 pints).

Meanwhile put the oil into another pan, and add the garlic and tomatoes. Cook over a medium heat for 5 to 10 minutes, pressing the tomatoes into a rough purée without too many large lumps. Add the mussel liquor and season with salt and pepper. Simmer for 15 minutes, then adjust the seasoning with sugar and tomato purée, if necessary. Add the mussels to reheat for a few seconds (not for long, or they will turn rubbery), and pour into a tureen. Serve with the croûtons, added at the last moment and sizzling hot, on top of the soup.

JANE GRIGSON
GOOD THINGS

New England Soup

Soupe de la Nouvelle Angleterre

This recipe is from Mrs Henry Cabot Lodge.

To serve 6

1 kg	cod or haddock fillets	2 to 2½ lb
1 litre	water	2 pints
500 g	potatoes, diced	1 lb
60 g	green bacon, diced	2 oz
125 g	onion, finely sliced	4 oz
½ litre	double cream	1 pint
	salt and white pepper	

Put the fish and the water into a saucepan; bring to the boil and cook over a medium heat for 15 minutes. Remove and flake the fish. Put the potatoes into the fish's cooking liquid and cook over a low heat for 10 minutes. The potatoes should be cooked but still firm.

Meanwhile, sauté the bacon in a frying pan. Add the onion and cook until golden. Pour in the cream and bring to the boil. Pour the mixture into the saucepan with the potatoes. Add the salt and pepper and the flaked fish. Reheat without boiling, check the seasoning, and serve.

LES PETITS PLATS ET LES GRANDS

Lobster Stew

To serve 3 or 4

3	live lobsters, 600 g (1¼ lb) each	3
125 g	butter	4 oz
1 litre	rich milk	2 pints

Steam the live lobsters in a small amount of water for 20 minutes. Leave to cool and, as soon as you can handle them, remove the meat and cut into bite-size pieces. Save the fat, tomalley (liver), and coral.

In a heavy saucepan heat the butter. Simmer the fat, tomalley and coral for 7 to 8 minutes. Add the pieces of lobster meat and cook over low heat for 10 minutes. Very slowly, pour in the milk, stirring constantly. Remove from the heat. Cool and refrigerate. Leave for at least 12 hours (some recommend 24). Reheat without boiling.

MARJORIE PAGE BLANCHARD
TREASURED RECIPES FROM EARLY NEW ENGLAND KITCHENS

Seafood Stew

Cioppino

According to the author, the name of this dish comes from the fishermen at the San Francisco wharf who used to "chip in" everything they had caught that day, but had not sold. They would make this marvellous stew, open a bottle of wine, put out some French bread, and have themselves a feast.

To serve 6 to 8

250 g	crab meat	8 oz
24	clams in their shells	24
24	large prawns	24
1 kg	firm-fleshed fish, cut into pieces	2 to 2½ lb
1	lobster, cut into pieces (optional)	1
2	large onions, cut into wedges	2
2	bunches spring onions, thickly sliced	2
2	sweet green peppers, seeded and diced	2
4	large garlic cloves, crushed	4
10 cl	olive oil	4 fl oz
½ litre	red wine	1 pint
¼ litre	puréed tomato	8 fl oz
1 litre	water	2 pints
1	bay leaf	1
1 tsp	oregano	1 tsp
1 tsp	basil	1 tsp
1 tsp	Tabasco sauce	1 tsp
	salt and pepper	

Sauté the onions, spring onions, green peppers and garlic in the oil for 5 minutes. Add the wine and simmer briskly. Add the puréed tomato, water and herbs. Cover and simmer the broth for about 1 hour.

Place the crab meat, clams, prawns, fish and lobster (if using) in a large kettle. Add the wine and tomato sauce and simmer for 20 to 30 minutes or until the clams are opened and the fish cooked. Season to taste with Tabasco sauce, salt and pepper, and serve immediately.

THE JUNIOR LEAGUE OF DALLAS
THE DALLAS JUNIOR LEAGUE COOKBOOK

Bread Soups

Saffron Soup

Le Mourtaïrol

The quality of this soup depends entirely on the richness of the chicken broth and the honesty of the bread. The quantity of saffron may be increased to taste.

To serve 4

¼ tsp	powdered saffron	¼ tsp
300 g	home-made bread (*page 165*), thinly sliced	10 oz
1 litre	chicken broth (*page 164*)	2 pints

Place the bread slices in an earthenware casserole. Bring the broth to the boil, and stir a spoonful into the saffron. When the saffron is dissolved, after about 5 minutes, pour it into the broth. Pour the saffron-flavoured broth over the bread until the bread refuses to absorb any more. Set the casserole to simmer in an oven preheated to 180°C (350°F or Mark 4) for about 30 minutes, adding some of the remaining hot broth from time to time, if necessary, to keep the bread moist. Serve the soup from the casserole in which it has been cooked.

LA FRANCE À TABLE

Almond Soup

Sopa de Almendras

To serve 4

24	almonds, blanched	24
2 tbsp	oil	2 tbsp
3	garlic cloves, chopped	3
2	slices bread, cubed	2
1	sweet red pepper, seeded and chopped	1
1 tsp	chopped parsley	1 tsp
3	peppercorns	3
1 tsp	powdered saffron	1 tsp
1 litre	boiling water	2 pints
	salt	

Fry the almonds in hot oil until they are golden, then remove and drain. In the same oil gently fry the garlic, bread, red pepper, parsley, peppercorns and saffron for 10 minutes or until lightly browned. Transfer this mixture to a mortar, add the almonds, and pound until smooth and blended. Place the mixture in a saucepan over a low heat, and gradually pour in the boiling water, stirring continuously. Season with salt to taste and serve when the soup is hot.

ELIZABETH CASS
SPANISH COOKING

Pumpkin Panade

Soupe au Potiron

To thicken the soup with bread rather than the potatoes used here, omit the potatoes and layer the pumpkin purée with sliced bread in the pumpkin shell.

To serve 10

One 3 kg	pumpkin	One 6 to 7 lb
2 litres	water	4 pints
500 g	potatoes, thickly sliced	1 lb
	salt and pepper	
10 cl	cream	4 fl oz
	croûtons made from 3 slices of bread	
50 g	Gruyère cheese, grated	2 oz

Cut out and discard a lid from the top of the pumpkin. Scoop out the seeds with a spoon. Remove the flesh from the interior, using a knife and a spoon, and being careful not to pierce the pumpkin shell. Put the shell on a heavy baking sheet.

Cut 500 g (1 lb) of the pumpkin flesh into pieces. (Use the rest for a tart or gratin.) Put the pieces in a pan with the water and the potatoes. Season with salt and pepper, bring to the boil, and cook, covered, over a low heat for 45 minutes.

Put the soup through a sieve or food mill. Add the cream. Pour the soup into the hollowed-out pumpkin shell and sprinkle the surface of the soup with the croûtons and the Gruyère. Put in an oven preheated to 220°C (425°F or Mark 7) and cook for 15 minutes. To serve, bring the pumpkin shell filled with the soup to the table.

ODETTE KAHN (EDITOR)
CUISINE ET VINS DE FRANCE

Bread Soup

Panade à l'Eau

For a richer result, this soup may be made with broth or milk instead of water; the method is the same.

To serve 6 to 8

500 g	bread, broken into pieces	1 lb
1.5 litres	water	3 pints
	salt	
100 g	butter	3½ oz
2	eggs	2

Put the bread in a saucepan with the water and leave to soak for 30 minutes. Then add a pinch of salt and half the butter and simmer for 20 minutes, stirring with a wooden spoon. When the bread is well mixed and the broth is smooth, break the eggs into a soup tureen and beat well with a fork. Add the remaining butter to the eggs. Pour in half the bread broth, mixing well with the spoon. Add the rest of the broth and continue to mix. Serve.

JULES GOUFFÉ
LE LIVRE DES SOUPES ET DES POTAGES

Asturian Garlic Soup

Sopa de Ajo Asturiana

This recipe was taught to me by a family from Asturias but there are many other variations from different parts of Spain, in which red chili pepper, or sweet pepper, or a beaten egg may be added just before serving.

To serve 4

4 or 5	garlic cloves, chopped	4 or 5
6 tbsp	olive oil	6 tbsp
About 250 g	stale bread, broken up into walnut-sized pieces	About 8 oz
1 litre	water	2 pints
½ tsp	salt	½ tsp
2 or 3	tomatoes, skinned and chopped (optional)	2 or 3

Heat the oil gently in a large saucepan, and allow the garlic to stew in the oil. Gradually add the bread to the oil and garlic, stirring well. Do not allow it to brown. Add the water and the salt. Throw in the tomatoes (which may be omitted if not available). Allow the soup to simmer gently for about 15 minutes, until the bread has become very soft but has not completely disintegrated.

ANNA MACMIADHACHÁIN
SPANISH REGIONAL COOKERY

Black Bread Soup, Franconian-Style

Brotsuppe

This soup has several variations. Two chopped pared apples may be sautéed with the onion, and a little grated lemon peel added to the broth. The leftover gravy may be replaced by soured or double cream. Five minutes before serving, sliced bratwurst *may be added to the soup.*

To serve 6 to 8

6	slices slightly stale dark rye bread, cubed	6
2 litres	beef broth or water, heated to boiling	4 pints
1	medium-sized onion, chopped	1
15 to 30 g	meat dripping	½ to 1 oz
	salt (optional)	
2 to 3 tbsp	leftover gravy (preferably pork)	2 to 3 tbsp

Cover the bread cubes with the boiling broth or water and let stand until the bread is soft, about 10 minutes. Meanwhile, in a saucepan, sauté the onion in the dripping until soft and yellow. Add the bread and broth, and simmer for 30 minutes. If water is used, add salt to taste. Stir in the gravy and serve.

BETTY WASON
THE ART OF GERMAN COOKING

Auvergne Bread and Cheese Soup

Soupe d'Auvergne au Fromage, Mitonnée

At the turn of the century, a French culinary magazine published this description by A. Colombié, a famous chef, of his childhood Christmases in the rugged Auvergne. Preserved goose, confit d'oie, *is a speciality of the region.*

To serve 6

	thinly sliced dark bread	
150 g	Cantal or white Cheshire cheese, thinly sliced	5 oz
1 kg	cabbage, cut into 5 cm (2 inch) pieces	2 to 2½ lb
1.5 litres	water	3 pints
	salt	
1	garlic clove	1
¼	goose, preserved, with some of its fat clinging to it	¼

Generally, the finest white-heart cabbage was left in the garden for the Christmas soup, and a marked, prime pot of preserved goose, pork or duck was carefully put aside. The sops, or slices of bread, were taken from the familiar round wholemeal loaf and propped against the tilted wrought iron grill to be toasted in front of the fire.

The cabbage, water, salt, garlic and the preserved goose with a little of its fat, were put together in the soup pot, which was hung over the fire. When it came to the boil, Mother let it boil for 30 to 40 minutes while she toasted the bread and cut the cheese; she layered grilled bread and the cheese in the brown earthenware soup tureen, interspersed with ladles of cabbage. She poured over the liquid, setting the piece of goose aside to eat cold, covered the tureen and put it on the glowing cinders at the side of the fire so that it would simmer very gently until we returned from midnight mass. The result was a sort of cream that formed strand after strand and how happy I was to see these strands stretch from the plate to my mouth. A happy age and how little it took to delight children then!

MME. JEANNE SAVARIN (EDITOR)
LA CUISINE DES FAMILLES

Portuguese Panade

Açorda Alentejana

This soup often accompanies grilled fresh sardines.

To serve 6 to 8

250 g	dry bread, broken up	8 oz
1	sprig coriander	1
3 to 4	garlic cloves	3 to 4
½ tsp	salt	½ tsp
3 tbsp	olive oil	3 tbsp
2 litres	boiling water	4 pints

In a mortar, pound to a paste the coriander, garlic and salt. Put the mixture in a serving bowl and add the oil, stirring well. Pour in the boiling water and add the broken up bread. Mix together well until smooth.

CAROL WRIGHT
PORTUGUESE FOOD

Soup of Mallorca

Sopa a la Mallorquina

To serve 6

3 tbsp	oil	3 tbsp
3	onions, finely sliced	3
3	sweet red peppers, seeded and chopped	3
1	small green cabbage, cored and chopped	1
2	garlic cloves, chopped	2
3	tomatoes, skinned, seeded and chopped	3
1 tbsp	chopped parsley	1 tbsp
1 litre	boiling water	2 pints
	salt	
12	thin slices bread	12

Heat the oil in a large saucepan; add the onions, peppers, cabbage and garlic and allow them to cook gently. When the onion begins to soften, add the tomatoes and parsley. Cover the pan and allow the vegetables to cook gently for about 15 minutes. Now add the water, bring to the boil and simmer until the cabbage is soft, about 15 minutes. Season to taste.

Cover the bottom of a casserole, in which the soup will be served, with a layer of bread slices. Then ladle some of the cooked vegetables on to the bread. Add another layer of bread and another of vegetables until all the vegetables have been taken out of the stock. Pour over the stock and simmer slowly until all the stock is absorbed, making a very solid purée.

ELIZABETH CASS
SPANISH COOKING

Spanish Egg Soup

Sainserelle à l'Espagnole

This recipe is from a book published anonymously, but attributed to Louis-Auguste de Bourbon, Prince de Dombes.

To serve 4

3	eggs	3
50 g	fresh breadcrumbs	2 oz
50 g	Parmesan cheese, grated	2 oz
1 litre	broth, warmed (*pages 163-164*)	2 pints

Mix the breadcrumbs and Parmesan, and beat in the eggs. Stir this mixture into the warmed broth and heat gently, stirring constantly, until the soup is thickened. Serve the soup immediately.

LE CUISINIER GASCON

Soup with Eggs

Zuppa Pavese

To serve 2

4	eggs	4
8	thin slices bread, buttered	8
60 g	Parmesan cheese, freshly grated	2 oz
½ litre	boiling stock	1 pint
	freshly ground white pepper	

Sprinkle the bread with the cheese and place the slices in two individual ovenproof casseroles. Pour over the stock, and gently break the eggs into the casseroles, taking care to keep the yolks whole. Season with a dash of pepper and put into a hot oven, preheated to 230°C (450°F or Mark 8), for 10 minutes or long enough to set the eggs. Serve very hot, accompanied by additional grated cheese.

GIANNI BRERA AND LUIGI VERONELLI
LA PACCIADA

Onion Soup

The English cookery writer, Hannah Glasse, published this recipe in the 1747 volume she signed only "By a Lady".

To serve 4 to 6

10 to 12	medium-sized onions, chopped	10 to 12
250 g	butter	8 oz
2 tbsp	flour	2 tbsp
1 to 1.5 litres	boiling water	2 to 3 pints
100 g	stale bread, cut into small pieces or crumbled	3½ oz
	salt	
2	egg yolks	2
2 tsp	vinegar	2 tsp

Take the butter, put it into a stew-pan on the heat, let it all melt, and boil it till it has done making any noise; then have ready the onions, throw them into the butter, and let them fry for 15 minutes. Shake in the flour, and stir the onions round; shake your pan, and let them do a few minutes longer. Pour in the boiling water, stir round, take the bread and throw it in. Season with salt to your taste. Let it boil for 10 minutes, stirring it often; then take it off the heat, and have ready the egg yolks beaten with the vinegar; mix some of the soup with them, then stir this into your soup and mix it well, and pour it into your dish. This is a delicious dish.

THE ART OF COOKERY MADE PLAIN AND EASY

Onion Soup

Soupe à l'Oignon

Simple and inexpensive, this soup is excellent for breakfast; it is restorative and light.

To serve 5 or 6

250 g	white onions, quartered lengthwise and thinly sliced crosswise	8 oz
60 g	butter	2 oz
	salt	
	sugar	
1 tbsp	flour	1 tbsp
1.5 litres	boiling water	3 pints
½	bay leaf	½
2 or 3	egg yolks (optional)	2 or 3
10 cl	cream (optional)	4 fl oz
15 to 20	thin slices white French bread or baguette, dried in a cool oven	15 to 20
	pepper	

Put the onions in a saucepan with 30 g (1 oz) of the butter, and stew them over a very low heat, stirring frequently with a wooden spoon. Add a pinch of salt and a pinch of sugar, and cook until the onions are golden. Sprinkle with the flour; 2 minutes later, pour on the boiling water. Stir until the mixture comes to the boil, then move the saucepan half way off the heat and add the bay leaf and salt to taste. Cook gently for 10 to 12 minutes; remove the bay leaf at the last minute.

The soup may be served as it is or bound with a *liaison* of egg yolks and cream, whisked together and stirred in just before serving. In either case, arrange the slices of dried bread in a soup tureen, grind some pepper over them, dot with the remaining butter, and pour over the soup.

URBAIN DUBOIS
ÉCOLE DES CUISINIÈRES

Onion Soup

Soupe à l'Oignon

Instead of pouring the soup over the bread, you may float bread slices and grated cheese on top of the soup and brown it under the grill.

This soup has a reputation for dispelling the effects of intoxication; thus it is justly called drunkard's soup. If it is to be used for this purpose, the cheese is best omitted.

To serve 4

2 or 3	large onions, finely chopped	2 or 3
30 g	butter	1 oz
2 tsp	flour	2 tsp
1 litre	water	2 pints
90 g	bread, sliced	3 oz
75 g	Gruyère or Parmesan cheese, grated (optional)	2½ oz
	salt	

Melt the butter in a saucepan, and sauté the onions until lightly coloured. Stir in the flour, and continue to cook until the onion mixture has turned as brown as it can become without burning. Add the water, cover and simmer for 30 minutes. Put the slices of bread into a warmed soup tureen. If you are using cheese as well, alternate layers of bread with layers of cheese. Season the soup with salt, pour it into the tureen and serve. If using cheese, add only a very little salt.

JULES BRETEUIL
LE CUISINIER EUROPÉEN

Bread and Tomato Soup

Pappa al Pomodoro

It is most important that the bread is not soggy. It should be sufficiently old, several days at least, rather hard, and, if possible, dark rather than light.

Though considered a soup, the consistency of this dish is not liquid at all. It may be eaten hot, lukewarm or cold, or reheated the following day.

To serve 4

500 g	bread, cut into small pieces (*page 165*)	1 lb
500 g	very ripe tomatoes, skinned, seeded and quartered	1 lb
10 cl	olive oil	4 fl oz
3	large garlic cloves, coarsely chopped	3
	dried hot pepper flakes	
¾ litre	hot chicken or meat broth (*page 164*)	1½ pints
	salt and freshly ground black pepper	
4 or 5	basil leaves	4 or 5

Place half the oil in a stockpot, preferably flameproof terra-cotta, and add the garlic and a pinch of pepper flakes. Sauté them very gently for 10 to 12 minutes. Add the tomatoes to the pot and simmer for a further 15 minutes.

Add the bread to the pot, along with the broth, salt, pepper and basil leaves. Stir the mixture very well and simmer for 15 minutes longer, then remove the pot from the heat, cover, and leave to rest for 1 to 2 hours.

When ready to serve, stir very well and spoon the soup into individual soup bowls. At the table, sprinkle 1 tablespoon of the remaining olive oil on each serving, and grind some fresh black pepper into each bowl.

GUILIANO BUGIALLI
THE FINE ART OF ITALIAN COOKING

Fisherman's Soup

Soupe du Pêcheur

This is not a fish soup, but a special onion soup obtained by the author from a fisherman friend. For a less rich soup, the tomato and the butter spread on the bread may be omitted.

	To serve 4	
250 g	home-made bread (*recipe, page 165*), sliced 1 cm (½ inch) thick	½ lb
100 g	butter	3½ oz
150 g	Gruyère cheese, grated	5 oz
4	medium-sized onions, thinly sliced	4
3 tbsp	puréed tomato	3 tbsp
About 1 litre	boiling water	About 2 pints
	salt	

Grill the slices of bread. Leave them to get quite cold, then spread them with 90 g (3 oz) of the butter. Cover with a generous coating of cheese. (The layers of butter and cheese together must be the same thickness as the bread.) Sauté the onions in the remaining butter until golden-brown.

Arrange a layer of the bread slices spread with butter and cheese at the bottom of a fireproof earthenware casserole, and sprinkle with a third of the onions. Make another layer of bread and onions, and sprinkle with 2 tablespoons of the puréed tomato. Layer the remaining bread and onions, and add the remaining tomato. Cover with grated cheese. Since the bread swells considerably during cooking, it is important that the casserole be no more than two-thirds full.

Take a funnel and push the stem into the casserole so that it touches the base. Pour boiling water slowly through the funnel until the contents of the casserole just begin to float upwards. Salt should be added to the hot water unless the cheese is very salty. Place the casserole on top of the stove, uncovered, and let it simmer over a low heat for 30 minutes. Add enough additional boiling water at the end of this time to keep the bread from drying out.

Put the casserole into a warm oven, preheated to 170°C (325°F or Mark 3), for 1 hour, adding more water and more salt during the cooking if necessary. The soup is cooked when the cheese topping forms a nicely golden, rather crisp, crust. By this time the interior will have been reduced to a purée. Each guest is served with a portion of the smooth, thick interior, and with a section of the crisp crust.

B. RENAUDET
LES SECRETS DE LA BONNE TABLE

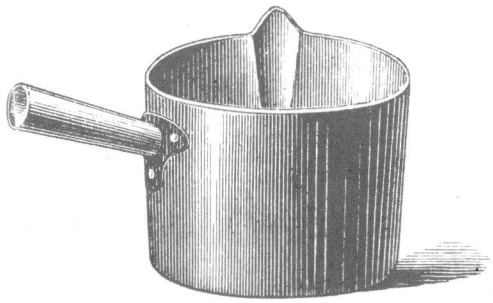

La Soupe au Fromage et au Pain Bis

Pain bis ***is a large round loaf of peasant-style bread, usually made from a mixture of unbleached white flour, wholemeal, and rye, leavened with a sourdough yeast. For this recipe, cut a large wedge from the round loaf and slice it. For a bread recipe that can be adapted to make*** pain bis, ***see page 165. If Cantal cheese is unavailable, substitute a sharp, mature Cheddar.***

	To serve 4	
24	thin slices stale or dry bread	24
200 g	Cantal cheese, grated	7 oz
6	onion, sliced	6
3	garlic cloves, sliced	3
30 g	butter	1 oz
	salt	
1 litre	water	2 pints

Sauté the onions and garlic in the butter. Season with a little salt, then pour on the water and bring to the boil. Allow to simmer while you prepare the soup tureen. Warm an oven-proof tureen (preferably of the bulbous shape used in Auvergne), and cover the bottom with a layer of bread slices. Cover the bread with grated cheese. Repeat, alternating layers of bread and cheese, until both are used up and the tureen is full. Pour the onion broth into the tureen, and put the tureen—uncovered—into an oven preheated to 180°C (350°F or Mark 4) for 45 minutes to 1 hour. The soup should be thick enough for a spoon to stand upright in the middle, and there should be a golden crust on top.

SUZANNE ROBAGLIA
MARGARIDOU: JOURNAL ET RECETTES
D'UNE CUISINIÈRE AU PAYS D'AUVERGNE

Italian Bread Soup

Zuppa Mitunà

As a variation on this recipe, 150 g (5 oz) of *fontina* or other soft Italian cheese may be sliced and placed on the bread.

	To serve 6	
300 g	stale home-made bread, thinly sliced (*page 165*)	10 oz
2	garlic cloves, halved	2
2 litres	chicken or beef broth, heated (*page 164*)	4 pints
2 tbsp	finely chopped parsley	2 tbsp

Place the bread on a baking sheet and put into an oven preheated to 180°C (350°F or Mark 4) until thoroughly dried. Rub the slices with the cut sides of the garlic cloves. Place the bread in an ovenproof tureen, and pour over the hot broth a little at a time so that it is absorbed by the bread. Put the tureen into a hot oven, preheated to 220°C (425°F or Mark 7), and let the soup brown for 10 to 15 minutes. Sprinkle the parsley over the soup just before serving.

LAURA GRAS PORTINARI
CUCINA E VINI DEL PIEMONTE E DELLA VALLE D'AOSTA

Stuffed Bread Soup

Zuppa di Pane Farcito

For instructions on extracting beef marrow from a marrow-bone, see page 18.

	To serve 6	
1	small square loaf of bread, thinly sliced	1
250 g	cooked chicken, boned and skinned	8 oz
60 g	*prosciutto*, thinly sliced	2 oz
30 g	beef marrow	1 oz
1	egg, lightly beaten	1
½ tsp	salt	½ tsp
⅛ tsp	freshly ground pepper	⅛ tsp
40 g	Parmesan cheese, grated	1½ oz
About 90 g	butter	About 3 oz
2 litres	boiling broth (*pages 163-164*)	4 pints

Chop and mix thoroughly (or put through the medium blade of a meat grinder) the chicken, *prosciutto* and marrow; add the egg, salt, pepper and 1 tablespoon of the cheese, and mix thoroughly until smooth. Cut out rounds from the slices of bread, using a pastry cutter, 4 cm (1½ inches) in diameter. Spread half the rounds with the chicken mixture and cover with the remaining rounds, pinching the edges of these sandwiches together firmly. Melt 30 g (1 oz) of the butter in a frying pan and fry the stuffed sandwiches to a golden-brown on both sides, adding more butter as necessary. Distribute the sandwiches in deep soup plates, pour over them the boiling broth, and serve, passing the grated cheese separately.

LUIGI CARNACINA
GREAT ITALIAN COOKING

Panade with Sorrel or Leek

La Panade avec Oseille ou Blanc de Poireau

The bread used must always be nearly stale. Ideally, one should only use the "upper crust", that is the upper half of the loaf, this being lighter and better cooked than the underside. Any burnt or dark-coloured parts should be cut off. If the bread is not very dry, lay the pieces on a tray and put in a very low oven for a few minutes. Instead of water, you may use a degreased veal stock or a mixture of water and milk.

	To serve 6 to 8	
250 g	dry bread, cut into small pieces	8 oz
100 g	sorrel, roughly chopped, or 75 g (2½ oz) leek, white part only, very finely chopped	3½ oz
90 g	butter	3 oz
2 litres	water, warmed	4 pints
6	egg yolks, lightly beaten	6
	salt	

Melt 30 g (1 oz) of the butter in a deep, thick-bottomed saucepan and lightly sauté the sorrel or leek over a low heat for 10 minutes. If using leeks, do not allow them to colour. Add the bread and pour on the water. Cover and let stand off the heat for 10 minutes to allow the bread to absorb the water.

Bring the soup to the boil, stirring constantly with a wooden spoon. Cover and simmer very gently for at least 30 minutes. Do not stir during the cooking period, as stirring will make the bread stick to the pan.

When the soup is cooked, stir vigorously to break up any remaining lumps. You should have a very smooth purée or cream. Off the heat, whisk in the egg yolks, the remaining butter, and salt to taste. Return the pan to a gentle heat and whisk the soup until it thickens. Serve.

MADAME SAINT-ANGE
LA CUISINE DE MADAME SAINT-ANGE

Panade with Sorrel

To serve 6

250 g	stale white bread, cut into pieces	8 oz
200 g	sorrel, shredded	7 oz
30 g	butter	1 oz
1 litre	warm water	2 pints
1 tsp	salt	1 tsp
½ litre	milk, or milk and cream if available	1 pint
1	large, or 2 small, eggs, lightly beaten	1

Put the sorrel in a saucepan with half of the butter. Cover and cook slowly until the sorrel is cooked down to about a quarter of its original volume. Add the water, salt and bread. Mix well so that the bread will become thoroughly soaked, then bring the mixture to the boil, stirring all the time. Cook slowly for 30 minutes longer, stirring from time to time. At this point beat briskly with a whisk to make the mixture smooth. Add the milk to the eggs and combine with the hot mixture. Add the remaining butter. Bring back to boiling point, but do not allow to boil. Correct the seasoning and serve.

LOUIS DIAT
FRENCH COOKING FOR AMERICANS

Fried Breadcrumb Soup

Soupe à la Mie de Pain Frite

To serve 4

100 g	fresh breadcrumbs	3½ oz
60 g	butter	2 oz
1 litre	boiling milk	2 pints
15 cl	raspberry syrup, or puréed fresh raspberries, sweetened to taste	¼ pint

Brown the breadcrumbs in the butter and drain them; place them in a warmed soup tureen. Pour in half of the milk, cover the tureen and let stand for 5 minutes. Pour in the raspberry syrup and the remaining milk, stir gently, and serve.

JEAN DE GOUY
LA CUISINE ET LA PATISSERIE BOURGEOISES

Cold Soups

Avocado Summer Soup

To serve 4 to 6

4	ripe, unblemished avocados, peeled, stoned and sieved	4
¼ litre	chicken stock or broth (*page 164*)	8 fl oz
¼ litre	double cream	8 fl oz
10 cl	dry white wine (optional)	4 fl oz
2 tsp	lemon juice	2 tsp
	salt and pepper	
	cayenne pepper	
	chives or dill	

Add the chicken stock to the sieved avocado. Mix well and strain through a sieve, then combine with the cream, and white wine, if you are using it. Add the lemon juice, salt and pepper and a tiny speck of cayenne pepper. Cover the container and chill well. Chop the chives or dill and sprinkle them over the soup just before serving.

HELEN EVANS BROWN
HELEN BROWN'S WEST COAST COOK BOOK

Avocado Bisque

To serve 2

1	large avocado, peeled and stoned	1
10 cl	lemon juice	4 fl oz
	salt and freshly ground pepper	
35 cl	rich chicken broth (*page 164*)	12 fl oz
15 to 20 cl	double cream	6 fl oz

Pour the lemon juice into a deep bowl. Cut the avocado into large chunks and immediately dip them into the lemon juice. With a fork, mash the avocado into the lemon juice—not too finely, as you want some of the pulp to remain in nuggets about the size of a pea. Season with salt and pepper. Turn the mixture into a saucepan, preferably one with an enamel lining, and place over low heat. Slowly add the chicken broth, stirring to blend, then add the cream. Bring the soup just to the boil and simmer for 2 minutes. Serve hot or chill in the refrigerator for several hours.

DORIS TOBIAS AND MARY MERRIS
THE GOLDEN LEMON

Cucumber and Cream Soup

Minestra di Cetriolo alla Crema

To serve 2 to 4

1	large cucumber, peeled and cut into pieces	1 1
1	large or 2 small dill pickled cucumbers, cut into pieces	1
3 tbsp	lemon juice	3 tbsp
3 tbsp	grated onion	3 tbsp
15 to 20 cl	double cream	6 fl oz
	salt and pepper	
1 tbsp	chopped dill	1 tbsp

Put the cucumber pieces in a liquidizer, reserving 2 tablespoons for garnish, and blend with the pickled cucumber, lemon juice and onion. When the mixture is smooth, pour into a chilled tureen and stir in the cream, salt and pepper and dill. Garnish with the reserved cucumber and serve chilled.

JANET ROSS AND MICHAEL WATERFIELD
LEAVES FROM OUR TUSCAN KITCHEN

White Garlic Soup with Grapes

Sopa de Ajo Blanco con Uvas

The original version of this Malagan soup is made with fresh almonds, that is, not green almonds but simply ripe ones recently removed from their shells and not kept for months. They are skinned, dried slightly in the oven and ground down in a mortar. Powdered almonds can be used instead, but something of the flavour is lost.

To serve 6

5	garlic cloves	5
500 g	grapes, skinned, halved and seeded	1 lb
2 tbsp	ground almonds or 30 fresh almonds	2 tbsp
60 g	brown breadcrumbs	2 oz
	salt	
2 tbsp	olive oil	2 tbsp
1 tbsp	vinegar	1 tbsp
½ litre	water	1 pint
6	ice cubes	6

Pound the almonds, garlic, breadcrumbs and salt together in a mortar. Add the oil gradually, mixing well, then add the vinegar. Put this mixture into a soup tureen and pour in the water. Add the grapes and the ice and leave in a cool place for about 30 minutes before serving.

ELIZABETH CASS
SPANISH COOKING

Iced Soup, Simplified

Soupe à la Glace Simplifiée

The author of this recipe suggests that melon can be substituted for the cucumber. To extract the cucumber juice, grate or grind a large cucumber, salt it, and leave to drain in a muslin-lined colander. Squeeze and twist the muslin to extract all the liquid. The curdled milk can be either naturally soured milk or fresh milk to which rennet has been added—alternatively, buttermilk may be substituted.

To serve 4

100 g	sorrel, chopped	3½ oz
15 g	butter	½ oz
1 litre	curdled milk	2 pints
10 cl	cucumber juice	4 fl oz
3 tbsp	chopped fennel or dill leaves	3 tbsp
2 tbsp	chopped chives	2 tbsp
1	small cucumber, peeled, seeded and thinly sliced	1
2	eggs, hard-boiled and sliced	2
	salt	
6 to 8	ice cubes, crushed in a cloth	6 to 8

Melt the sorrel in the butter over a low heat for 3 to 4 minutes. Put it into a soup tureen and mix with the milk, cucumber juice, fennel, chives, and sliced cucumber and eggs. Salt to taste. Just before serving, stir in the crushed ice.

L. E. AUDOT
LA CUISINIÈRE DE LA CAMPAGNE ET DE LA VILLE

Yogurt Soup

Tarator: Soupe de Yaourt à la Bulgare

To serve 6

1.5 litres	yogurt	3 pints
500 g	cucumbers, cut into small dice	1 lb
150 g	shelled walnuts, pounded in a mortar	5 oz
10 cl	olive oil	4 fl oz
1 tbsp	chopped fresh dill	1 tbsp
1	garlic clove, crushed	1
	salt	

Put the yogurt into a chilled soup tureen and stir in all the other ingredients. If the soup is not sufficiently chilled, add a few ice cubes just before serving.

LES PETITS PLATS ET LES GRANDS

Cream of California Herbs

Any combination of harmonious herbs will do for this soup; just do not overdo them.

	To serve 6	
125 g	lettuce leaves, chopped	4 oz
30 g	parsley or chervil, finely chopped	1 oz
4	shallots, or 1 small onion, finely chopped	4
1 tsp each	finely chopped tarragon and finely chopped rosemary	1 tsp each
1 litre	white stock	2 pints
	salt and pepper	
¼ litre	single cream	8 fl oz
3	egg yolks	3
	chopped chives	
3 or 4	spinach leaves (optional)	3 or 4

Simmer the lettuce in the stock, along with the parsley or chervil, shallots or onion, and the tarragon and rosemary. Simmer gently for 10 minutes, then press through a strainer. If the colour is not good, add a few leaves of spinach, ground to a paste in a mortar. Correct the seasoning, then bind with the cream and egg yolks. Serve hot or cold, topped with chives.

HELEN EVANS BROWN
HELEN BROWN'S WEST COAST COOK BOOK

Chilled Consommé Madrilène

Consommé Glacé à la Madrilène

The addition of chopped chicken parts, particularly feet, provides extra gelatine to help set the broth.

	To serve 8 to 10	
3 litres	beef or chicken broth (*page 164*)	5½ pints
750 g	lean chuck beef, finely chopped	1½ lb
1	egg white	1
50 g	carrot, finely diced	2 oz
100 g	leek, finely diced	3½ oz
12 to 15	tomatoes, halved, seeded and chopped	12 to 15
3 tbsp	tomato purée (optional)	3 tbsp
	cayenne pepper (optional)	

In a tall saucepan, mix the broth with the chopped beef, egg white, carrot, leek and tomatoes. Bring to the boil, stirring. Reduce the heat, partially cover, and allow to simmer very slowly for 1 to 1½ hours. Add the tomato purée, if you are using it, at this point. Strain the consommé through a colander lined with a napkin, or several layers of muslin, wrung out in cold water. Degrease the consommé thoroughly, and season with a little cayenne pepper if liked. Chill until lightly set, and serve in chilled porcelain cups.

PROSPER MONTAGNÉ
MON MENU

Andalusian Consommé

Consommé Andalou

This recipe, a variety of the Spanish soup gazpacho, is from the Café de Paris at Biarritz.

	To serve 4	
500 g	tomatoes, skinned, seeded and chopped	1 lb
3	small onions, chopped	3
1	small cucumber, peeled, seeded and thinly sliced	1
1	sweet red pepper, grilled, peeled, seeded and chopped	1
20 cl	olive oil	7 fl oz
150 g	day-old bread, crusts removed, crumbled	5 oz
2	garlic cloves, finely chopped and pounded to a paste	2
	salt and freshly ground pepper	
¼ tsp	paprika	¼ tsp
¼ tsp	ground cumin	¼ tsp
1 to 2 tbsp	vinegar	1 to 2 tbsp
1.5 litres	iced water	3 pints
	Garnishes	
3 or 4	sour gherkins, coarsely chopped	3 or 4
2	small onions, very finely sliced	2
250 g	tomatoes, skinned, seeded and diced	8 oz
1	small cucumber, peeled, seeded and diced	1
50 g	bread, diced	2 oz

Pound the tomatoes, onions, cucumber and sweet pepper in a mortar. Alternatively, put the mixture through the fine blade of a food mill, or blend them—very briefly—in a liquidizer. Add the olive oil, crumbled bread, garlic, salt and pepper, paprika and cumin. Pound together until the mixture has reached the consistency of a smooth paste. Add vinegar to taste, then stir in the water. Chill the soup thoroughly. Serve accompanied by the garnishes, each in a separate side dish.

LES PRINCES DE LA GASTRONOMIE

Andalusian Gazpacho

To serve 4

1	garlic clove	1
2 to 3 tbsp	olive oil	2 to 3 tbsp
5	tomatoes, sliced	5
1	onion, sliced	1
½ tsp	salt	½ tsp
¼ tsp	pepper	¼ tsp
¼ tsp	paprika	¼ tsp
1½ tbsp	vinegar	1½ tbsp
¼ litre	cold water	8 fl oz
200 g	cucumber, peeled, seeded and chopped	7 oz
4	slices bread	4
	ice cubes	

Pound the garlic clove with a wooden spoon in a salad bowl. Stir in the oil to form a paste. Add the tomatoes, onion, salt, pepper, paprika, vinegar and water. Leave for half an hour. Ten minutes before serving, add the chopped cucumber, slices of bread, more water if necessary and the ice cubes.

MARINA PEREYRA DE AZNAR AND NINA FROUD
THE HOME BOOK OF SPANISH COOKERY

Senegalese Soup

To serve 6

2 tbsp	chopped onion	2 tbsp
30 g	butter	1 oz
2 tsp	curry powder	2 tsp
1 tbsp	flour	1 tbsp
1 litre	chicken stock or broth (*page 164*)	2 pints
4	egg yolks	4
½ litre	double cream	1 pint
100 g	cooked white meat of chicken, finely diced, or cooked, peeled shrimps	3½ oz

Sauté the onion in the butter until soft, but do not brown. Add the curry powder and flour, and cook slowly for 5 minutes. Add the stock and bring to the boil, stirring until smooth. Beat a few spoonfuls of soup into the egg yolks and return the yolk mixture to the soup, stirring constantly. Cook for 1 minute without allowing the soup to boil. Pour the soup through a sieve into a tureen, and chill thoroughly. Add the cream and diced chicken (or peeled shrimps). Serve very cold in bowls surrounded by crushed ice.

HELEN CORBITT
HELEN CORBITT'S COOKBOOK

Iced Soup for a Very Hot Day

Soupe Glacée pour Grosse Chaleur

This recipe, using raw tomatoes, is by Gérard Vié, chef at Les Trois Marches in Versailles.

To serve 1

2	tomatoes	2
	salt and freshly ground pepper	
1 tbsp	lemon juice	1 tbsp
1 tbsp	olive oil	1 tbsp
1 tsp	coarsely chopped *fines herbes*	1 tsp

Put the tomatoes in a liquidizer with the salt and pepper, lemon juice and oil. Blend at high speed for 2 minutes. Serve the soup chilled, with the herbs sprinkled on top.

LA CUISINE NATURELLE À L'HUILE D'OLIVE

Cold Fish and Vegetable Soup

Chlodnik z Ryby

This is a refreshing summer dish, but also a filling one. I have suggested using redfish, but almost any white fish with firm flesh will do. Cod or hake would be quite suitable. You will need enough to provide at least 750 g (1½ lb) cleaned flesh.

To serve 6

1 kg	redfish, cleaned and scaled	2 to 2½ lb
3	carrots, coarsely grated	3
1	turnip, coarsely grated	1
1	onion, coarsely grated	1
1	large beetroot, coarsely grated	1
1	Hamburg parsley root, coarsely grated (optional)	1
1 litre	water	2 pints
	salt and pepper	
	sugar	
1	large cucumber, peeled and cut into strips	1
1 tbsp each	finely chopped chives, dill and parsley	1 tbsp each
3 tbsp	lemon juice	3 tbsp
3	eggs, hard-boiled and quartered	3
10 cl	soured cream	4 fl oz

Put the grated vegetables into a large saucepan with the water and cook over a moderate heat for 30 minutes. If you wish to have a clear broth, strain out the vegetables at this point. Add salt, pepper and sugar to taste, and put in the fish.

Cook for another 20 minutes or so, covered, until the fish is cooked through. Take the pan off the heat, lift out the fish, let it cool, remove all skin and bones and break the flesh into fairly small pieces. Chill the liquid and then add the cucumber and the chopped herbs to the soup, and season to taste with lemon juice. Stir well.

Arrange some pieces of fish and 2 quarters of a hard-boiled egg on each soup plate. Bring the soup to the table in a tureen and ladle it over the fish. Let each person add a dollop of soured cream to his own portion.

ALAN DAVIDSON
NORTH ATLANTIC SEAFOOD

Cold Fish Soup

Botvinya

White wine or cider may be substituted for kvas, ***the Russian rye beer included in this recipe. In place of the sorrel and spinach you may use 750 g (1½ lb) young beetroot or chard leaves, parboiled and very finely chopped.***

	To serve 12	
1 kg	salmon, sea trout or firm-fleshed white fish	2 to 2½ lb
250 g	sorrel, stemmed, chopped and cooked in 1 tbsp butter until melted into a purée	8 oz
500 g	spinach, parboiled, squeezed and very finely chopped	1 lb
1	cucumber, peeled, seeded and diced	1
4	spring onions, chopped	4
2 tbsp	finely chopped fresh dill	2 tbsp
3 tbsp	chopped parsley	3 tbsp
	salt	
10 cl	black treacle	4 fl oz
	grated horseradish	
25	crayfish tails or prawns (optional)	25
	Kvas	
250 g	stale rye bread, dried out and broken into pieces	8 oz
2 litres	boiling water	4 pints
4 tbsp	black treacle	4 tbsp
7 g	fresh yeast, or ½ tsp dried yeast	¼ oz
½ tsp	malted barley flour (optional)	½ tsp
	raisins	

To make the *kvas*, put the bread into a bowl and pour on the boiling water. Cover immediately with a thick cloth and leave to cool until lukewarm. Strain through a sieve lined with a clean cloth into another bowl; do not squeeze the cloth. Add the treacle to the strained liquid, stirring well to dissolve. Mix the yeast with the flour, dissolve to a thin paste with a bit of the liquid, and stir into the bowl. Cover and leave to stand in a warm room for 12 hours. Strain the liquid again and bottle it, putting 2 raisins in each bottle. Cork the bottles well and store them in a cool place. The *kvas* will be ready for use in 3 to 4 days, and should be used within about 2 months.

To make the soup, poach the fish in salted water for about 10 minutes or until it flakes easily. Drain the fish, cool, remove any skin or bone, and cut into bite-sized pieces. Put the sorrel and spinach into a cold soup tureen and add the cucumber, spring onion, dill, parsley, salt and treacle. Stir in 2 litres (4 pints) of *kvas*, and chill the soup thoroughly.

At serving time, add the pieces of fish to the soup, with the prawns or crayfish tails, if using. Serve a bowl of grated horseradish separately.

ELENA MOLOKHOVETS
PODAROK MOLODŶM KHOZYAÏKAM

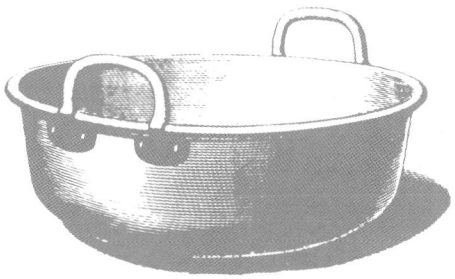

Cold Cherry and Rice Soup

This soup may be served with small cherry pirozhki—***rounds of pastry each folded in half to enclose a stoned cherry, the edges sealed, and baked in a hot oven until crisp.***

	To serve 6	
250 g	cherries, stoned and stones reserved	8 oz
60 g	rice	2 oz
1.5 litres	water	3 pints
30 g	sugar	1 oz
4 tbsp	double cream	4 tbsp

Put the cherry stones in the water, bring to the boil, and boil for 10 minutes. Strain. Put the rice and sugar into the cherry-stone stock and simmer for 30 minutes or until the rice is very soft. Five minutes before the end of the cooking time add the cherries. Cool the soup and serve it very cold with a spoonful of cream on each serving.

SOFKA SKIPWITH
EAT RUSSIAN

Hungarian Cherry Soup

Meggy Leves

This recipe, using morello cherries and white wine, comes from the Gay Hussar restaurant in London's Soho.

	To serve 6	
500 g	morello cherries, stoned, stones and stalks reserved	1 lb
¾ litre	Riesling or other white wine	1¼ pints
60 g	sugar	2 oz
	2.5 cm (1 inch) cinnamon stick	
2	lemons, rind of 1 grated and reserved	2
10 cl	brandy (optional)	4 fl oz
½ litre	soured cream	1 pint

Crush a few of the cherry stones, then put all the stones and stalks into a pan with the wine, sugar, cinnamon stick and the juice of both lemons and the grated rind of one. Simmer for 5 minutes, then leave to infuse for at least 15 minutes. Strain, bring back to the boil, and add the cherries and their juice. Remove from the heat immediately, and allow to cool to tepid. Stir in the brandy, if using. Put the soured cream into a tureen, then gradually pour in the cherry soup, mixing thoroughly. Serve chilled.

JANE GRIGSON
OBSERVER MAGAZINE

Cold Pear and Watercress Soup

This recipe is by the San Francisco chef and restaurateur Jeremiah Tower.

	To serve 4	
8	ripe pears, peeled, quartered and cored, skins and cores reserved	8
125 g	watercress, leaves and stems chopped	4 oz
25 g	watercress leaves	1 oz
1 litre	chicken broth (*page 164*)	2 pints
2 to 3 tbsp	lemon juice	2 to 3 tbsp
	salt and pepper	
15 to 20 cl	double cream	6 fl oz

As you prepare the pear quarters, plunge them into half the chicken broth to prevent them from discolouring. Boil the pear skins and cores in the remaining broth for a few minutes to extract their maximum flavour, then strain the broth into another saucepan. Add the chopped watercress to the strained broth, simmer for 10 minutes, then purée the mixture in a liquidizer or food mill.

Purée the pear quarters with their broth through a sieve or in a liquidizer and combine the two purées. (More chicken broth may be stirred in at this point to bring the purée to the desired consistency.) Add a little lemon juice and mill in salt and pepper to taste. Chill the mixture thoroughly.

Plunge the remaining watercress leaves into boiling water to wilt them and brighten their green hue, then quickly refresh them in cold water. To serve, whisk double cream to taste into the soup, check the seasoning, pour into a tureen, and float the watercress leaves on top.

PETITS PROPOS CULINAIRES

Cold Strawberry Soup

Soupe Froide aux Fraises

The sugar syrup in this recipe is made by boiling 500 g (1 lb) sugar with 2 litres (4 pints) water for a few minutes until completely dissolved. Cool before using.

	To serve 12	
2.5 litres	wild strawberries	5 pints
2 litres	cold sugar syrup	4 pints
1 bottle	white Rhine wine	1 bottle
2 tbsp	lemon juice (or more to taste)	2 tbsp
1 bottle	champagne, well chilled	1 bottle

Put 2 litres (4 pints) of the strawberries through a fine nylon drum sieve or a muslin strainer into a porcelain bowl. Add the sugar syrup, the wine and the lemon juice. Cover tightly and refrigerate until well chilled. Just before serving, add the remaining strawberries, left whole, and the champagne.

ÉDOUARD NIGNON
LES PLAISIRS DE LA TABLE

Whole Meal Soups

Borscht

Borisch

This is the authentic recipe for the borscht served at the court of Tsar Nicholas II. As a modern variation, the vegetables with a shorter cooking time—onion, cabbage, leek—may be added later, so that they are just cooked at the end. The parsley roots may be added whole and removed before serving.

To serve 8

1 kg	beetroot	2 to 2½ lb
500 g	leeks	1 lb
1	celeriac	1
2	Hamburg parsley roots or parsnips	2
1	onion	1
1	small Savoy cabbage	1
75 g	butter	2½ oz
2 litres	pot au feu broth (*page 149*) or veal stock	4 pints
15 cl	fermented beetroot liquid (*page 84*), or vinegar or lemon juice	¼ pint
1	duckling, three-quarters roasted	1
1 kg	beef brisket	2 to 2½ lb
1	bouquet garni (including marjoram, bay leaf, clove)	1
	salt and pepper	
10 cl	soured cream	4 fl oz
1 tbsp	chopped parsley	1 tbsp
1 tbsp	chopped dill leaves	1 tbsp
500 g	chipolata sausages, grilled and skinned	1 lb

Reserve two of the beetroots, and cut the remainder into *julienne*. Cut the leeks, celeriac, parsley roots, onion and cabbage into *julienne*. Melt the butter in a large saucepan and sauté the vegetables until they are lightly coloured. Stir in the broth and the fermented beetroot liquid; then add the duckling, the beef, and the bouquet garni. Cover and simmer very gently over a low heat.

Remove the duckling when cooked, after about 1 hour; continue to simmer until the beef is cooked, about another 1½ hours. Remove the beef; remove and discard the bouquet garni; degrease the soup and season with salt and pepper. Grate the remaining beetroots and press out the juice; mix the juice with the soured cream and stir into the soup with the chopped parsley and dill leaves.

Cut the duckling and the beef into serving pieces, and arrange on a warmed platter with the chipolatas. If necessary, reheat in an oven at 180°C (350°F or Mark 4). Pour over a ladle of the soup and serve the rest of the soup separately from a tureen. Alternatively, the meats can be arranged in a deep dish and all the soup poured over for serving.

MME JEANNE SAVARIN (EDITOR)
LA CUISINE DES FAMILLES

Ukrainian Borscht

Borscht Malorossiiskiĭ

This soup is traditionally served with a variety of garnishes: small, fried chipolata sausages, small meat dumplings, pirozhki, *or roasted buckwheat* kasha. *A bowl of soured cream also is passed as a side dish. To make the fermented beetroot liquid called for in the recipe, see page 84. Vinegar may be substituted, but much less is needed as it is more pungent.*

To serve 8

1.5 kg	beef plate or shin, or pork or a mixture of beef and smoked ham	3 lb
2.5 litres	water	5 pints
2	onions	2
1	bay leaf	1
	salt and pepper	
1	cabbage, cored and coarsely chopped	1
About ½ litre	fermented beetroot liquid	About 18 fl oz
6	beetroots	6
1½ tbsp	flour	1½ tbsp
	finely chopped parsley	

Put the meat into a large pot with the water, onions, bay leaf, salt and pepper. Bring to the boil, skim, partially cover, and simmer for 2 to 3 hours. Strain the stock, reserving the meat, and return the stock to a clean pan. Add the cabbage and fermented beetroot liquid to taste, and simmer for 1 hour.

Meanwhile, bake 5 of the beetroots in a moderate oven, 180°C (350°F or Mark 4) for about 2 to 3 hours or until soft; or boil the beetroots in water for the same length of time. Drain, peel and chop them, and mix with the flour. Add them to the stock and return it to the boil. Correct the seasoning.

Grate the remaining beetroot and press out the juice. Cut up the meat used for the stock and return it to the pot to reheat to simmering point. Put the parsley into a warmed tureen, add the juice from the grated beetroot, and pour in the soup. Serve the borscht accompanied by a choice of garnishes.

ELENA MOLOKHOVETS
PODAROK MOLODŶM KHOZYAĬKAM

Polish Borscht

Borshch Pol'skii

For instructions on making fermented beetroot juice, see page 84. A dash of vinegar is often substituted. The beetroots for this soup may be either baked or boiled. Beetroots will require 1 to 3 hours of baking time, or 1 to 2 hours of boiling time, depending on their age and size. Borscht is often served with various garnishes such as buckwheat kasha, ***meat dumplings, or*** pirozhki. ***For recipes, see pages 90 to 92.***

	To serve 6	
5	beetroots, baked or boiled	5
3 tbsp	fermented beetroot liquid	3 tbsp
¼ to ½ litre	soured cream	8 to 18 fl oz
	salt	
2 tbsp	finely chopped parsley	2 tbsp
2 tbsp	finely chopped dill	2 tbsp

	Stock	
1 to 1.5 kg	beef brisket or chuck	2 to 3 lb
1.5 litres	water	3 pints
5 or 6	peppercorns	5 or 6
1 or 2	bay leaves	1 or 2
500 g	ham hock or shoulder (optional)	1 lb
2	onions (optional)	2
50 g	dried mushrooms, soaked and drained (optional)	2 oz

To make the stock, place all the stock ingredients in a large saucepan, bring to the boil, and skim. Simmer, partly covered, very slowly for 3 to 4 hours. Strain the stock, reserving the meats, and allow to cool slightly. Skim off the fat.

Peel the baked or boiled beetroots and cut them into very fine strips. Put the strips into a saucepan and add the strained stock, the fermented beetroot liquid, and the soured cream. Season with salt, parsley and dill. Finely chop the reserved ham, if used, and add it to the soup. Heat the soup, but do not allow it to boil lest it lose its colour.

The beef may be served as a main course after the soup, or made into salad for another meal.

ELENA MOLOKHOVETS
PODAROK MOLODYM KHOZYAIKAM

Poached Chicken Soup

Poule au Pot

This is the broth for holidays, and it is a point of honour with the good housewife to prepare it herself. The cooking is usually begun the evening before, because the quality of the broth is dependent on the slowness of the simmer. The chicken can be served together with its stuffing and vegetables, or as a separate course. Or it may be served on a bed of rice, cooked separately in broth from the pot; or again it may be cooled in the broth, and served cold with mayonnaise and salad. The bread slices may be replaced by vermicelli or small soup pasta. The knuckle of veal gives sweetness to the broth, but leg of beef or ham shank may be used instead.

	To serve 8	
2 kg	plump fowl, singed and trussed with the liver reserved	4 lb
1 kg	veal knuckle	2 to 2½ lb
4 litres	water	7 pints
1 tbsp	salt	1 tbsp
4	carrots	4
4	leeks	4
1	turnip	1
1	large onion, stuck with 5 to 7 cloves	1
1	bouquet garni, including a 2.5 cm (1 inch) cinnamon stick	1
	slices dry bread	

	Stuffing	
200 g	bread, crusts removed, soaked in milk and squeezed dry	7 oz
1 or 2	cloves garlic, finely chopped	1 or 2
	the reserved chicken liver, finely chopped	
100 g	ham or green bacon, finely chopped or lean sausage meat	3½ oz
2	eggs	2
	salt, pepper, herbs and mixed spice	

Put the veal knuckle into a large pot with the water. Bring very slowly to the boil, skimming often. When the scum has almost ceased to rise, add the salt. Skim again. If you are finishing the soup the following day, leave to simmer overnight as slowly as possible. If serving it the same day, add the vegetables and bouquet garni. Simmer for about 2 hours.

Meanwhile, to make the stuffing, mix together all the ingredients until well blended. Stuff the fowl with this mixture and sew up the opening with strong thread. Put the chicken into the pot and continue to simmer very gently for 2 to 3 hours or until the chicken is cooked.

Remove the chicken, carve it, and serve at the same time as the broth or separately. The stuffing is sliced and served separately. The broth is served ladled over slices of dry bread.

SIMIN PALAY
LA CUISINE DU PAYS

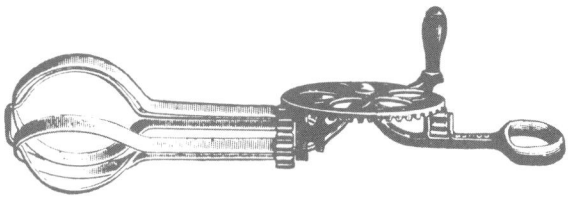

The Catalan Pot au Feu

Escudella: Carn d'Olla

This is a very elaborate pot au feu. *Botifarra* is the name for several different kinds of Catalan sausages. The dark sausage is something like a *boudin noir* (black pudding), while the white is milder in flavour.

	To serve 8	
½	chicken	½
500 g	stewing veal	1 lb
1	small ham bone	1
250 g	chick peas, soaked overnight in water	8 oz
2.5 litres	water	5 pints
2	onions	2
4	carrots	4
2	sticks celery	2
2	leeks	2
1	small green cabbage, halved and cored	1
1 kg	potatoes	2 to 2½ lb
2	*botifarra,* 1 white and 1 dark	2
250 g	small macaroni	8 oz
	Pilota (dumplings)	
2	garlic cloves, finely chopped	2
1 tbsp	chopped parsley	1 tbsp
1	egg	1
30 g	breadcrumbs	1 oz
250 g	sausage meat	½ lb
	flour	

Rinse the chick peas and simmer them in water to cover for 2 hours. Drain them and put them in a tall deep saucepan (a marmite, if possible). Add the water, bring to the boil, and put in the chicken, veal, ham bone, onions, carrots, celery and leeks. Cook gently, covered, for 1½ hours, then add the cabbage, potatoes and *botifarra.*

Meanwhile, prepare the *pilota* by combining all the *pilota* ingredients (except the flour) in a bowl. Mix well and form into the shape of two small rolls of bread. Flour them, then add them to the soup 5 minutes after you add the *botifarra,* and cook for 15 minutes more.

Strain the soup from the pot into another pan, and cook the macaroni in it for 15 minutes or until done, while keeping the meats and vegetables warm. Serve the soup first, then the meat and vegetables.

IRVING DAVIS
A CATALAN COOKERY BOOK

Pot au Feu

As a rule, enough meat and vegetables are put in the pot au feu to last two meals and there is usually stock left for the base of soups or sauces to follow on other days. Rump of beef, short rib or chuck are the best cuts of meat for pot au feu. In addition, every good housewife saves the carcasses of chickens she may have served and adds them to the pot. Or, if the chicken salad, vol-au-vent or other cooked chicken dish is planned for another day, the fowl is cooked in the pot au feu because the chicken flavour makes the stock extra delicious.

	To serve 10 to 12	
1.5 kg	beef (meat and bones)	3 lb
4.5 litres	water	8 pints
2 tbsp	salt	2 tbsp
2 or 3	carrots	2 or 3
1	turnip	1
1	small parsnip	1
5 or 6	leeks	5 or 6
2	sticks celery	2
1	onion	1
	thyme	
½	bay leaf	½
1	clove	1
	thin slices dry crusty rolls	

Cover the meat and bones with water, bring to the boil and parboil for 5 minutes. Remove the meat and bones, discard the water, and clean the pot. Put back the meat and bones, add the cooking water and salt, and bring very slowly to the boil, skimming all the time until the scum stops rising to the top. Alternatively, the meat and bones may be placed directly in the cooking water, reserving ½ litre (1 pint) to be added after the soup has come to the boil. This brings the scum more quickly to the top of the pot.

Simmer the soup very gently for 1½ hours, with the lid half on. Add the vegetables—cut into pieces of any desired size—and the seasonings, and cook for about 2½ hours longer or until the meat is tender. Skim off the fat and correct the seasoning. Remove as much stock as desired for serving, remove the meat, slicing enough for serving, and the vegetables. Strain the remaining stock through cheesecloth or a fine sieve, let cool and keep in the refrigerator for use in soups or sauces.

The meat, vegetables and soup may be served all together in the same bowl, or the soup may be eaten separately and followed by the sliced meat and vegetables. But always very, very thin slices of small dry crusty rolls are eaten in the soup.

LOUIS DIAT
FRENCH COOKING FOR AMERICANS

Beef and Lamb Soup Roman-Style

Brodetto alla Romana

This dish is traditionally served at Easter.

	To serve 6	
1 kg	boiling beef (brisket, shin, thin rib, etc.)	2 to 2½ lb
1 kg	lamb breast	2 to 2½ lb
6 litres	water	11 pints
1	small onion, stuck with 2 cloves	1
1	small carrot	1
1	stick celery	1
1	sprig parsley	1
30 g	coarse salt	1 oz
6	egg yolks	6
100 g	Parmesan cheese, grated	3½ oz
2 tbsp	lemon juice	2 tbsp
	white pepper	
1 tbsp	chopped marjoram	1 tbsp
	bread slices, dried in the oven	

Put the meats into a fireproof, earthenware pot with the water, and bring to the boil over a medium heat. Skim and add the vegetables, parsley and salt. Simmer, uncovered, over a very low heat. After about 1½ hours, remove the lamb and, after another 1½ hours, the beef; set the meats aside, cover with some of the stock, and keep warm.

Beat the egg yolks with 2 tablespoons of the cheese and the lemon juice. Strain the stock and return it to the pan. Pour in the egg mixture, stirring briskly. Return the pot to a low heat; stir the soup until the eggs thicken it slightly. Add the pepper and marjoram. Arrange the bread slices in soup bowls and pour on the soup; serve with the remaining cheese. Serve the meats as a second course, accompanied by fresh vegetables.

LUIGI CARNACINA
GREAT ITALIAN COOKING

Genoese Veal Soup with Fine Noodles

Zuppa di Cima alla Genovese con Linguine Fine

	To serve 4 to 6	
1½ kg	breast of veal, boned	3 lb
125 g	fine noodles, broken into 5 cm (2 inch) pieces	4 oz
1	large carrot, chopped	1
1	large onion, chopped	1
1	bay leaf	1
	salt	
1 tbsp	finely chopped fresh marjoram	1 tbsp
2	eggs	2
	Stuffing	
250 g	lean pork, minced	8 oz
125 g	*prosciutto*, minced	4 oz
4	slices bread, soaked in milk and squeezed dry	4
1 tbsp	grated Parmesan cheese	1 tbsp
1 tbsp	finely chopped pistachios	1 tbsp
1½ tsp	salt	1½ tsp
	freshly ground pepper	
	grated nutmeg	
3	eggs, beaten	3

To make the stuffing, combine all the stuffing ingredients and mix together well. Spread the breast of veal flat; spoon the stuffing on to the centre of veal. Fold the meat in half over the stuffing, sewing it together to seal in the stuffing completely. Then tie with string. Place the roll in a 5 litre (9 pint) pot and cover with water. Stir in the carrot, onion, bay leaf and salt. Cover and simmer for 1½ hours, or until the meat is tender. Remove the meat to a platter and place a heavy weight on top to press the meat into a flat shape.

Add the marjoram to the liquid remaining in the pot. Simmer, uncovered, for 20 minutes. Add the noodles to the pot and cook 5 to 10 minutes or until *al dente*. Beat the eggs and stir them into the broth; bring it to the boil, and when the eggs have curdled into streaky threads or *stracciatelle*, remove the soup from the heat and ladle it immediately into hot bowls. Serve the stuffed meat, thinly sliced, as a main course, accompanied by a vegetable.

JACK DENTON SCOTT
THE COMPLETE BOOK OF PASTA

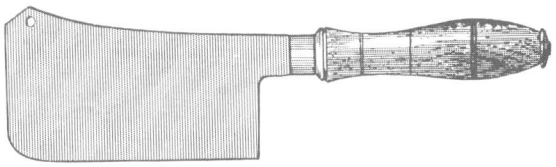

Gourmets' Pot au Feu

Pot-au-Feu des Gourmets

To serve 6 to 8

2 kg	plump fowl	4 lb
1 kg	brisket or leg of beef, cut in a square, boned and tied, bones reserved	2 to 2½ lb
1	veal knuckle bone	1
4 to 5 litres	water	7 to 9 pints
	salt	
2	carrots	2
1	turnip	1
1	large onion, stuck with 2 cloves	1
1	leek	1
1	lettuce	1
1	sprig chervil	1
400 g	rice, blanched	14 oz
	powdered saffron	
	Sausage stuffing	
125 g	lean sausage meat, seasoned with dried herbs	4 oz
60 g	bread, crusts removed, soaked in broth and squeezed	2 oz
	salt and pepper	
2 tbsp	chopped parsley	2 tbsp

Mix all the stuffing ingredients together, blend well, and stuff the fowl with the mixture. Truss the fowl and sew up the opening with strong thread.

Put the beef and beef bones, if any, into a pot (preferably a fireproof earthenware marmite) with the veal bone, the water, and a little salt; bring to the boil and skim, then partially cover and reduce the heat to maintain a slow simmer. After 1½ to 2 hours, add the fowl with carrots, turnip and onion and the leek tied in a bundle with the lettuce and chervil. Simmer slowly until the beef and fowl are cooked, about 1½ hours or longer depending on the age of the fowl.

Strain the broth through a cloth-lined sieve into a bowl and pour 2 litres (4 pints) of the broth into a saucepan without degreasing it. Bring to the boil, and add the rice and a pinch of saffron. Cook the rice slowly over a moderate heat, adding more broth if this soup becomes too thick. When the rice is cooked, the soup—though thick—should be much more liquid than a risotto. You must be able to see the broth.

To serve, pour the rice soup into a warmed tureen. Place the beef on a warmed platter, surrounded by some of the vegetables from the pot. Serve the fowl on another platter.

URBAIN DUBOIS
ÉCOLE DES CUISINIÈRES

Bean Soup

Zuppa di Fagioli

This soup may be enriched by adding other meats—for example, a piece of ham, pig's ears, or a fresh pork boiling sausage. Adjust the cooking time accordingly; some meats may need to simmer for 2 to 3 hours to be tender. To ensure that the flavouring vegetables do not lose their fresh taste, the onion, garlic, tomato, and chopped parsley may be sautéed in oil and added to the soup a few minutes before serving. The meats may be sliced and served separately.

To serve 4

250 g	haricot beans, soaked overnight and drained	8 oz
250 g	bacon, diced	8 oz
1	onion, finely chopped	1
1	garlic clove, finely chopped	1
1	stick celery, chopped	1
3 tbsp	oil	3 tbsp
3	tomatoes, skinned, seeded and chopped	3
About 1 litre	water	About 2 pints
	salt and pepper	
1 tbsp	chopped parsley	1 tbsp

Cook the bacon, onion, garlic and celery in the hot oil until they begin to brown, then add the tomatoes, the beans, the water, salt and pepper. Simmer gently until the beans are very well cooked. The time will depend on the type of beans and whether they are the new season's or the last. The cooking could take anything from 1½ to 3 hours. Serve the soup sprinkled with the chopped parsley.

BERYL GOULD-MARKS
THE HOME BOOK OF ITALIAN COOKERY

Chicken and Fresh Corn Chowder

Accompaniments in keeping with the clear freshness and simplicity of this stew are fresh, ripe tomato wedges and freshly baked biscuits with unsalted butter.

To serve 6

1.75 kg	chicken, jointed	3½ lb
8	ears fresh sweetcorn	8
1 litre	water	2 pints
1 tsp	salt	1 tsp
1	stick celery, with leaves	1
1	sprig parsley	1
1	onion, quartered	1
1	bay leaf	1
10	peppercorns	10
6	eggs, hard-boiled and chopped	6
	freshly ground black pepper	
60 g	parsley, chopped	2 oz
¼ litre	double cream	8 fl oz

Put the chicken pieces into a kettle with the water, salt, celery, parsley, onion, bay leaf and peppercorns. Bring to the boil, cover and simmer for 1 hour or until the meat is tender.

Lift the chicken from the broth, discard the skin and bones and break the meat into large pieces. Strain the broth and return it to the kettle. Add the meat. Scrape the kernels from the ears of corn. Heat the broth to a simmer, add the corn, and cook just until tender, about 5 minutes. Add the chopped eggs, and correct the seasoning with salt and pepper. Stir in the parsley. Salt the cream lightly, and whip it until soft peaks are formed. Ladle the soup into warmed bowls, and top each serving with a spoonful of whipped cream.

SHIRLEY SARVIS
SIMPLY STEWS

Swedish Pea Soup

Ärter med Fläsk

If split peas are substituted for whole dried yellow ones, the soaking time should be reduced to 2 to 3 hours and the cooking time to that of the pork.

To serve 6

250 g	yellow dried peas, rinsed and soaked overnight	8 oz
1.5 litres	water	3 pints
500 g	pork, fresh or slightly cured	1 lb
2 tsp	salt	2 tsp
¼ tsp	ground ginger	¼ tsp

Put the peas in a saucepan with the water, let them come to the boil slowly, then cook vigorously for the first hour, to make the skins come off more easily. As the skins float to the surface, skim them off. When the peas have cooked for 1 hour, put in the pork and simmer for about another 2 hours. Season with the salt and ginger. Remove the pork, slice it and serve separately from the soup.

If the water is hard, add a pinch of bicarbonate of soda or else boil the water and let it cool again before using it.

Leftover pea soup is very good made into a purée.

INGA NORBERG
GOOD FOOD FROM SWEDEN

Dutch Green Pea Soup

Hollandse Erwtensoep

Lightly smoked boiling sausage, spareribs or kidneys may be added to this soup with the vegetables.

To serve 4

500 g	split peas, soaked overnight in 4 litres (7 pints) water	1 lb
2	well-scrubbed, meaty pig's trotters	2
	salt	
1	small celeriac, peeled and cut into 5 mm (¼ inch) cubes	1
60 g	fresh green celery leaves, chopped	2 oz
4	potatoes, cut into 5 mm (¼ inch) cubes	4
250 g	fresh pork sausages	8 oz
250 g	green bacon	8 oz
	savory	
	pepper	

Bring the split peas to the boil in their soaking water. Add the pig's trotters and salt and simmer for 3 hours in a covered soup kettle. Then add the celeriac, celery leaves, potatoes, sausages and bacon and simmer, stirring occasionally, for 30 minutes or until the soup is well thickened and the meat from the pig's trotters comes off the bone easily. Transfer the pig's trotters, sausages and bacon to a cutting board; discard the bones from the pig's trotters. Slice the meat, sausages and bacon. Return the cut-up trotters and sausages to the soup. Season with savory and pepper, and heat the soup through for a few minutes, constantly stirring.

Serve the soup in big bowls accompanied by slices of crusty white bread, slices of black rye bread, the sliced bacon and a pot of hot mustard.

C.A.H. HAITSMA MULIER-VAN BEUSEKOM (EDITOR)
CULINAIRE ENCYCLOPÉDIE

Mary's Portuguese Soup

To serve 8

1.5 kg	boned chuck beef in one piece	3 lb
	salt and freshly ground black pepper	
2 tbsp	oil	2 tbsp
3	onions, sliced	3
1.5 litres	water	3 pints
150 g each	dried red kidney beans and white haricot beans, soaked overnight	5 oz each
3 or 4	*chourico* (Portuguese sausage) or *chorizo* (Spanish sausage)	3 or 4
500 g	cabbage, halved, cored and shredded	1 lb
500 g	small florets broccoli	1 lb
500 g	spinach, roughly shredded	1 lb

Sprinkle the meat generously with salt and pepper and, with your fingers, rub in the seasoning. Cover the meat and let it stand in the refrigerator overnight or up to 3 days.

Heat the oil in a large, heavy casserole or kettle, add the meat and brown quickly on all sides. Add the onions and water, bring to the boil, cover and simmer slowly for about 1 hour. Drain the beans and add to the casserole. Bring to the boil, cover and simmer for 45 minutes or until the meat and beans are tender. Remove the meat, dice it finely, and then return it to the casserole.

Add the sausages and cook for 5 minutes. Stir in the cabbage and cook, covered, for 5 minutes; stir in the broccoli and cook, covered, for 5 minutes; add the spinach and cook, covered, for 3 minutes. Check the seasoning and serve.

JEAN HEWITT
THE NEW YORK TIMES WEEKEND COOKBOOK

Spanish One-Pot Meal

Puchero

Puchero *is the Spanish word for cooking pot and by extension means the stew cooked in the pot.* Chorizo *is a dry and highly spiced sausage typical of Spain but now widely available.*

To serve 6

500 g	leg or shin of beef	1 lb
1	boiling fowl	1
1	pig's ear	1
100 g	green bacon	3½ oz
200 g	chick peas, soaked overnight	7 oz
4 litres	water	7 pints
1 tsp	salt	1 tsp
1	bouquet garni	1
200 g	pumpkin or winter squash, peeled and seeded	7 oz
200 g	cabbage, cored, coarsely chopped and blanched	7 oz
200 g	carrots	7 oz
200 g	turnips	7 oz
500 g	*chorizo*	1 lb
	bread, sliced and grilled	

In a very large saucepan place the beef, chicken, pig's ear, bacon, chick peas, water and salt. Bring to the boil. Skim carefully and add the bouquet garni and the vegetables. Leave to simmer, covered, for 4 hours over a low heat, adding the *chorizo* 20 minutes before the end.

Put the slices of bread into a warmed soup tureen. Strain the broth and pour it over the bread. Serve the meats and vegetables separately from the soup.

LÉON ISNARD
LA CUISINE FRANÇAISE ET AFRICAINE

Fish Soup with Garlic Mayonnaise

Bourride

To serve 4

500 g	angler-fish, cleaned and sliced	1 lb
1	small bass, cleaned and sliced	1
250 g	whiting, cleaned and sliced	8 oz
1	onion, thinly sliced	1
1	sprig thyme	1
1	branch fennel	1
1	bay leaf	1
1	strip dried orange peel	1
	salt and pepper	
10	slices bread	10
4	egg yolks	4
	Aïoli	
4	garlic cloves	4
	salt	
1	egg yolk, at room temperature	1
40 cl	olive oil, at room temperature	¾ pint
2 to 3 tbsp	lemon juice	2 to 3 tbsp
1 to 2 tsp	water	1 to 2 tsp

To make the *aïoli*, or garlic mayonnaise, put the garlic cloves in a large mortar. Reduce to a paste with the pestle, add a pinch of salt and the egg yolk and begin pouring in the oil in a thin stream, turning the mixture with the pestle. Pour the oil very slowly, and never stop turning the pestle. You should obtain a thick mayonnaise.

After pouring in the first 3 or 4 tablespoons of oil, add the lemon juice and a teaspoonful of tepid water. Continue to add the oil, little by little, until the mayonnaise is again too stiff to turn easily. Add a little more water. If the *aïoli* breaks, and the oil separates out, pour the whole mixture out of the mortar. Clean the mortar and put in another egg yolk and a few drops of lemon juice. Little by little, add the broken mayonnaise, turning continuously. This time, it should be successful. This is known as "lifting" the mayonnaise.

To make the soup, put the fish into a saucepan with the onion, thyme, fennel, bay leaf and orange peel. Add enough hot water to slightly more than cover the fish. Season with salt and pepper and cook rapidly for 10 minutes.

Meanwhile, arrange the bread slices in a deep bowl or tureen. When the fish is cooked, remove it from the pan and keep it warm. Strain the broth into a bowl. Moisten the bread with a few spoonfuls of broth, without letting the bread float.

In a clean saucepan, blend the egg yolks with 10 cl (4 fl oz) of the *aïoli*. Add the remaining broth very slowly to this mixture, stirring continuously. Cook over a low heat until the soup begins to thicken. When it has thickened, the soup should coat a spoon. Be careful that the soup does not boil, because there is no hope of "lifting" it.

As soon as the soup is smooth and velvety, pour it over the soaked bread. The soup may be served first, and followed by the fish slices served with the remaining *aïoli*, or both courses may be served together.

J. B. REBOUL
LA CUISINIÈRE PROVENÇALE

Fish Soup from Provence

Une Soupe Provençale

To serve 8

1 kg	conger eel, cut into 8 slices	2 to 2½ lb
1 litre	live mussels, scrubbed	2 pints
8 cl	olive oil	3 fl oz
1	small onion, finely sliced	1
4	tomatoes, skinned and chopped	4
2	garlic cloves, crushed	2
1	large bouquet garni	1
1	small strip dried orange peel	1
2 litres	water	4 pints
	salt and pepper	
	powdered saffron	
	slices of home-made bread (*page 165*)	
	chopped parsley	

In a large saucepan, heat half of the olive oil and cook the onion gently without letting it colour. When it is soft, add the tomatoes, garlic, bouquet garni, orange peel and water. Season with salt, pepper and a pinch of saffron. Boil rapidly for 15 minutes. Pass the broth through a fine sieve into a bowl, pressing the vegetables to extract all their juices.

Put the pieces of eel in the cleaned saucepan and season the eel with salt and pepper. Sprinkle on the remaining oil, then pour on the strained broth. Cook rapidly for 10 minutes. Meanwhile, put the mussels into a pan, cover, and cook over a high heat until they have all opened. Shell the mussels and strain their cooking liquor.

Add the mussels and their liquor to the saucepan and cook for 3 minutes. Arrange the fish and the mussels on a warmed serving platter. Put several large, thick slices of bread into a soup tureen, and pour in the soup. Sprinkle with chopped parsley. The fish may be served at the same time as the soup, or as a second course.

70 MÉDECINS DE FRANCE
LE TRÉSOR DE LA CUISINE DU BASSIN MÉDITERRANÉEN

Leghorn Fish Stew

Cacciucco alla Livornese

In this famous fish dish, all or any of the fish mentioned here could be included: eel, squid, a delicate crustacean—*squilla mantis*—for which shrimps or prawns could well be substituted, gurnard, whiting, hake, red mullet, small octopus, John Dory, and cuttlefish.

To serve 6

2 to 2.5 kg	assorted fish, cleaned, heads removed and reserved, larger fish cut into pieces	4 to 5 lb
30 cl	olive oil	½ pint
	salt and pepper	
1	onion, finely chopped	1
1	carrot, finely chopped	1
2	sticks celery, finely chopped	2
3 tbsp	finely chopped parsley	3 tbsp
2	garlic cloves	2
2	small hot dried chili peppers	2
2	bay leaves	2
1	sprig thyme	1
30 cl	red wine	½ pint
1 kg	tomatoes, skinned and chopped	2 to 2½ lb
1.25 litres	water	2½ pints
	bread slices, fried in oil or browned in the oven	

Put the fish into a shallow dish and sprinkle them with 4 tablespoons of the olive oil and with salt and pepper. Leave for 30 minutes. Meanwhile, heat 10 cl (4 fl oz) of the olive oil in a large pan. Add the aromatic vegetables, parsley, garlic, chili peppers, bay leaves, thyme and, finally, the fish heads. Brown the heads well, moisten with the wine, and continue cooking until the wine has reduced to a thick sauce. Add the tomatoes and water. Season and continue cooking for 30 minutes. Rub the soup through a fine sieve.

In another large pan, preferably an earthenware one, heat the remaining olive oil. Add the squid, cuttlefish and octopus, and cook these for 15 minutes. Add the *squilla mantis* (or shrimps or prawns), and, 5 minutes later, the remaining fish. Add salt, if necessary, and plenty of pepper, and continue cooking for another 10 minutes.

Put 2 or 3 slices of bread per person into the bottom of a large soup tureen or into large individual soup bowls. Add the fish and pour the soup over the top.

ADA BONI
ITALIAN REGIONAL COOKING

Norman Fish Stew

Bouillabaisse Normande

To serve 8

1 litre	mussels, scrubbed and bearded	2 pints
750 g	sole, cleaned and cut into pieces	1½ lb
750 g	turbot, cleaned and cut into pieces	1½ lb
750 g	brill, cleaned and cut into pieces	1½ lb
2 tsp	ground saffron or saffron threads	2 tsp
200 g	butter	7 oz
1	large onion, sliced	1
2	garlic, cloves crushed	2
1	carrot, finely sliced	1
	crushed white pepper	
	ground nutmeg	
	salt	
2 litres	water	4 pints
1	bouquet garni	1
16	thin slices French bread, toasted	16

Steam the mussels in a covered pan over a high heat until they open. Strain the liquid through muslin into a bowl and reserve. Shell the mussels. In a small bowl, dissolve the saffron in a little of the liquid.

Melt the butter in a large pan, and add the onion, garlic, carrot, pepper, nutmeg and salt. Cook over a medium heat for 5 minutes. Add the water, bouquet garni, and the mussel cooking liquid. Return to the boil, and add the fish pieces. When the fish is cooked, in about 10 minutes, drain the pieces and place them on a warmed serving dish, surrounded by the mussels. Arrange the toasted bread around the edge of the dish. Strain the broth into a warmed tureen, add the saffron mixture and serve it at the same time as the platter of fish.

JULES GOUFFÉ
LE LIVRE DES SOUPES ET DES POTAGES

Greek Fish Soup

Kakavia

To serve 8 to 10

2 kg	3 or 4 kinds of mixed fish (bass, cod, hake, haddock, halibut, pollack, snapper, trout, whiting, wrasse, etc.), cleaned and sliced	4 lb
1	lobster, cut up, claws cracked (optional)	1
500 g	shrimps, peeled and de-veined	1 lb
500 g	scallops or mussels in their shells, scrubbed (optional)	1 lb
125 g	onions, spring onions or leeks, sliced	4 oz
10 cl	olive oil	4 fl oz
4	tomatoes, skinned, seeded and chopped	4
1	stalk fennel or celery, sliced	1
3	sprigs parsley	3
1	bay leaf	1
2	sprigs thyme	2
¼ litre	dry white wine	8 fl oz
1.5 litres	water	3 pints
	salt and pepper	
8 to 10	thick slices bread, toasted	8 to 10
	croûtons	

In a soup pot with a wide bottom, sauté the onions or leeks in the oil, without browning, until soft. Add the tomatoes, fennel or celery, herbs, wine and water and bring to the boil. Season with salt and pepper to taste and simmer for 45 minutes. Pour the stock into a large bowl through a sieve, squeezing all the pulp from the cooked vegetables before discarding the fibres remaining in the sieve. Return the soup stock to the pot and bring it to the boil.

Meanwhile, lightly salt the fish and let stand for 10 minutes, then rinse with water and lower into the soup, adding water only if needed to cover the fish. Reduce the heat and simmer for 5 minutes, then add the lobster, if using it. Cover and simmer for 5 minutes longer, then add the shrimps and scallops or mussels and simmer for an additional 10 minutes. Taste and adjust the seasonings.

Arrange the toast slices in large, warmed soup plates. Ladle in the various fish, shellfish, and the broth. Serve hot, with the croûtons on a separate plate.

VILMA LIACOURAS CHANTILES
THE FOOD OF GREECE

Breton Chowder

La Cotriade

Fish for this dish may include conger, mackerel, pollack, saithe; and (of the soft-fleshed varieties) sardines, skate, cod, ballan and wrasse.

This soup is at its best in its place of origin—the western coast of Cape Finistère. The fish should be perfectly fresh, and still wet with sea water. There are as many *cotriades* as there are varieties of fish and they vary with the seasons.

To serve 4 to 6

1 kg	mixed fish, cleaned and cut into slices if large	2 to 2½ lb
3 tbsp	olive oil, butter or chopped green bacon fat	3 tbsp
500 g	onions, quartered	1 lb
1 kg	potatoes, roughly cut up	2 to 2½ lb
1	bouquet garni	1
2 litres	boiling water, lightly salted	4 pints
30 g	coarse salt	1 oz
	dried bread slices	
2 tbsp	peppercorns, crushed	2 tbsp
¼ litre	wine vinegar	8 fl oz

In a large, heavy saucepan, heat the oil or fat and add the onions. Cook over a medium heat for 1 to 2 minutes, add the potatoes and bouquet garni and continue cooking, stirring occasionally, for 10 minutes or until the onions begin to turn golden. Pour on the boiling water and cook for about 15 minutes or until the potatoes are just beginning to turn tender. Add the fish, reserving any soft-fleshed varieties to add 5 minutes later. Cook at a light boil for another 10 to 15 minutes. Remove the fish and vegetables to a hot serving dish, discarding the bouquet.

Dissolve the coarse salt in half of the broth, and pour this mixture over the fish. Pour it off again. Pour it on to the fish twice more, working carefully so that the fish absorb the salt but are not broken up. Alternatively, serve bowls of the salted broth for the diners to dip their fish into. Pour the remaining unsalted broth into a tureen lined with the bread slices. Mix the peppercorns with the vinegar, and serve as a dipping sauce for the fish and potatoes. A bite of fish and potato may be dipped first into the brine, then into the vinegar. Serve the soup after the fish is eaten.

CURNONSKY
À L'INFORTUNE DU POT

Bahama Seafood Chowder

The conch and coquina called for in this recipe are Caribbean shellfish unavailable in Europe. But the soup may, of course, be made with a selection of locally available seafood.

To serve 8

1 kg	assorted fillets red snapper, mullet, jack and bluefish, cut into 4 cm (1½ inch) pieces	2 to 2½ lb
1 kg	cleaned, shelled conch, crab, coquina, mussels, clams, squid, cut into bite-size pieces	2 to 2½ lb
	juice of 1 large Seville orange or 2 large limes	
2	dried red chili peppers	2
125 g	fat green bacon, coarsely minced	4 oz
6	yellow onions, diced	6
1	large green pepper, diced	1
3	small garlic cloves, crushed	3
750 g	potatoes, diced	1½ lb
3.5 litres	water	6 pints
½ tbsp	dried thyme	½ tbsp
1	small bay leaf	1
	grated mace	
5 or 6 drops	Angostura bitters	5 or 6 drops
½ litre	single cream	18 fl oz
	salt	
15 g	fresh coriander, finely chopped	½ oz

Put the fish and shellfish into a large non-metallic bowl and add the orange or lime juice and chili peppers. Mix gently but thoroughly and let the mixture stand at room temperature for 1 hour. Toss occasionally.

Fry the green bacon in a large soup kettle until golden. Remove the solid bits and reserve. In the fat in the kettle, sauté the onions, green pepper and garlic until soft but not brown. Add the potatoes, water, thyme, bay leaf, a pinch of mace and the bitters. Bring to the boil, then cover and simmer for 40 minutes. Add the drained seafood and simmer for 20 minutes. (If conch or squid is used, simmer for about 15 minutes before adding the rest.) Stir in the cream and the bacon bits. Season with salt to taste, and add the coriander.

JACQUELINE E. KNIGHT
THE COOK'S FISH GUIDE

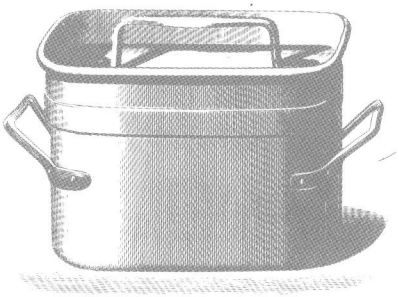

Fish Chowder Roman Tavern-Style

Zuppa di Pesce delle Osterie Romane

To serve 4

2 kg	mixed fish (red mullet, flounder, halibut, eel, sole, etc.), cleaned, boned, sliced, heads removed, fish heads and bones reserved	4 lb
24	live mussels, scrubbed	24
250 g	squid, cleaned and sliced	8 oz
2 tbsp	chopped onion	2 tbsp
30 g	parsley, chopped	1 oz
1 tbsp	salt	1 tbsp
6	peppercorns	6
¾ litre	water	1½ pints
½ litre	dry white wine	1 pint
15 cl	olive oil	¼ pint
2	leeks, chopped	2
2	heads cabbage-type lettuce, halved, cored and shredded	2
	thyme	
1	bay leaf	1
	pepper	
4	anchovy fillets, pounded to a paste	4
2	garlic cloves, chopped	2
4	slices French bread, toasted	4

Put the fish heads and bones into a pot with the onion, half the parsley, the salt and peppercorns, water, and 45 cl (16 fl oz) of the wine. Simmer this court-bouillon for 30 minutes, then strain through a fine sieve.

In a heavy pan, heat 4 tablespoons of the oil, put in the mussels, cover and cook them over a medium heat until they open. Remove the mussels from their shells and strain the pan juices over them. Heat 4 tablespoons more of the oil in a soup kettle, and sauté the sliced squid for 5 minutes. Add the leeks, lettuce, a pinch of thyme, the bay leaf, salt and pepper. Cook over moderate heat for about 30 minutes. When the squid are almost cooked, pour in the remaining wine. Simmer until the wine evaporates. Add the anchovies and sliced fish. Simmer for a few minutes, stirring constantly. Add the court-bouillon and continue cooking the chowder for 10 minutes. Finally add the mussels and their juice.

In a small pan, sauté the garlic in the remaining oil until golden. Remove and discard the garlic, then pour the oil into the chowder. Put the bread into soup dishes, pour the chowder over it, and sprinkle with the remaining parsley.

WAVERLEY ROOT
THE BEST OF ITALIAN COOKING

Barcares Fish Soup

Boullinada du Barcares

For this recipe from the Ariège, a wide variety of fish may be used. Possibilities are red mullet, whiting, plaice, flounder, hake, angler-fish, conger eel, and small squid. The original recipe specifies "slightly rancid" lard—typical of the cooking of this region, but an acquired taste.

To serve 6

2 kg	mixed fish, cleaned, whole or cut up depending on size	4 lb
90 g	lard, diced	3 oz
4 tbsp	finely chopped parsley	4 tbsp
3	garlic cloves, finely chopped	3
	salt	
	cayenne pepper	
2 kg	potatoes, finely sliced	4 lb
2 tbsp	flour	2 tbsp
3 tbsp	olive oil	3 tbsp

Spread the lard in a large saucepan or fireproof earthenware pot. Mix the parsley and garlic, and scatter over, then season with salt and cayenne pepper. Cover this base with a layer of potatoes, followed by a layer of fish. Sprinkle over the flour. Continue alternating layers of potatoes and fish until the pot is filled. Add enough cold water to reach the top layer of fish.

Cover the pot and place it over a high heat. Bring quickly to the boil; this will bind the sauce and give flavour to the dish. As soon as it has come to the boil, add the oil, cover, and continue to cook rapidly for 15 to 20 minutes, or until the potatoes are just cooked. Serve hot.

CURNONSKY
RECETTES DES PROVINCES DE FRANCE

Russian Fish Soup

Oukha

This soup is traditionally served as a meal in itself, accompanied by rastegai ***(herring-filled yeast pastries) or*** koulebiaka ***(a large pasty usually made with puff pastry and filled with a mixture of salmon and rice).***

To serve 4

500 g	mixed fish (cod, hake, haddock, plaice, sole), cleaned, boned, trimmed and cut into pieces, bones and trimmings reserved	1 lb
1.5 litre	water	3 pints
1	onion	1
1	large leek	1
1	sprig parsley, with root	1
1	stick celery	1
10	peppercorns	10
10	juniper berries	10
½	bay leaf	½
4 tbsp	dry white wine (optional)	4 tbsp
100 g	scampi or prawns (optional)	3½ oz
	salt	

Put the fish bones and trimmings into a pot with the water, onion, leek, parsley, celery, peppercorns, juniper berries and bay leaf. Simmer for about 30 minutes, then strain the stock and return it to the pan. Put in the fish pieces, and the wine and scampi, if using. Simmer for 15 to 20 minutes. Salt to taste and serve, with a few pieces of fish in each plate.

SOFKA SKIPWITH
EAT RUSSIAN

Peasant Vegetable Soup

Garbure

Each season determines what goes into this fine soup, for only freshly picked vegetables may be used. The classic ***garbure*** should contain, along with the vegetables, some preserved meat (goose, duck or pork) or at least some kind of salted meat (ham, salt pork, sausage or the carcasses of salted poultry). Traditionally, the soup is cooked on a wood fire. As it simmers gently in the hearth, a very thin layer of fat is spread on the surface of the soup and ignited; this creats a gratin which is reinforced by putting a metal cover on the tureen and placing glowing embers on top of the cover.

	To serve 8	
500 g	potatoes, thickly sliced	1 lb
250 g	broad beans, skinned	8 oz
250 g	large shelled peas	8 oz
250 g	fresh white beans	8 oz
2 litres	water	4 pints
	salt and pepper (preferably cayenne pepper)	
3	garlic cloves	3
1	bouquet garni of thyme, parsley and marjoram	1
1	large green cabbage	1
500 g	preserved or salted meat	1 lb
	stale dark bread, very thinly sliced	

Put the water into a fireproof earthenware pot and bring it to a rolling boil. Throw in the potatoes, peas and beans, and season with salt and pepper. Add the garlic and the bouquet garni. Cook, covered, for about an hour, making sure that the water never stops boiling.

Meanwhile, core the cabbage and separate the leaves. Cut the ribs out of the leaves, roll up the leaves and cut them crosswise into a *chiffonade*. Add to the boiling soup, and cover the pot. As soon as the cabbage has begun to cook, which should be about half an hour before serving time, put in the preserved or salted meat, with its adhering fat. If you are not using preserved goose, a spoonful of goose fat added with the meat will greatly improve the soup.

Put the bread into a soup tureen. If you are using a poultry carcass, remove it from the soup. Cut the meat into portions and serve on a platter with the vegetables. Pour the broth over the bread in the tureen, and serve separately. Tradition demands that when the meat is finished, one empties one's glass of red wine into the remains of the bread and broth.

SIMIN PALAY
LA CUISINE DU PAYS

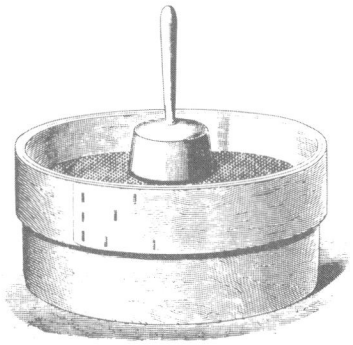

Cabbage Soup with a Meat Crust

Koolsoep van Anneke

	To serve 4	
350 g	white cabbage, quartered, cored and cut into chunks	12 oz
15 g	butter	½ oz
2 tbsp	olive oil	2 tbsp
2 tsp	paprika	2 tsp
	salt and pepper	
2 tbsp	flour	2 tbsp
1 litre	stock or broth (*pages 163-164*)	2 pints
	Meat crust	
30 g	butter	1 oz
1	small onion, chopped	1
300 g	mixed minced pork and beef	10 oz
	salt and pepper	
½ tsp	caraway seeds, crushed or ground	½ tsp
1	small red sweet pepper, diced	1
	breadcrumbs	

In a heavy soup pot, sauté the cabbage in the butter and oil for about 5 minutes. Stir in the paprika, salt and pepper, then the flour. Stir and sauté for 5 minutes. Add the stock and simmer until the cabbage is just tender, about 15 minutes.

To make the crust, melt the butter and sauté the onion until transparent. Add the minced meat and crush it with a fork. Cook over a medium heat, stirring, for about 5 minutes, or until evenly browned. Add the salt, pepper, the caraway seeds and the diced red pepper.

Pour the soup into four fireproof, earthenware soup bowls and spread the meat mixture on top. Sprinkle lightly with breadcrumbs and put the bowls in a fairly hot oven, preheated to 200°C (400°F or Mark 6), or under a grill for 5 to 10 minutes to brown the crust. Serve with thick slices of French bread.

HUGH JANS
BISTRO KOKEN

Wrexham Soup

For the "bladder" used in this recipe to cover the top of the jar, the modern cook may substitute a piece of aluminium foil. The vegetables should be prepared according to their type—root vegetables cut into small pieces, onions and leeks sliced, lettuce shredded. No water is added. The jar or deep bowl of soup should be simmered gently in a water bath over a low heat or baked at a temperature of 130 °C (250 °F or Mark 1/2).

To serve 4

500 g	lean stewing beef	1 lb
1 kg	mixed vegetables (carrot, turnip, celery, potato, leek, onion, peas, lettuce, etc), prepared	2 to 2½ lb
	salt and pepper	

Cut the beef into very small pieces; put them into a 2 litre (½ gal.) stoneware jar, fill it up with every description of vegetable, even lettuces. Tie the jar over with a bladder, and put it over the fire in a deep saucepan of boiling water, or cook in the oven, which is far better, for at least 6 hours.

This generally makes sufficient soup for 4 persons. A little salt and pepper must be added.

MARY JEWRY
WARNE'S MODEL COOKERY AND HOUSEKEEPING BOOK

Beef, Okra, and Tomato Soup

To serve 8

1.5 kg	beef shin bone with meat, sawn into several pieces	3 lb
350 g	okra, sliced	12 oz
350 g	tomatoes, skinned and diced	12 oz
2 litres	cold water	4 pints
1	bouquet garni of bay leaf, oregano and parsley	1
1	onion, diced	1
150 g	French beans, diced	5 oz
90 g	celery, diced	3 oz
½	sweet green pepper, seeded and diced	½
90 g	carrots, diced	3 oz
½ tsp	salt	½ tsp
¼ tsp	pepper	¼ tsp
	boiled rice	

Put the meat in a soup kettle with the water. Slowly bring to the boil, and after 5 minutes of hard boiling, reduce the heat and skim thoroughly. Add the bouquet garni and continue simmering, partially covered, for 2 hours or until the broth is flavourful and the meat nearly tender. Add the okra, tomatoes and all the other vegetables, and salt and pepper. Cover and let simmer gently for about 45 minutes. Remove the meat from the soup, dice it, and return it to the soup kettle, discarding the bones. Cook gently for 10 minutes longer. Taste and adjust the seasoning, and serve in heated soup plates with a side dish of plain boiled rice.

LOUIS P. DE GOUY
THE SOUP BOOK

Bacon Broth

In some parts of Wales and of northern England soup is made in a kettle. This is a sort of stew-pan, having a short wide spout and a lid large enough to cover the whole of the top surface, with a handle like an ordinary kettle rather than that of a saucepan. It is very practical, for one can pour off the soup through the spout and leave meat, bones and vegetables in the kettle. It is ideal for bacon, mutton, beef or rabbit broth.

To serve 8

750 g	bacon, or bacon hock, or salted or pickled pork knuckle, soaked overnight and drained	1½ lb
500 g	shin of beef	1 lb
1	white cabbage, quartered, cored and sliced	1
250 g	parsnips, chopped	8 oz
250 g	carrots, chopped	8 oz
½	small swede, sliced	½
500 g	potatoes, diced	1 lb
	salt and pepper	
1	large leek, sliced	1
2 tbsp	oatmeal	2 tbsp

Put the bacon, beef, cabbage, parsnips, carrots, swede and potatoes into a large soup kettle or stew-pan. Cover them with water. Add salt and pepper. Bring to the boil and let them simmer with the lid on for 3 hours or longer (almost as long as you like, within reason) either in a slow oven or on the hob of an open fire. Ten minutes before eating the soup, add the leek. Mix the oatmeal to a paste with cold water and stir this into the soup. Let the soup boil until thickened, then serve. The meat and vegetables are served separately, after the broth.

SHEILA HUTCHINS
ENGLISH RECIPES AND OTHERS FROM SCOTLAND, WALES AND IRELAND

Marbled Partridge Soup

Potage de Perdrix Marbrées

To serve 4

2	old partridges, trussed and barded	2
1.5 litres	veal or chicken stock	3 pints
	salt	
100 g	stale bread, crusts removed	3½ oz
125 g	mushrooms, sliced	4 oz
¼ litre	water	8 fl oz
125 g	almonds, ground	4 oz
10 cl	mutton or lamb roasting juices, degreased, or reduced lamb stock	4 fl oz
60 g	pistachios, blanched	2 oz
2 tbsp	lemon juice	2 tbsp

Half roast the partridges for 15 minutes at 230°C (450°F or Mark 8). Bring the stock to the boil, salt to taste, and put in the partridges. Simmer until the partridges are tender—1 hour or more, depending on their age. Add the bread and simmer gently until it becomes a pulp; add the mushrooms and cook a few minutes longer. Pour the water over the ground almonds, allow to steep for a few minutes, and drain the liquid through a cloth, squeezing the cloth to extract all the almond milk. Remove the partridges from the soup, split them, and arrange the halves on a deep serving dish. Combine the almond milk, mutton juice, pistachios and lemon juice and add the mixture to the soup. Pour the soup over the partridges and serve.

LA VARENNE
LE VRAY CUISINIER FRANÇOIS

Duck Soup: Farmhouse

To serve 8

2	ducks	2
3.5 litres	water	6 pints
1	carrot	1
1	small turnip	1
3	onions	3
½	head celery	½
4	potatoes	4
1	bunch parsley	1
	salt and pepper	
1	large marrowbone	1
30 cl	orange juice	½ pint

Put the ducks into a large pot with the water, vegetables, parsley, salt and pepper. Bring to the boil and simmer for 30 minutes, skimming well during that time. Then add the marrowbone and skim no further: the delicate globules of marrow fat are a delicacy.

When the birds are very tender, after about 2 hours, lift them from the pot. Put the soup through a sieve but do not rub through any of the vegetables. Return the stock to the pot. Cut the meat off the birds and chop finely. (Do *not* use a mincer.)

Give the meat a dust of salt and pepper and add to the stock. Bring to the boil and no more. Taste the soup and add more salt or pepper if necessary. Draw to the side of the fire and add orange juice to taste. Serve with boiled potatoes.

JANET MURRAY
WITH A FINE FEELING FOR FOOD

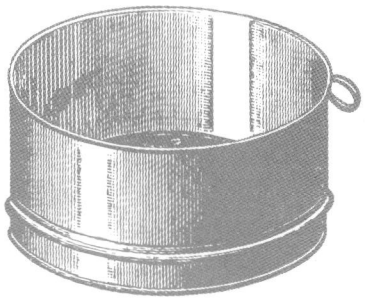

Irish Farm Broth

To serve this soup country fashion, a pot of boiled potatoes was in readiness. The meat was removed from the pot, cut in small pieces and distributed round the plates (or bowls most likely) to which the broth was added. Two or three peeled potatoes were broken up in each plate, and all was eaten with a spoon, the whole forming a warm and substantial meal.

To serve 8

1 kg	boiling beef	2 to 2½ lb
2 to 3 litres	water	4 to 5½ pints
200 g	split peas	7 oz
200 g	barley	7 oz
1	small head cabbage, cored and shredded	1
60 g	celery tops, shredded	2 oz
2	leeks, thinly sliced,	2
1	carrot, diced	1
1	small turnip, diced	1
	salt and pepper	

Put the beef into the pot with the amount of water required for the broth, add the peas and the barley. Put on the lid and cook slowly, while you prepare the vegetables. Add the vegetables to the pot and simmer all for 2 or 3 hours on a low heat. (As a rule none of the fat was skimmed off—a practice which was dietetically sound. People leading an outdoor life could digest it.) Season with salt and pepper to taste and serve.

FLORENCE IRWIN
IRISH COUNTRY RECIPES

Nettle Broth

This used to be the peasants' Christmas dinner, perhaps the only day in the year on which fresh meat was eaten.

To serve 8

100 g	nettle tops, chopped	3½ oz
1 kg	stewing beef or mutton	2 to 2½ lb
2 litres	water	4 pints
150 g	barley	5 oz
1	bunch Welsh or spring onions, chopped	1
2 tbsp	flour (optional)	2 tbsp
	salt and pepper	

Put the meat, water and barley in the pot and simmer, partially covered, for 2 hours. Add the chopped onions and nettles and simmer another hour. Thicken if liked, by blending the flour to a paste with a little of the broth, then stirring it into the soup. When the meat is tender, the broth is ready. Season to taste. The meat can be cut up and returned to the broth to serve, or it may be served separately after the soup.

FLORENCE IRWIN
IRISH COUNTRY RECIPES

Broad Bean and Mutton Soup

Soupe de Fèves au Collet de Mouton

To serve 8 to 10

1 kg	broad beans, shelled and skinned	2 to 2½ lb
2 kg	neck of mutton or lamb	4 lb
4 litres	water	7 pints
40 g	salt	1½ oz
1	bouquet garni of thyme and bay leaf	1
60 g	butter	2 oz
	pepper	
1 tbsp	chopped fresh winter savory	1 tbsp
12	slices day-old French bread	12

Put the mutton in a large saucepan with the water, salt and bouquet garni. Bring to the boil and skim. Simmer for 2 hours with the lid half on. Add the beans and raise the heat. As soon as the soup has come to the boil, turn the heat right down so that the soup will do no more than simmer gently. When the beans are cooked, in 10 to 20 minutes, transfer the meat to a warmed serving dish. Drain the beans and toss them briefly in a saucepan over moderate heat with the butter, pepper, salt, if necessary, and the savory. Remove the bouquet garni.

Put the bread in a warmed soup tureen and pour in the soup. Arrange the beans in the serving dish around the meat, and serve as a second course after the soup.

JULES GOUFFÉ
LE LIVRE DES SOUPES ET DES POTAGES

Thick Mutton Soup

Soupe Courte

To serve 4 to 6

750 g	mutton or lamb, one thick slice from top of leg	1½ lb
30 g	lard	1 oz
100 g	green streaky bacon, cut into lardons	3½ oz
1	onion, chopped	1
2 or 3 tbsp	broth or water	2 or 3 tbsp
	salt and pepper	
1.5 litres	hot water	3 pints
250 g	rice	8 oz
¼ tsp	powdered saffron	¼ tsp
1	onion, studded with 3 cloves	1
1	bouquet garni of 1 stick celery, 1 sprig chervil, 1 bay leaf	1

Put the mutton in a copper pan with the lard and the bacon; brown the meat on both sides, add the chopped onion, stir, and moisten with 1 tablespoon of the broth. Season with salt and pepper, cover and cook over a very low heat, occasionally turning the meat and moistening it lightly, if necessary, with additional broth. When you judge the meat to be cooked (normally this takes not less than 2 hours, but it will depend on the thickness of the meat), add the water. Increase the heat and, when the water is boiling, throw in the rice, saffron, as much salt as is necessary, the clove-studded onion and the bouquet garni. Cook, covered, over a low heat for at least 25 minutes, or longer if you like the rice well cooked. This soup should be almost as thick as a pilaff. Remove the bouquet garni and the whole onion. Serve the meat separately.

J. B. REBOUL
LA CUISINIÈRE PROVENÇALE

Garlic Soup

Soupe Languedocienne

To serve 4

20	garlic cloves, crushed	20
3 tbsp	goose fat	3 tbsp
2	large slices gammon or raw cured ham	2
1 tbsp	flour	1 tbsp
2.5 litres	water or broth (*pages 163-164*)	5 pints
2	large tomatoes, sieved	2
	salt and pepper	
1	sprig thyme	1
3	egg yolks	3
5 tbsp	olive oil	5 tbsp
	thick slices home-made bread (*page 165*)	
	grated Gruyère or Parmesan cheese	

Melt the goose fat in a large sauté pan, and sauté the ham slices until they are golden on both sides. Remove the ham and keep it warm between two plates.

Put the garlic in the pan and cook gently, without letting it brown. Sprinkle the garlic with the flour, and cook until the flour is absorbed. Pour in the water or broth, and add the sieved tomatoes. Season lightly with salt and generously with pepper. Add the thyme and boil the soup rapidly, uncovered, for 12 to 15 minutes. Beat the egg yolks with the oil in a tureen, and pour in the soup, mixing well.

Serve the soup accompanied by slices of bread sprinkled with grated cheese and lightly browned in the oven. Serve the ham, sliced, and arranged on a warmed plate with the bread, at the same time.

70 MÉDECINS DE FRANCE
LE TRÉSOR DE LA CUISINE DU BASSIN MÉDITERRANÉEN

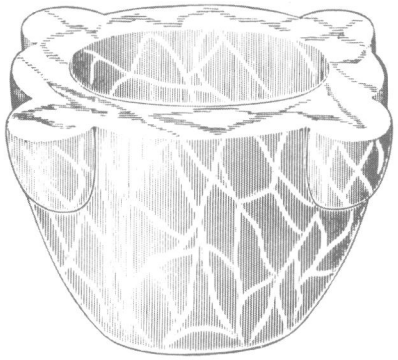

Standard Preparations

Vegetable Broth

To make 1.5 litres (3 pints) broth

2	leeks, thinly sliced	2
2	sticks celery with leaves, chopped	2
2	onions, thinly sliced	2
4	carrots, chopped	4
2	cabbage leaves, cut in *chiffonade*	2
1	lettuce, cut in *chiffonade*	1
4	sprigs flat-leafed parsley with stems, chopped	4
1 tsp	thyme	1 tsp
1	bay leaf	1
	salt	
1.5 litres	water	3 pints

Place all the ingredients in a large saucepan and bring very slowly to the boil. Skim, then cover with the lid ajar, and allow the broth to simmer undisturbed, for about 45 minutes.

Strain the broth through a sieve into a bowl, without pressing any of the vegetables through the sieve.

Fish Broth

To make 1.5 litres (3 pints) broth

1 kg	fish heads, bones and trimmings, rinsed and broken into pieces	2 to 2½ lb
1 each	onion, carrot and leek, sliced	1 each
1	stick celery, diced	1
1	bouquet garni	1
2 litres	water	4 pints
	salt	

Place the fish, vegetables and herbs in a stock pot or large saucepan. Add the water and season lightly with salt. Bring to the boil over a low heat. With a large spoon or ladle, skim off the scum that rises to the surface as the liquid begins to simmer. Keep skimming until no more scum rises, then cover, with the lid slightly ajar, and simmer for 30 minutes. Without pressing, strain the broth through a colander into a bowl.

Game Broth

Game broth may be prepared in the same way as the beef broth enriched with chicken pieces (*below*), except for the addition of game birds such as stewing pheasants or partridges. Partially roast the pheasants for 25 minutes, the partridges for 15 minutes in a very hot oven, 230°C (450°F or Mark 8). Add them to the broth with the aromatic vegetables.

Alternatively, you can add game trimmings and carcasses, raw or cooked, to a richly flavoured beef or chicken broth. Add fresh aromatic vegetables at the same time, and simmer the broth for 2 to 3 hours before straining.

Meat Broth

This basic broth, of beef with the addition of chicken and veal, may be used in any recipe calling for beef broth, stock, consommé or pot au feu bouillon. Almost any veal, chicken or beef bones may be included; the exceptions are large marrow-bones that take up too much room in the pot, obliging you to add too much water and thus weaken the resulting broth.

To make 4 litres (7 pints)

1 kg	shin or leg of beef	2 to 2½ lb
1 kg	plate or short ribs of beef	2 to 2½ lb
1 kg	chicken pieces (backs, necks, wing tips)	2 to 2½ lb
1	chicken carcass, raw or cooked (optional)	1
1	meaty veal knuckle, chopped (optional)	1
5 litres	water	9 pints
300 g	carrots	10 oz
1	large onion, stuck with 3 cloves	1
1	large head of garlic	1
1	bouquet garni	1
	salt	

Place a round metal grill in the bottom of your stock pot, to prevent the ingredients from sticking. Tie thin cuts of meat into compact shapes with string. Starting with the largest pieces, fit all the beef, chicken and veal into the pot. Add the water and bring very slowly to the boil; it should take at least 1 hour for the water to reach boiling point. With a spoon or ladle, carefully lift off the surface scum as the liquid comes to the boil. Add the carrots, onion, garlic, bouquet garni and salt, and skim once more as the broth returns to the boil.

Turn the heat down, cover the pot with the lid ajar, and leave to simmer undisturbed for 3½ hours if you wish to serve the beef afterwards, or for 5 hours if you wish to extract all the goodness of the beef into the broth.

Strain the finished broth through a colander, lined with dampened muslin. Degrease thoroughly with a paper towel, or allow the broth to cool completely and then remove the solidified fat from the top.

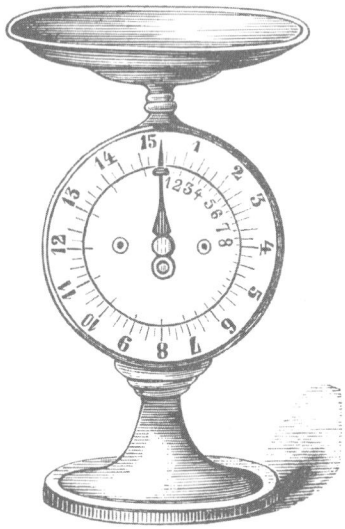

Chicken Broth

To make 4 litres (7 pints)

2.5 to 3 kg	boiling fowl, trussed	5 to 7 lb
1	large onion, stuck with 3 cloves	1
2	carrots	2
1	large head of garlic	1
1	bouquet garni	1
About 5 litres	water or broth	About 9 pints
	coarse salt	

Place the fowl, breast uppermost, in the bottom of an oval pot just large enough to hold the ingredients. Place the vegetables and the bouquet garni around it. Pour on water or broth to cover, and slowly bring to the boil. Skim until no more scum forms on the top. As the fat from the bird melts and rises to the top, skim that off, too. When the boiling point is reached, add the salt and cover the pan, with the lid ajar. Reduce the heat and cook undisturbed at a slow simmer for 1½ to 3 hours, depending on the age of the bird. Remove the bird and the vegetables from the pot, and strain the broth through a colander, lined with dampened muslin.

Quenelles

This mixture can be made with chicken, partridge or pheasant breast, lean veal or skinned fish fillets, instead of the chicken. A food processor may be used instead of a mortar, but the purée should still be sieved after processing.

To serve 6

200g	raw breast of chicken, skinned	7 oz
	salt and white pepper	
	grated nutmeg	
	cayenne pepper	
1	egg white	1
15 cl	double cream	¼ pint

In a large mortar, pound the meat with the seasonings until a smooth paste is formed. Add the egg white, continuing to pound until it is amalgamated. Pass the mixture through a sieve, and pack into a metal bowl, set in crushed ice. Let it chill for 1 hour. Then, with the bowl still over ice, work the cream into the sieved meat. Put the mixture into a pastry bag with a metal tip, or a cone of greaseproof paper with the end snipped off. Press out small, oval quenelles into a buttered shallow pan. Carefully pour in boiling water to cover, and place over a low heat so that the water continues to not quite simmer. When the quenelles float to the surface of the water, they are done and may be transferred to a hot broth for serving.

Pasta Dough

To make green pasta, parboil 250 g (8 oz) of spinach or chard for 3 to 5 minutes, or until just tender. Drain, squeeze completely dry with your hands, and chop finely, or purée in the liquidizer. You should have about 50 g (2 oz) of purée. Omit the saffron from the recipe and use the purée to replace one of the eggs in the recipe. To stuff and cook pasta see the demonstration on page 17.

To serve 6 to 8 as a garnish

250 g	flour	8 oz
	powdered saffron (optional)	
2	large eggs	2
1 tsp	olive oil	1 tsp
½ tsp	salt	½ tsp
	semolina	

Put three-quarters of the flour into a bowl, and blend with a pinch of saffron, if using. Add the eggs, oil and salt, and mix with a fork, adding more flour if necessary and kneading with your fingers until a pliable dough forms. Wrap the dough in a damp cloth or a piece of plastic wrap, and allow it to rest at room temperature for 30 minutes.

On a floured board, with a rolling pin, roll and stretch the dough until it is very thin. During the rolling, it will absorb the remaining flour. Alternatively, put it through a pasta machine until it will go through the desired setting.

If making stuffed pasta, stamp out small rounds with a cutter and stack them to prevent them from drying out.

If making noodles, roll the sheet of dough up loosely from both sides until the two rolls meet in the centre. Cut across with a sharp knife to make noodles of the desired thickness. Separate the noodles and allow them to dry for a few minutes on a cloth or board, lightly sprinkled with semolina. Cook in a large pot of boiling, salted water before adding to soup.

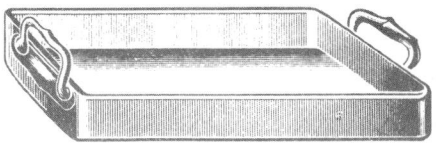

Bread

This recipe is for a basic crusty loaf, similar to French country bread (*pain de campagne*). It can be varied by including dark flour (for example, 1 part wholemeal and 1 part rye, to 2 parts unbleached white flour) and by allowing the yeast to ferment for 24 hours before making the bread. For a finer flavour, dissolve the yeast in ¼ litre (8 fl oz) of warm water, and stir in 250 g (8 oz) of flour. Beat until smooth, cover the mixture with plastic wrap, and leave the bowl in a warm place overnight. Then add the remaining ingredients and continue with the recipe as below.

To make 1 large or 2 small loaves

1½ tsp	dried yeast or 15 g (½ oz) fresh yeast	1½ tsp
½ litre	warm water	1 pint
	salt	
750 g	strong plain bread flour	1½ lb
	semolina, cornmeal, or cracked wheat (optional)	

Dissolve the yeast in 10 cl (4 fl oz) of the water and leave for about 15 minutes, or until foamy. Add the remaining water and the salt, and begin stirring in the flour. When the dough is stiff and starts to pull away from the sides of the bowl, turn it out on to a floured board. Knead, folding the dough towards you, pushing it away with the heels of your hands, and giving it a quarter-turn; and repeat vigorously until the dough is smooth and shiny and not sticky—after at least 10 minutes. Sprinkle with more flour as necessary during kneading.

Gather the dough into a ball, dust with flour and return the dough to the bowl; cover with a cloth and leave in a warm place until the dough has more than doubled in bulk, 1 to 2 hours.

Turn the dough on to the floured board and punch it down to expel all the air. Knead again briefly and form into a large round loaf, or tapered, long, cylindrical French loaves on a lightly floured baking sheet. Or form into 1 large or 2 small cylinders and put into loaf tins. Leave to rise, covered loosely with a tea towel, until doubled in size, about 1 hour.

Preheat the oven to fairly hot, 200°C (400°F or Mark 6). To create steam, put a baking tin containing about 2.5 cm (1 inch) of hot water on the floor of the oven or lowest shelf.

If you are baking a large round loaf, you may leave it to rise for the second time on a board generously sprinkled with semolina, cornmeal, or cracked wheat. Place the baking sheet in the oven while it is preheating. To bake the bread, slash the surface with a razor blade, and transfer it with a rapid jerk to the heated baking sheet. After the first 20 minutes of baking, remove the pan of water and turn the oven down to moderate, 180°C (350°F or Mark 4). The bread will take about 1 hour to bake, depending on the size and shape of the loaves. When it is done, it will be golden-brown all over and the bottom crust will sound hollow when tapped. Cool on a wire rack.

If it is to be used in soups, this bread should be kept for at least 1 to 2 days after it has been baked.

Crêpes

For crêpes to cut into strips as a soup garnish, 1 to 2 tablespoons of chopped parsley or *fines herbes* may be added, or a pinch of powdered saffron may be dissolved in a little hot water and the mixture used as part of the liquid for the batter.

To serve 8

50 g	flour	2 oz
3	eggs	3
3 tbsp	melted butter	3 tbsp
2 tbsp	cognac (optional)	2 tbsp
	salt (optional)	
About ¼ litre	milk or water	About ½ pint

In a bowl, make a well in the centre of the flour and add the eggs, butter, and the cognac and/or the salt if used. Whisk while gradually adding enough of the milk or water to make a batter with the consistency of single cream. Do not whisk the mixture more than necessary.

To make the crêpes, heat a crêpe pan or small frying pan over a medium-low heat and grease it lightly, with butter for the first crêpe only. Pour in a small ladleful of the batter, tilting the pan to form a thin layer all over the bottom. Cook the crêpe for 1 to 2 minutes or until the edges separate from the pan, then turn the crêpe and briefly cook the other side. The crêpes may be stacked on a plate and kept warm in the oven, or they may be stacked and covered with plastic wrap to be refrigerated until needed.

Rouille

There are many versions of this classic red pepper sauce; some omit the basil and sweet red pepper, others moisten the sauce with fish broth as well as olive oil. To make a less highly spiced sauce, the seeds of the dried chili peppers may be removed.

To make 30 cl (½ pint) rouille

2	small dried chili peppers	2
	coarse salt	
	pepper	
1	small bunch basil leaves	1
2 or 3	garlic cloves	2 or 3
1	thick slice white bread, crust removed, soaked in warm water and squeezed dry	1
1	sweet red pepper, grilled, skinned, and seeded	1
	olive oil	

In a large mortar, pound the dried peppers until they are reduced to a powder. Add salt and pepper and the basil and garlic and continue to pound until the mixture is crushed to a paste. Add the bread, then the sweet pepper, pounding well to mix all the ingredients into a smooth purée. Add the oil in a thin, steady stream while turning or stirring the mixture with the pestle. The finished *rouille* should be a smooth sauce with the consistency of mayonnaise.

Royales

These custard garnishes for consommé may be coloured and flavoured in a variety of ways. About 50 g (2 oz) of puréed, cooked peas or spinach will make green *royales;* the same quantity of puréed tomato will turn them red. If spinach or tomato are added, the amount of broth should be reduced, to keep the proportion of egg to liquid the same.

To serve 6 to 8

1	egg	1
3	egg yolks	3
20 cl	hot broth (*pages 163-164*)	7 fl oz

Beat the egg and the yolks together, and gradually beat in the hot broth. Pass the mixture through a fine sieve, and use to fill small buttered moulds. Place the moulds on a grill set in a wide saucepan, and pour enough hot water into the pan to come half way up the sides of the moulds. Cover the pan and poach the custards, either in a cool oven at 150°C (300°F or Mark 2), or over a low heat. Cook for 12 to 15 minutes, or until set, never letting the water in the pan come to the boil. Remove the moulds, allow them to cool, then turn out the custards and cut them into dice with a knife, or into ornamental shapes with special cutters.

White Sauce

This sauce, in which the cooking liquid is milk, can be used in purées which require an additional starchy element. The recipe can be used whenever béchamel sauce is required.

To make about 45 cl (¾ pint)

30 g	butter	1 oz
2 tbsp	flour	2 tbsp
60 cl	milk	1 pint
	salt	
	white pepper	
	freshly grated nutmeg (optional)	
	double cream (optional)	

Melt the butter in a heavy saucepan. Stir in the flour and cook, stirring, over a low heat for 2 to 5 minutes. Pour in all of the milk, whisking constantly to blend the mixture smoothly. Raise the heat and continue whisking while the sauce comes to the boil. Season with a very little salt. Reduce the heat to very low, and simmer for about 40 minutes, stirring every so often to prevent the sauce from sticking to the bottom of the pan. Add white pepper and a pinch of nutmeg if desired; taste for seasoning. Whisk again until the sauce is perfectly smooth, and add cream if you prefer a richer and whiter sauce.

Egg Threads

To serve 4

1	egg	1
1½ to 2 tbsp	flour	1½ to 2 tbsp
	salt	
1 litre	broth (*pages 163-164*)	2 pints

Put the flour and salt in a bowl, break in the egg, and whisk to amalgamate. Strain the batter through a fine sieve. Bring the broth to the boil in a saucepan. When it is bubbling, hold a perforated spoon over the pan and pour the batter from the bowl through the spoon. The batter will solidify as it goes into the broth. Cook for 2 to 3 minutes more, then serve.

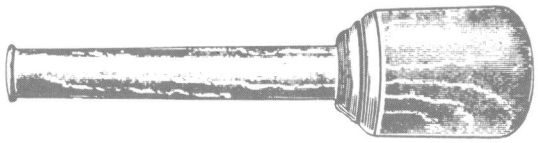

Velouté Sauce

This sauce is the basis of many puréed soups. It may be made with any of the broths in this standard preparations section, depending on the other ingredients used in the purée.

To make about 30 cl (½ pint) sauce

60 cl	broth (*pages 163-164*)	1 pint
30 g	butter	1 oz
2 tbsp	flour	2 tbsp

Melt the butter in a heavy saucepan over a low heat. Stir in the flour to make a roux and cook, stirring, for 2 to 3 minutes. Pour the broth into the saucepan, whisking constantly. Raise the heat and continue to whisk the mixture until the sauce comes to the boil. Reduce the heat to low, and move the saucepan half off the heat so that the liquid on only one side of the pan simmers. A skin of impurities will form on the other, still side. Remove the skin periodically with a spoon. Cook the sauce for at least 40 minutes in order to reduce it and to eliminate the taste of flour.

Recipe Index

English recipe titles are listed by categories such as "Bean", "Beef", "Fish" or "Fruit", and within those categories appear alphabetically. Foreign recipe titles are listed alphabetically without regard to category.

Açorda *Alentejana*, 136
Aïgo Boulido, 88
Aïoli, 154
Almond Soup, 134
  see also Fennel
Angler-Fish, *see* Fish and Shellfish
Apple, *see* Fruit
Apricot, *see* Fruit
Ärter med Fläsk, 152
Artichoke, Jerusalem, *see* Jerusalem artichoke
Asparagus Soups:
  Asparagus, 108
  Cream of, 101
Aubergine or Marrow Soup, 119
Avocado Soups:
  Bisque, 141
  Summer, 141
Bacon, *see* Pork
Baudroie à l'Aigo Sau, 128
Bean Soups:
  Bean, 151
  Black Bean, 97
  Broad Bean, 95
  Broad Bean and Mutton, 162
  Fresh Haricot Bean, 107
  Red Kidney Bean, 120
  Red Pottage, 97
  Three-Helping, 126
Beef Soups:
  Catalan, 121
  and Lamb Soup Roman-Style, 150
  Okra, and Tomato, 160
  Oxtail, 117
  see also Broths; Consommé; Meat; Meat and Vegetables; Pot au Feu
Beer Soup, Swedish, 88
Beetroot, *see* Borscht
Bisque d'Écrevisses, 102
Bisques:
  Avocado, 141
  Crayfish, 102
Black Bean, *see* Bean
Boiled Water, 88
Borchtch Vert, 118
Borisch, 147
Borscht:
  Borscht, 147
  Green, 118
  Polish, 148
  with Squid, 129
  Ukrainian, 147
Borscht Malorossiiskii, 147
Borshch Pol'skii, 148
Borshch S Kal'Marami, 129
Botvinya, 145
Bouillabaisse Normande, 155
Boullinada du Barcares, 158
Bouillon de Legumes, 98
  d'une Heure, 89
Bourride, 154
Bread, 165
  Balls, 91
BREAD SOUPS, 134-141:
  Almond, 134
  Asturian Garlic, 135
  Auvergne, and Cheese, 136
  Black, Franconian-Style, 136
  Bread, 135
  and Cheese, 139
  with Eggs, 137
  Fisherman's, 139
  Fried Breadcrumb, 141
  Italian, 140
  of Mallorca, 137
  Onion, 137,138
  Panade with Sorrel, 141
  Panade with Sorrel or Leek, 140
  Portuguese Panade, 136
  Pumpkin Panade, 135
  Saffron, 134
  Spanish Egg, 137
  Stuffed, 140
  and Tomato, 138
Broad Beans, *see* Beans
Broccoli, *see* Cauliflower
Brodetto alla Romana, 150
Brotchen Roy, 116
Broth:
  Bacon, 160
  Basic, 164
  Boiled Water, 88
  Chicken, 164
  Chicken Mousse in, 123
  Fife, 115
  Fish, 163
  Game, 164
  Green Soup with Fish, 106
  Irish Farm, 161
  Japanese Soup, 89
  Leek and Oatmeal, 116
  Meat, 164
  Nettle, 162
  for Pickled Cucumber and Kidney Soup, 122
  Rapid, 89
  Rich Country, 112
  Scotch, 115
  Vegetable, 98,163
BROTHS, COMPOUND, 105-134
  SIMPLE, 88,89
Brotsuppe, 136
Bruine Bonensoep, 120
Buckwheat, 90
Budino di Pollo in Brodo, 123
Burgonyagombóc, 91
Cabbage Soups:
  with Cream, 109
  Fresh Mushroom and, 110
  with Meat Crust, 159
  Sweet and Sour, 110
Cacciucco alla Livornese, 155
Carrot Soup, 94
  and Orange, 94
Catalan, 121
Cauliflower and Broccoli Soup, with Parsley, 107
Cheese Soups:
  Auvergne Bread and, 136
  Bread and, 139
Cherbah, 111
Cherry, *see* Fruit
Chestnut Soups:
  Chestnut, 96
  in Milk, 113
  and Rice, 114
Chicken Soups:
  Broth, 164
  Cock-a-Leekie, 116
  and Cress, 108
  with Flakes of Egg and Cheese, 93
  and Fresh Corn Chowder, 152
  Mousse in Broth, 123
  Mulligatawny, 119
  Poached, 148
  Purée of, 104
  Puréed, 104
  Rice and Chicken Liver, 123
  Senegalese, 144
  see also Meat; Meat and Vegetables; Pot au Feu
Ch'ing Ts'ai Ma Ku T'ang, 110
Chlodnik z Ryby, 144
Chowders:
  Bahama Seafood, 157
  Breton, 156
  Chicken and Fresh Corn, 152
  Fish, Roman Tavern-Style, 157
  Manhattan Clam, 131
  New England Clam, 131
  Old-Fashioned Fish, 132
  Smoked Fish, 131
Cioppino, 134
Clam, *see* Chowder
Cock-a-Leekie, 116
Cockie-Leekie, 116
Cod, *see* Fish and Shellfish
COLD SOUPS, 141-146
COMPOUND BROTHS, 105-134
Consommé:
  Andalusian, 143
  Chilled, Madrilène, 143
  Consommé, 88
  with Threads of Egg, 92
Consommé Andalou, 143
  aux Oeufs Filés, 92
  Glacé à la Madrilène, 143
Cotriade, 156
Crayfish, *see* Bisque
Cream Soups:
  of California Herbs, 143
  Cucumber and, 142
  of Pumpkin and Shrimp, 103
  Sorrel and, 100
  Thick, 100
  of Turnips, 96
Crème:
  Bonne Femme, 105
  d'Emeraude, 101
  de Tomate, 98
  à la Vierge, 96
Crêpes, 166
Cucumber Soups:
  and Cream, 142
  Pickled, and Kidney, 122
Curry Seasoning, 119; *see also* Senegalese
Dashi, 89
Don Far Tong, 108
Duck Soup: Farmhouse, 161
Dumplings:
  Brain, 91
  for Hamburg Eel Soup, 130
  Leek Soup with, 122
  Liver, 92
  Marrow, 93
  Meat, 92
  Pilota, 149
  Pomeranian, 92
  Potato, 91

Suet, 125
Eel, *see* Fish and Shellfish
Eggs:
Consommé with Egg Threads, 92
Egg Balls, 91
Royales, 167
Egg Threads, 167
Soup with Eggs, 137
Spanish Egg Soup, 137
Escudella: Carn d'Olla, 149
Fennel and Almond Fish Soup, 103
Fife Broth, 115
Fish and Shellfish Soups:
Angler-Fish, 128
Barcares Fish, 158
Cod, Fruit Soup with, 129
Cold Fish, 145
Cold Fish and Vegetable, 144
Eel, 130
Eel, Hamburg, 130
Fennel and Almond Fish, 103
Fish Broth, 163
Fish, from Provence, 154
Fish, with Garlic Mayonnaise, 154
Greek Fish, 156
Green, with Fish Broth, 106
Leghorn Fish Stew, 155
Lobster Stew, 133
Mackerel, 127
Mussel, with Milk, 132
Mussel and Tomato, 133
Mussel, Velouté of, 132
New England, 133
Norman Fish Stew, 155
Octopus, 129
Prawns, Cream of, 102
Rock Fish, 128
Russian Fish, 158
Scallop, 103
Seafood Stew, 134
Shrimp, Cream of Pumpkin and, 103
Sole, 127
Squid, Borscht with, 129
see also Bisques; Chowders
Frikadel'ki iz Gouyadiny, 92
Fruit Soups:
Apple, 93
Apricot and Vegetable Marrow, 98
Cherry, Hungarian, 146
Cherry and Rice, Cold, 145
Fruit, with Cod, 129
Grapes, White Garlic, with, 142
Melon and Potato, 101
Orange, Carrot and, 94
Pear and Watercress, Cold, 146
Raspberry, 93
Strawberry, Cold, 146
Game Soups:
Broth, 164
Brown Rabbit, 89
Game, 104
Grouse, 116
Marbled Partridge, 161
Pigeon, with Barley, 117
Garbure, 159
Garlic Mayonnaise, 154
Garlic Soups:
Asturian, 135
Garlic, 163
White, with Grapes, 142
GARNISHES, 90-93
Brain Dumplings, 91
Bread Balls, 91
Buckwheat (*Kasha*), 90
Crêpes, 166
Crostini, 110
Egg Balls, 91
Egg Threads, 167
Little Russian Meat Pies (*Pirozhki*), 90
Liver Dumplings, 92
Meat Balls, 120
Meat Dumplings, 92
Pasta, Dough for, 165
Potato Dumplings, 91
Quenelles, 165
Ravioli with Ricotta and Spinach, 90
Royales, 167
Suet Dumplings, 125
Gazpacho, Andalusian, 144
Grapes, *see* Fruit
Grouse, *see* Game
Haddock, Smoked, *see* Chowders
Ham, *see* Pork
Hamburger Aalsuppe, 130
Harcho, 122
Herb Soups:
Cream of California, 143
Green, 106
Green, with Fish Broth, 106
Soup of Green, 106
Hollandse Erwtensoep, 152
Iced Soups:
Simplified, 142
for a Very Hot Day, 144
Japanese Soup Broth, 89
Jerusalem Artichoke Soup, 95
Julienne aux Champignons, 110
K*akavia*, 156
Kasha, 90
Kidney Beans, *see* Beans
Kidney, Pickled Cucumber and, 122
Koolsoep van Anneke, 159
Kraeklingasupa úr Mjólk, 132
Kvas, 145
Lamb, *see* Beef; Scotch Broth
Leek:
Cook-a-Leekie, 116
Cockie-Leekie, 116
with Dumplings, 122
and Oatmeal Broth, 116
Panade with, 140
and Potato, 105
Potato and, 105
Lettuce Soup, 107
Purée, 95
Lights, Soup of, 123
"Little Chickens" Soup Antonio, 121
Lobster, *see* Fish and Shellfish
Mackerel, *see* Fish and Shellfish
Markklösschensuppe, 93
Marrow, *see* Vegetable Marrow
Meat:
Balls, 120
Broth, 164
Crust, 159
Dumplings, 92
Pies, Little Russian, 90
Meat-Rice Barrel, 120
see also Broth; Consommé; Meat and Vegetables; and individual meats
Meat and Vegetable Soups:
Beef, Okra and Tomato, 160
Broad Bean and Mutton, 162
Ham and Winter Melon, 108
Irish Farm Broth, 161
Jamaica Pepperpot, 126
Mary's Portuguese, 153
Mockturtle, 118
Nettle Broth, 162
Pickled Cucumber and Kidney, 122
Scotch Broth, 115
Soup Made in the Gruzian Way, 122
Spanish One-Pot Meal, 153
Spinach and Pork, 108
Wrexham, 160
see also Bortsch; Broths; Meat; Pot au Feu; Vegetable, Mixed
Meggy Leves, 146
Melon, *see* Fruit
Melon, Winter, *see* Pork
Menudo, 125
Minestra:
de Carciofi di Giudea, 95
di Castagne e Riso, 114
di Cetriolo alla Crema, 142
di Pomidoro, 110
di Riso e Fegatini, 123
di Trippe alla Milanese, 124
Minestrone alla Contadina, 113
alla Milanese, 111
Mixed Vegetables, *see* Vegetables, Mixed
Mockturtle Soup, 118
Mother Onésime's Soup, 114
Mourtaïrol, 134
Mulligatawny, 119
Mushroom Soups:
and Barley, 109
Cream of, 99
Fresh, and Cabbage, 110
Vegetable, 110
Wild, 109
Mussels, *see* Fish and Shellfish
Mutton Soups:
Broad Bean, 162
Scotch Broth, 115
Thick, 162
N*asi Tim Voor 2 Zieken*, 120
Nettle Broth, 162
New England Soup, 133
Nouzillards, 113
Nuts, *see* Almond; Chestnut
Oatmeal Broth, Leek and, 116
Octopus, *see* Fish and Shellfish
Okra, Beef and Tomato Soup, 160
Onion Soups:
Creamy, 105
Fisherman's, 139
Onion, 137, 138
White Soubise, 99
Orange, *see* Fruit
Oukha, 158
Oxtail, *see* Beef
Panade, *see* Bread Soups
Panade:
à l'Eau, 135
avec Oseille ou Blanc de Poireau, 140
Pappa al Pomodoro, 138
Partridge, *see* Game
Pasta Dough, 165
Pea Soups:
Dutch Green, 152
Fresh, 95
Pea, 94

Swedish, 152
Turnip, with Green, 107
Pear, *see* Fruit
Pepper Pot, Philadelphia, 125
Pepperpot, Jamaica, 126
Picada, 121
Pig's Ear, *see* Pork
Pigeon, *see* Game
Pilota, 149
Pilz- oder Schwammerlsuppe, 109
Pirozhki, 90
Pistou, 112
Pommersche Kliebensuppe, 92
Pork Soups:
Bacon Broth, 160
Fife Broth, 115
Ham and Winter Melon, 108
Pig's Ear, 127
Spinach and, 108
Portuguese Soup, Mary's, 153
Potage:
de Chou-Fleurs et de Broccolis au Persil, 107
Crème de Potiron aux Crevettes, 103
aux Fèves de Marais, 95
de Framboises, 93
Germiny, 100
aux Herbes dit Hourtète, 106
aux Herbes Maigres, 106
de Navets aux Petits Pois, 107
de Perdrix Marbrées, 161
de Petits Haricots Verts et Blancs, 107
aux Pointes de Grosses Asperges, 108
de Poireaux aux Kliotzki, 122
aux Poireaux et Pommes de Terre, 105
de Poisson aux Herbes, 106
Printannié en Maigre, 100
Purée de Volaille à la Reine, 104
à la Reine, 104
St. Germain, 94
Saint-Hubert, 104
Santé, 99
aux Soles, 127
Potages Velouté, 100
Potato:
Dumplings, 91
Grated, Soup, 105
and Leek Soup, 105
Melon and, Soup, 101
Purée, 99
Pot au Feu:
Catalan, 149
Gourmets', 151
Pot au Feu, 149
Pot-au-Feu des Gourmets, 151
Poule au Pot, 148
Poultry *see* Chicken; Duck; Turkey
Prawns, *see* Fish and Shellfish
Puchero, 153
Pulcini Zuppa all'Antonio, 121
Pumpkin Soups:
Blossom Soup, 96
Cream of, and Shrimp, 103
Panade, 135
Pumpkin, 97
Puré de Gambas, 102
Purée Leontine, 96
PURÉES, 93-104
Quenelles, 165
Rabbit, *see* Game
Raspberry, *see* Fruit
Ravioli with Ricotta and Spinach, 90
Ravioli con Ricotta e Spinaci, 90
Razsolnik, 122
Rice Soup:
Chestnut and, 114
and Chicken Liver, 123
Cold Cherry and, 145
Indonesian, 120
Meat-Rice Barrel, 120
Rice, 121
Rock Fish, *see* Fish and Shellfish
Rouille, 166
Royales, 167
Saffron Soup, 134
Sainserelle à l'Espagnole, 137
Sajur Terung Atau Labu, 119
Sauces:
Aïoli, 154
Rouille, 166
Velouté, 167
White, 167
Scallop, *see* Fish and Shellfish
Schwedische Biersuppe, 88
Scotch Broth, 115
Senegalese, 144
Shellfish, *see* Fish and Shellfish
Shrimp, *see* Fish and Shellfish
SIMPLE BROTHS *see* BROTHS
Søbronade, 112
Sodsuppe, 129
Sole, *see* Fish and Shellfish
Sopa:
de Ajo Asturiana, 135
de Ajo Blanco con Uvas, 142
de Almendras, 134
de Apatzingán, 101
de Flor de Calabaza, 96
a la Mallorquina, 137
de Mandonghuilles a la Casolana, 121
de Patata Rallada, 105
de Pulpo, 129
Soppi Mondongo, 124
Sorrel Soups:
and Cream, 100
Panade with, 140,141
Soupa Rizi Avgholemono, 121
Soupe:
d'Auvergne au Fromage, Mitonnée, 136
aux Choux à la Crème, 109
Courte, 162
Fausse Tortue, 118
de Fèves au Collet de Mouton, 162
Froide aux Fraises, 146
au Fromage et au Pain Bis, 139
à la Glacé Simplifiée, 142
Glacée pour Grosse Chaleur, 144
Languedocienne, 163
des Maures, 97
de la Mère Onésime, 114
à la Mie de Pain Frite, 141
de la Nouvelle Angleterre, 133
à l'Oignon, 138
aux Oreilles de Porc, 127
du Pêcheur, 139
de Poisson du Moulin de Mougins, 128
au Potiron, 135
aux Poumons de Porc ou de Veau, 123
du Père Tranquille, 95
de Pigeon a l'Orge, 117
au Pistou, 112
Provençale, 154
Soupes de la Bonne Ménagère, 114
Spanish One-Pot Meal, 153
Spinach Soups:
and Pork, 108
Spinach, 101
Squid, Borscht with, 129
STANDARD PREPARATIONS, 163-167
Stock, 148
Stracciatella, 93
Strawberry, *see* Fruit
***T**avator: Soupe de Yaourt à la Bulgare*, 142
Tomatensuppe, 98
Tomato Soups:
Algerian, 111
Beef, Okra and, 160
Bread and, 138
Cream of, 98
Iced, for a Very Hot Day, 144
Italian, 110
Mussel and, 133
Tomato, 98
Tourin Bordelais, 105
Tripe Soups:
Mexican, 125
Milanese, 124
Philadelphia Pepper Pot, 125
Tripe, 124
Turkey Soup, 115
Turnip Soups:
Cream of, 96
with Green Peas, 107
Veal: Genoese, Soup with Fine Noodles, 150
Vegetable Marrow Soups:
Apricot and, 98
Vegetable Marrow, 119
Vegetables, Mixed:
Andalusian Gazpacho, 144
with Basil and Garlic, 112
Cold Fish and Vegetable, 144
Fife Broth, 115
Iced Soup, Simplified, 142
Mixed Vegetable, 111
Mother Onésime's Soup, 114
Mushroom Vegetable, 110
Peasant Vegetable, 159
Purée, 96
Red Pottage, 97
Rich Country Broth, 112
Soup of Mallorca, 137
Spring Vegetable, 100
Three-Helping Bean, 126
Thrifty Housewife's Soups, 114
Tuscan Minestrone Country-Style, 113
Wrexham, 160
see also: Borscht; Broths; Meat and Vegetables; Pot au Feu; and individual vegetables
Velouté, *see* Sauces
Vichyssoise, 105
Watercress Soups:
Chicken and Cress, 108
Cold Pear and, 146
WHOLE MEAL SOUPS, 147-163
Wrexham Soup, 160
Yogurt Soup, 142
Yuvarelakia Soupa Avgolemono, 120
***Z**uppa:*
di Cima alla Genovese con Linguine Fine, 150
di Fagioli, 151
Mituna, 140
di Pane Farcito, 140
Pavese, 137
di Pesce delle Osterie Romane, 157

General Index/Glossary

Included in this index are definitions of many of the culinary terms used in this book; definitions are in italics. The recipes in the Anthology are listed in the Recipe Index on page 168.

Açordas, 55
Aïoli, 80
Al dente: *Italian, literally translated as "to the tooth". Used to describe the texture of cooked pasta or vegetables, when they are firm to the bite, not too soft on the outside, and barely cooked through.*
Albumin, 5, 10, 64
Allspice: *the dried berry—used whole or ground—of a member of the myrtle family. Called allspice because its aroma suggests a combination of clove, cinnamon and nutmeg.*
Apples, 72
Apricots, 72
Aromatics: *all substances—such as vegetables, herbs and spices—that add aroma and flavour to food when used in cooking;* 8, 10
Artichokes, 23, 38
Asparagus, 38; leftover, 30
Avocado, 66; uncooked soup, 66-67
Bacon and bean soup, 4, 75, 78-79
Bain-marie: *a large pot or vessel in which water is heated so that a smaller pot can be placed inside and its contents cooked or re-heated. Used for sauces and other preparations that are too delicate to withstand direct contact with a stove's burner.*
Barding, 36
Barley, 44
Beans, 38; with bacon, 75, 78-79; broad, in purée, 24; French, 42-43; in garbure, 82-83; as garnish, 14; haricot, 42-43; purée chart, 38-39; soaking, 78
Beef, 6; cuts for basic broth, 8, 10; in jellied consommé, 64; leftover, 46-47; in poule au pot, 75-76
Beetroot, 38; in borscht, 75, 84-85; in chilled borscht, 86; liquor, 84
Bisque, 6, 32; crayfish, 32-33
Bivalves, 52
Blanch: *to plunge food into boiling water for a short period. Done for a number of reasons: to remove strong flavours, such as the excess saltiness of some bacon; to soften vegetables before further cooking; to facilitate the removal of skins or shells. Another meaning is "to whiten".*
Blanched almonds: *almonds that have been peeled by blanching (q.v.).*
Borscht, 75, 84-85; chilled leftover, 86; served at the court of Tsar Nicholas II, 75; Ukrainian, 75, 84-85
Botvinya, 63, 68-69
Boulanger, M., 5
Bouquet garni: *a bunch of mixed herbs—the classic three being parsley, thyme and bay leaf—used for flavouring and perfuming sauces, soups and stews;* 8, 44
Bourride, 75, 80-81
Bread, 5, 12-13, 16; baked, flavoured with garlic and olive oil, 16; croûtons, 16; with garbure, 82; as thickener, 32-33, 34, 38; type for soup making, 55
Bread soups, 7, 55-61; with leeks, 56-57; mourtaïrol, 55, 56-57; with onion and cheese, 58-59; pumpkin panade, 60-61
Broccoli, 38
Broth, 5-6; basic method, 8; chicken, 8; compound, 7, 41-53; cooking, 9; cooking time, 9; freezing, 11; meat, 8, 10-11, 44-47; mixed vegetable, 42-43; partridge, 36-37; Scotch, 41, 44-45; 75; skimming, 9, 10, 76; straining, 11; vegetable, 8-9
Brunoise, 12, 14
Brussels sprouts, 38
Buckwheat: *a variety of grain much used in Russian cooking; 84*
Butter, as enrichment, 23, 25, 30, 38
Cabbage, 75; in garbure, 82-83; stuffing leaves, 76-77
Caramelize: *to heat sugar until it turns brown and syrupy. Also to evaporate meat or vegetable juices to leave a brown "caramel" residue on the bottom of the pan;* onions, 58; oxtail soup, 46
Cardoon, 39
Carême, Antonin, 7
Carrots, 24-25; in basic broths, 8-9; as garnish, 12, 14
Cauliflower, 38
Celeriac, 23, 24
Celery, 39
Chard, 38
Cheese, for onion soup, 58
Cherries, 63, 72, 73; metal discolouring, 73
Chervil, as garnish, 12
Chestnuts, 39
Chicken, 8; broth, 6, 8; mourtaïrol, 55, 56-57; potage à la reine, 34-35; poule au pot, 75, 76-77; purée chart, 38-39; stuffing 77; trussing 77
Chicory, 38
Chiffonade, 12, 14
Chili pepper, see Peppers
Chili powder: *hot, pungent spice made from several varieties of dried, ground chili peppers*
Chilled soups, 63, 86
Chives, 12
Chowders, 41; clam, 52-53
Clam chowder, 52-53
Clarification, 6
Cleansing, 9, 10, 76
Cockie-leekie, 41
Coconut, in Senegalese, 70
Cold soups, 63-73, 86
Compound broths, 7, 41-53; liquid for, 41
Consommés, 5-6; clarification, 6; garnishing, 6; jellied, 64-65; à la Madrilène, 64-65; serving, 64; serving chilled, 63; with wine, 7
Corned beef: *salted beef*
Courgettes, 39
Court-bouillon: *cooking liquid flavoured with aromatic vegetables and wine.*
Crayfish bisque, 32-33
Cream, 6, 23, 27, 30; with eggs as enrichment, 28-29, 38
Crêpes, 13, 21
Croûtons, 16, 30, 38, 61
Crustaceans, crayfish bisque, 32-33; purée chart, 39
Cucumbers, 39
Curry spices, 71
Cussy, Marquis de, 7
Custards, 12; colouring and cutting out, 15
De Gouy, Louis P., 5
Deglaze: *to pour a liquid—such as wine, stock, water or cream—into a pan in which meat or vegetables have been fried or roasted, in order to incorporate the particles remaining on the bottom of the pan in a sauce or soup;* 36, 47
Degrease: *to remove fat from cooking juices and broths.*
Dill, 12, 86
Dumplings, 13, 18-19; marrow, breadcrumb and herb, 18-19; meat, 18-19; potato, 18-19
Eggs, 12, 15; custards, colouring and cutting out, 15; as enrichment, 23, 28-29, 38; metal discolouring, 35; poaching, 15; threads, 15; use in clarification, 5, 64
Endive, 38
Equipment, for puréeing, 38
Escoffier, Auguste, 6, 7
Fennel, 12, 39
Fines herbes: *a mixture of finely chopped herbs that always incorporates parsley, plus one or more of a selection that includes chives, tarragon and chervil.*
Fish, 9; botvinya, 68-69; bourride, 75, 80-81; purée chart, 38-39; soup, Mediterranean, 50-51
Flour, as thickener, 23, 26-27, 38; in velouté, 28
Freezing, 11
Fruit soups, 72-73
Game, purée chart, 38-39
Garbure, 82-83
Garlic, 8; in aïoli, 80; in pistou, 43; in rouille, 51; sauce, 80
Garnishes, 12-21
Gazpacho, 63, 66-67
Goose, in garbure, 82; leftover, 46
Gratin: *the French term for a crust. Usually of cheese or breadcrumbs (though some gratins contain neither), it is formed by strewing the gratin ingredients over the food and placing the dish in a hot oven or under a grill so that the top crisps. The word is also used for a cooked dish—a "gratin"—that has such a finish.*
Green bacon: *unsmoked bacon.*
Grimod de la Reynière, Alexandre-Balthazar-Laurent, 7
Guide Culinaire, Le, 7
Hamburg parsley: *type of parsley with an*

edible, parsnip-like root.
Hangovers, cure for, 48
Hare, 39
Haricot beans, see Beans
Herbs, as garnish, 12
Hominy, 48
Horseradish, as garnish, 69
Jerusalem artichoke, 39
Julienne, 12,14
Kale, 38
Kasha, 84
Kohlrabi, 38
Kvas, 68
Lamb, 44-45
Leeks, panade with, 56-57; and potato purée, 26-27; and potato soup, 42; purée chart, 39
Leftovers, meat, 46-47; vegetables, 30-31
Lentils, 36-37; purée chart, 38
Lettuce, 38
Liaison: *French term for a thickening agent for sauces. Common liaisons include beaten egg yolks, a mixture of flour and butter, or butter alone.*
Madrilène, 64-65
Mange-tout, 38; leftover, 30
Marigold petals, 44
Marrow, breadcrumb and herb dumpling, 18-19
Mayonnaise, aïoli, 80
Meat, 8, 10-11; broth, 8, 10-11; dumplings, 18-19; leftovers, 46-47; purée chart, 38-39
Melon, 72
Menudo, 41, 48-49
Minestrone, 42, 43
Mixed spices: *mixture of spices and herbs, classically, equal proportions of nutmeg, mace, cinnamon, cayenne pepper, white pepper, cloves, ground bay leaf, thyme, marjoram and savory.*
Molluscs, 52-53; purée chart, 39
Moules à la marinière, 52
Mourtaïrol, 55, 56-57
Mulligatawny, 71
Mushrooms, 39; velouté, 28-29
Mussels, velouté, 52
Mutton, 44-45
Noodles, cooking, 50; making, 17
Onions, 58; bistro-style soup, 59; caramelizing, 58; onion, bread and cheese soup, 58-59; purée chart, 39; soup thickened with flour, 26-27
Oxtail soup, 46-47
Panade, 7, 55; with leeks, 56-57; pumpkin, 60-61
Pancakes, 13, 21
Parboil: *to cook food briefly in boiling water or stock in order to soften the food or to shorten its final cooking time.*
Parsley, 12; see also Hamburg parsley
Parsnips, 39
Partridge, broth, 36-37; velouté, 36-37
Pasta, cooking, 50; in fish soup, 50; as garnish, 13; leftover, 30-31; making, 17; shaping and stuffing, 17; as thickener, 38; with vegetables, 43
Pastries, 13, 21
Peaches, 72
Pear and watercress purée, 72
Peas, 24-25; purée chart, 39; split peas, 78
Pepper, seasoning with, 7
Pepperpot, 41
Peppers, Chili: *numerous varieties of small, finger-shaped hot peppers native to tropical America and the West Indies;* in gazpacho, 66-67; in menudo, 48-49; in rouille, 51; in Senegalese, 70-71
Peppers, Sweet, 12, 39; with cold borscht, 86; in gazpacho, 65-67; skinning, 14
Pig's ears, 75, 78
Pirozhki, 13, 21, 84
Pistou, 42, 43
Plums, 72
Pork and bean soup, 75, 78-79
Pork sausage, 75, 78
Pot au feu, 6, 76
Potage, 4; germiny, 28-29; à la reine, 34-35
Potatoes, dumplings, 18-19; leek and potato purée, 26-27; leek and potato soup, 42; as thickener, 23, 26-27, 38
Poule au pot, 75, 76-77
Pulses, as thickener, 38
Pumpkin, 38; panade, 60-61
Purées, 6, 23-39; carrot, 24-25; chart, 38-39; chicken, 34-35; chilled, 63; enrichment, 23; equipment for , 23, 38; leek and potato, 26-27; leftover vegetable, 30-31; onion, thickened with flour, 26-27; partridge velouté, 36-37; pear and watercress, cold, 72; serving chilled, 63; shellfish, 32-33; single vegetable, 24-25; sorrel thickened with egg yolks, 28-29; texture, 23; thickening, 23, 26, 38
Quenelles, 20; as garnish, 13
Rabbit, 39
Radishes, as garnish, 69
Ravioli, 13
Render: *to refine fat by melting the pure fat out of the fleshy tissues of meats or poultry. Rendered fat, such as that from pork or goose, is used for cooking.*
Rhubarb, 72
Rice, 38
Ricotta: *a fresh Italian curd cheese.*
Romano: *a hard, sharp, Italian cheese made from sheep's milk and used in the same way as* Parmesan; 13
Rouille, 50, 51
Roux: *cooked mixture of butter and flour used to thicken sauces;* 28
Saffron: *spice which comes from a species of crocus and used to impart a distinctive aroma and yellow colour to certain dishes. Sold in thread or powdered form;* 56
Salsify, 23, 39
Sauces, aïoli, 80; pistou, 42, 43; rouille, 51
Sauté: *to fry food in just enough oil or fat to prevent it from sticking.*
Schwarzbrotsuppe, 55
Scotch broth, 41, 44-45, 75
Scumming, 9, 10, 76
Seakale, 39
Seasoning, 7
Senegalese, 63, 70-71
Shellfish purée, 6, 32-33
Simmer: *to cook in liquid at just below boiling point, so that the surface of the liquid trembles and bubbles do not burst violently.*
Skimming, 9, 10, 76
Sofrito, 78
Sorrel, 38; purée thickened with egg yolks, 28-29
Soup, origins of word, 5; role in meal, 7; types, 5-7
Soup Book, The, 5
Soupe de poisson, 50-51
Spices, Curry, 71
Spinach, 38
Squash, panade, 60-61; preparing shell as dish, 60
Stock, 5-6
Swedes, 39
Sweet pepper, see Peppers
Sweet potatoes, 38
Sweetcorn, 39
Tarragon, as garnish, 12
Tomatoes, 39
Tortellini, 13
Tripe, broths, 41; menudo, 48-49; types, 48
Trussing, 36, 77
Turnips, 39
Uncooked soups, 66-67
Veal, 6
Vegetables, 8-9, 12, 14; garbure, 82-83; in gazpacho, 63, 66-67; leftover purée, 30-31; purée chart, 38-39; mixed, 42; wilting leaves, 12, 72
Veloutés, 6-7, 28; enriching, 38; making base, 28; mushroom, 28-29; mussel, 52; partridge, 36-37
Vichyssoise, 27, 63
Watercress, 38; and pear purée, 72
Whole meal soups, 7, 75-86
Wilting vegetable leaves, 12, 72
Wine to serve with soup, 7
Zuppa di fagioli, 78-79

Recipe Credits

The sources for the recipes in this volume are shown below. Page references in brackets indicate where the recipes appear in the Anthology.

Acton, Eliza, *Modern Cookery.* Published by Longman, Brown, Green and Longmans, London. 1856 edition (*pages 89, 93, and 117*).

Allen, Jana and Gin, Margaret, *Innards and other Variety Meats.* Copyright © 1974 Jana Allen & Margaret Gin. Published by 101 Productions, San Francisco. By permission of 101 Productions (*page 125*).

American Heritage, The editors of, *The American Heritage Cookbook* © 1964 American Heritage Publishing Co., Inc., New York. Reprinted by permission of American Heritage Publishing Co., Inc. (*page 131*).

The Art of Cookery, Made Plain and Easy. By a Lady. The Sixth Edition, 1758 (*page 137*).

Audot, L. E., *La Cuisinière de la Campagne et de la Ville, ou la Nouvelle Cuisine Économique.* Published by Librairie Audot, 1881 edition (*pages 114, 142*).

Aznar, Marina Pereyra de and Froud, Nina, *The Home Book of Spanish Cookery.* First published in 1956 by Faber and Faber Limited, London. New material © Marina Pereyra de Aznar and Nina Froud 1967, 1974. By permission of Nina Froud (*pages 102, 105, 129 and 144*).

Becker, Fritz, *Das Kochbuch aus Mecklenburg, Pommern und Ostpreussen.* Copyright © 1976 by Verlagsteam Wolfgang Hölker. Published by Verlag Wolfgang Hölker, Munster. Translated by permission of Verlag Wolfgang Hölker (*page 92*).

Berjane, J, *French Dishes for English Tables.* © Copyright F. Warne (Publishers) Ltd. Published by Frederick Warne & Co. Ltd., London. By permission of Frederick Warne & Co. Ltd. (*page 104*).

Besson, Joséphine, *La Mère Besson "Ma Cuisine Provençale".* © Éditions Albin Michel, 1977. Published by Éditions Albin Michel, Paris. Translated by permission of Éditions Albin Michel (*page 88*).

Blanchard, Marjorie Page, *Treasured Recipes from Early New England Kitchens.* Copyright 1975 by Harrington's In Vermont, Inc. Richmond, VT.05477. Published by Garden Way Publishing Co. in association with Harrington's of Richmond, Vermont, Inc. By permission of Writers House, Inc., author's agents (*pages 131, 133*).

Boni, Ada, *Italian Regional Cooking.* Copyright © 1969 s.c. by Arnoldo Mondadori. English translation, copyright © 1969 s.c. by Thomas Nelson & Sons Ltd. and E. P. Dutton and Co., Inc. Published by Bonanza Books, a division of Crown Publishers, Inc. By permission of Arnoldo Mondadori Editore (*page 155*).

Boulestin, X. Marcel, *Recipes of Boulestin.* © The Estate of X. M. Boulestin 1971. Published by William Heinemann Ltd., London. By permission of William Heinemann Ltd. (*page 100*).

Boulestin, X. Marcel, *The Finer Cooking.* Published by Cassell & Company Limited, London 1937. By permission of A. D. Peters and Co., Ltd. (*page 99*).

Brandon, Leila, *A Merry-Go-Round of Recipes from Jamaica.* Revised edition. Published by Novelty Trading Co., Ltd. Jamaica. By permission of Leila E. Brandon (*page 126*).

Brera, Gianni and Veronelli, Luigi, *La Pacciada.* © 1973 by Arnoldo Mondadori Editore. Published by Arnoldo Mondadori Editore, Milan. Translated by permission of Arnoldo Mondadori Editore (*pages 111, 123 and 137*).

Breteuil, Jules, *Le Cuisinier Européen.* Published by Garnier Frères Libraires-Éditeurs C.1860 (*pages 104, 138*).

Brissenden, Rosemary, *South East Asian Food.* Copyright © R. F. and R. L. Brissenden, 1970. Published by Penguin Books Ltd., London. By permission of Penguin Books Ltd. (*page 119*).

Brown, Helen Evans, *Helen Brown's West Coast Cook Book.* Copyright 1952, by Helen Evans Brown. Published by Little, Brown and Company, Boston. By permission of Little, Brown and Company (*pages 108, 141 and 143*).

Bugialli, Giuliano, *The Fine Art of Italian Cooking.* Copyright © 1977 by Giuliano Bugialli. Published by Times Books/Quadrangle—The New York Times Book Co. Inc., New York. Reprinted by permission of Times Books, A Division of Quadrangle/The New York Times Book Co. Inc. (*pages 113, 139*).

Carême, Antonin, *L'Art de la Cuisine Française au Dix-Neuvième Siècle.* Published in Paris 1833 (*pages 107, 108*).

Carnacina, Luigi, *Great Italian Cooking* (edited by Michael Sonino). Published in English by Abradale Press Inc., New York. By permission of Aldo Garzanti Editore and Abradale Press (*pages 124, 140 and 150*).

Cass, Elizabeth, *Spanish Cooking.* Copyright © Elizabeth Cass, 1957. First published by André Deutsch Ltd., 1957. Also published by Mayflower Books Ltd., 1970. By permission of André Deutsch Ltd. (*pages 134, 137 and 142*).

Chantiles, Vilma Liacouras, *The Food of Greece.* Copyright © 1975 by Vilma Liacouras Chantiles. Published by Atheneum Publishers, New York. By permission of Vilma Liacouras Chantiles (*pages 120, 156*).

Chen, Joyce, *Joyce Chen Cook Book.* Copyright © 1962 by Joyce Chen. Published by J. B. Lippincott Company, Philadelphia and New York. By permission of J. B. Lippincott Company (*page 108*).

Clarisse ou la Vieille Cuisinière. Copyright © 1922 by Éditions de l'Abeille d'Or. Published by Éditions de l'Abeille d'Or, Paris. Translated by permission of Éditions Rombaldi, Paris (*page 105*).

Conran, Terence and Kroll, Maria, *The Vegetable Book.* © Conran Ink 1976. Published by Collins Publishers, Glasgow and London. By permission of Collins Publishers and Crescent Books, New York (*pages 94, 101*).

Corbitt, Helen, *Helen Corbitt's Cookbook.* Copyright © 1957 by Helen Corbitt. Published by Houghton Mifflin Company, Boston. Reprinted by permission of Houghton Mifflin Company (*page 144*).

Costa, Margaret, *Margaret Costa's Four Seasons Cookery Book.* Copyright © Margaret Costa. Published by Thomas Nelson & Sons Ltd., 1970. By permission of Margaret Costa (*page 103*).

La Cuisine Naturelle à l'Huile d'Olive, © 1978 Éditions De Vecchi S. A. Paris. Published by Éditions De Vecchi, Paris. Translated by permission of Éditions De Vecchi S. A. Paris. (*pages 128, 144*).

Cuisinier Gascon, Le (1740). Reprinted by Éditions Daniel Morcrette, B.P. 26,95270, Luzarches, France. Translated by permission of Éditions Daniel Morcrette (*page 137*).

Curnonsky, *A l'Infortune du Pot.* Copyright Éditions de la Couronne 1946. Published by Éditions de la Couronne, Paris (*page 156*).

Curnonsky, *Recettes des Provinces de France.* Published by Les Productions de Paris (*page 158*).

Cutler, Carol, *The Six-Minute Soufflé and Other Culinary Delights.* Copyright © 1976 by Carol Cutler. Published by Crown Publishers Inc., USA. By permission of Clarkson N. Potter, Inc. (*page 103*).

David, Elizabeth, *A Book of Mediterranean Food.* Copyright © Elizabeth David, 1958, 1965. Published by Penguin Books Ltd., London. By permission of Penguin Books Ltd. (*page 96*).

David, Elizabeth, *French Provincial Cooking.* Copyright © Elizabeth David, 1960, 1962, 1967, 1970. First published by Michael Joseph Ltd., London 1960. Also published by Penguin Books Ltd., London. By permission of Elizabeth David (*page 103*).

David, Elizabeth, *Italian Food.* Copyright © Elizabeth David, 1954, 1963, 1969, 1977. Published by Penguin Books Ltd., London. By permission of Penguin Books Ltd. (*pages 110, 123*).

Davidson, Alan, *North Atlantic Seafood.* Copyright © Alan Davidson, 1979. Published by Penguin Books Ltd. and Macmillan London Ltd. By permission of Penguin Books Ltd. and Alan Davidson (*pages 129, 130 and 144*).

Davis, Irving, *A Catalan Cookery Book.* Published by Lucien Scheler, Paris. By permission of Lucien Scheler (*page 149*).

Diat, Louis, *French Cooking for Americans.* Copyright 1941, 1946 by Louis Diat. Copyright © renewed 1969, by Mrs. Louis D. Diat. Published by J. B. Lippincott Company, New York. Reprinted by permission of J. B. Lippincott Company (*pages 94, 98, 141 and 150*).

Dubois, Urbain, *École des Cuisinières.* Published by Dentu, Paris, 1876 (*pages 127, 138 and 151*).

Duff, Gail, *Fresh All the Year.* © Gail Duff 1976. First published by Macmillan London Ltd., 1976. Also published by Pan Books Ltd., 1977. By permission of Macmillan London Ltd. (*page 94*).

Durand, Charles, *Le Cuisinier Durand.* Privately published by the author, 1843 (*page 106*).

Escoffier, A., *Le Carnet d'Epicure.* (Magazine.) 1912, no. 12 and 1913, no. 15. Translated by permission of Pierre Escoffier (*page 117*).

Farmer, Fannie Merritt. (Revised by Wilma Lord Perkins), *The Fannie Farmer Cookbook.* Copyright 1896, 1900, 1901, 1902, 1903, 1904, 1905, 1906, 1912, 1914 by Fannie Merritt Farmer. Copyright 1915, 1918, 1923, 1924, 1928, 1929 by Cora D. Perkins. Copyright 1930, 1931, 1932, 1933, 1934, 1936, 1940, 1941, 1942, 1943, 1946, 1951, © 1959, 1964, 1965 by Dexter Perkins Corp. Published by Little, Brown and Co. Boston. By permission of The Fannie Farmer Cookbook Corporation, Massachusetts (*page 132*).

Firuski, Elva and Maurice (Editors), *The Best of Boulestin.* Published by William Heinemann Ltd., London 1932. By permission of William Heinemann Ltd. (*page 106*).

Foods of the World—The Cooking of Italy. © 1968 Time Inc. Published by Time-Life Books, Alexandria (*page 93*).

France à Table, La (French Magazine). No. 7 June 1935, No. 11 Feb. 1936 (*pages 112, 134*).

Froud, Nina and George, *The Home Book of Russian Cooking.* © Nina and George Froud. Published by Faber and Faber Limited, London. By permission of Nina Froud (*page 90*).

The Good Cooking School, *The Great Cooks Cookbook.* © 1974 by the Good Cooking School, Inc. Published by Doubleday and Ferguson, New York. By permission of J. G. Ferguson Publishing Company (*page 126*).

Gouffé, Jules, *Le Livre des Soupes et des Potages.* Published by Librairie Hachette et Cie. Paris, 1875 (*pages 135, 155 and 162*).

Gould-Marks, Beryl, *The Home Book of Italian Cookery.* © Beryl Gould-Marks 1969. Published by Faber

and Faber Limited, London. Reprinted by permission of Faber and Faber Limited (*page 151*).
Gouy, Louis P. De, *The Soup Book.* Copyright © 1949 by Mrs Louis P. De Gouy. Published by Dover Publications Inc., New York. By permission of Dover Publications, Inc. (*pages 125, 160*).
Gouy, Jean de, *La Cuisine et la Pâtisserie Bourgeoises.* Published by J. Lebègue & Cie., Libraires-Éditeurs, Paris 1896 (*pages 118, 123, and 141*).
Greenberg, Florence, *Jewish Cookery.* Copyright © The Jewish Chronicle Ltd. 1963. Published by Penguin Books Ltd., London. By permission of Penguin Books Ltd (*pages 91, 110*).
Grigson, Jane, *English Food.* Copyright © Jane Grigson, 1974. First published by Macmillan 1974. Published by Penguin Books Ltd., London, 1977. By permission of Macmillan London Ltd. (*page 119*).
Grigson, Jane, *Good Things.* Copyright © Jane Grigson, 1971. First published by Michael Joseph 1971. Published by Penguin Books Ltd., 1973. By permission of David Higham Associates Limited for the author (*page 133*).
Grigson, Jane, *Jane Grigson's Vegetable Book.* © 1978 by Jane Grigson. Published by Michael Joseph, London. By permission of David Higham Associates Limited for the author (*page 99*).
Grigson, Jane, *Observer Magazine* (26 June 1977). By permission of David Higham Associates Limited for the author (*page 146*).
Haitsma Mulier-van Beusekom, C.A.H., (Editor), *Culinaire Encyclopedie.* Published by Elsevier © 1957. Revised edition 1974 by N. V. Uitgeversmaatschappij Elsevier Nederland and E.H.A. Nakken-Rövekamp. Translated by permission of N. V. Uitgeversmaatschappij Elsevier Nederland (*pages 120, 152*).
Hazelton, Nika Standen, *The Continental Flavour.* Copyright © Nika Standen Hazelton, 1961. Published by Penguin Books Ltd., London. Reprinted by permission of Penguin Books Ltd. (*page 90*).
Hewitt, Jean, *The New York Times New England Heritage Cookbook.* Copyright © 1972 and 1977 by the New York Times Company. Published by G. P. Putnam's Sons, New York. Reprinted by permission of Curtis Brown, Ltd. (*page 95*).
Hewitt, Jean, *The New York Times Weekend Cookbook.* Copyright © 1975 by Jean Hewitt. Translated by permission of Times Books a division of Quadrangle/The New York Times Book Co. Inc. (*page 153*).
Hutchins, Sheila, *English Recipes and Others from Scotland, Wales and Ireland.* © 1967 by Sheila Hutchins. Published by The Cookery Book Club. By permission of Sheila Hutchins (*page 160*).
Irish Recipes Traditional and Modern. Published by Mount Salus Press Limited, Dublin. By permission of Mount Salus Press Limited (*page 107*).
Irwin, Florence, *Irish Country Recipes.* Published by The Northern Whig Limited, Belfast (*pages 116, 161 and 162*).
Isnard, Léon, *La Cuisine Française et Africaine.* Copyright 1949, by Éditions Albin Michel. Published by Éditions Albin Michel, Paris. Translated by permission of Éditions Albin Michel (*pages 88, 92, 101 and 153*).
Jakobsson, Oskar, *Good Food in Sweden.* © 1968 G. L. A. and Oskar Jakobsson. Published by Generalstabens Litografiska Anstalt, Stockholm. By permission of G. L. A. and Oskar Jakobsson (*page 130*).
Jans, Hugh, *Bistro Koken.* © Unieboek/B.V./C.A.J. van Dishoeck. Published by Unieboek/C. A. J. van Dishoeck. Translated by permission of Unieboek B.V. (*page 159*).
Jans, Hugh, *Vrij Nederlands Kookboek.* © 1973 Unieboek/C. A. J. van Dishoeck, Bussum. Published by Unieboek/C.A.J. van Dishoeck, Bussum. Translated by permission of Unieboek B.V. (*page 120*).
Jarratt, Enrica and Vernon, *The Complete Book of Pasta.* © 1969 by Enrica and Vernon Jarratt. English translation © 1975 by Vernon Jarratt. Published by Michael Joseph, London. By permission of Michael Joseph (*page 90*).
Jewry, Mary (Editor), *Warne's Model Cookery and Housekeeping Book.* © Copyright F. Warne (Publishers) Ltd. Published by Frederick Warne & Co. Ltd., London. By permission of Frederick Warne & Co. Ltd. (*pages 97, 160*).
The Junior League of Dallas, *The Dallas Junior League Cookbook.* © 1976 by The Junior League of Dallas. Published by Junior League of Dallas, Dallas. By permission of Junior League of Dallas (*page 134*).
Kahn, Odette (Editor), *Cuisine et Vins de France (Magazine).* Published by Société Française d'Éditions Vinicoles. Translated by permission of Odette Kahn (*page 135*).
Kennedy, Diana, *The Cuisines of Mexico.* Copyright © 1972 by Diana Kennedy. Published by Harper and Row Publishers, Inc. Reprinted by permission of Harper and Row Publishers, Inc. (*pages 96, 101*).
Knight, Jacqueline, E., *The Cook's Fish Guide.* Copyright © 1973 by Jacqueline E. Knight. Published by E. P. Dutton & Co. Inc., New York. By permission of E. P. Dutton & Co. (*page 157*).
Lallemand, Roger, *La Vraie Cuisine de L'Anjou et de la Touraine.* Published by Quartier Latin, La Rochelle. Translated by permission of Quartier Latin (*page 113*).
Lallemand, Roger, *La Vraie Cuisine de la Normandie.* Published by Quartier Latin, La Rochelle. Translated by permission of Quartier Latin (*page 127*).
Lassalle, George, *The Adventurous Fish Cook.* © Caroline Lassalle 1976. Published by Pan Books Ltd., London. By permission of Pan Books Ltd. (*page 133*).
Leyel, Mrs C. F. and Hartley, Miss Olga, *The Gentle Art of Cookery.* © The Executors of Mrs C. F. Leyel 1925. Published by Chatto & Windus Ltd., London. By permission of Chatto & Windus Ltd. (*pages 98, 99 and 111*).
Lin, Florence, *Florence Lin's Chinese Vegetarian Cookbook.* Copyright © 1976 Florence S. Lin. Published by Hawthorn Books, Inc., New York. By permission of Hawthorn Books, Inc. (*page 110*).
MacMiadhacháin, Anna, *Spanish Regional Cookery.* Copyright © Anna MacMiadhacháin, 1976. Published by Penguin Books Ltd., London. By permission of Penguin Books Ltd. (*pages 121, 135*).
Macnicol, Fred, *Hungarian Cookery.* Copyright © Fred Macnicol, 1978. Published by Penguin Books Ltd., London. By permission of Penguin Books Ltd. (*page 91*).
Martin, Peter and Joan, *Japanese Cooking.* Copyright © 1970 Peter and Joan Martin. Published by André Deutsch Limited, London. By permission of André Deutsch Limited (*pages 89, 108*).
McNeill, F. Marian, *The Scots Kitchen.* Published by Blackie and Son Limited, London. By permission of Blackie and Son Limited (*pages 97, 115 and 116*).
70 Médecins de France, *Le Trésor de la Cuisine du Bassin Méditerranéen* (*pages 97, 154 and 163*).
Menon, *La Cuisiniere Bourgeoise.* 1746 (*page 100*).
Molokhovets, Elena, *Podarok Molodým Khozyaikam.* Published in St. Petersburg, 1892 (*pages 92, 145, 147 and 148*).
Montagné, Prosper, *Larousse Gastronomique.* © copyright The Hamlyn Publishing Group Limited, 1961. Published by The Hamlyn Publishing Group Limited, London. By permission of The Hamlyn Publishing Group Limited (*page 104*).
Montagné, Prosper and Gottschalk, A., *Mon Menu—Guide d'Hygiène Alimentaire.* Published by Société d'Applications Scientifiques, Paris (*page 143*).
Murray, Janet, *With a Fine Feeling for Food.* Copyright © Janet Murray, 1972. By permission of Janet Murray (*pages 115, 116 and 161*).
Nignon, Edouard, *Les Plaisirs de la Table.* Published by the author c.1920. Translated by permission of Daniel Morcrette, B. P. 26, 95270-Luzarches, France (*pages 89, 146*).
Norberg, Inga, *Good Food from Sweden.* Published in 1935 by Chatto & Windus, London. By permission of Curtis Brown Ltd. (*page 152*).
Ohio USA Housewives Companion, *1876* (*page 115*).
Olney, Richard, *Simple French Food.* Copyright © 1974 by Richard Olney. Published by Atheneum Publishers, New York. By permission of Penguin Books Ltd. (*pages 105, 112*).
Ortiz, Elisabeth Lambert, *Caribbean Cooking.* Copyright © Elisabeth Lambert Ortiz, 1973, 1975. Published by Penguin Books Ltd., London. By permission of Penguin Books Ltd. (*page 124*).
Palay, Simin, *La Cuisine du Pays.* © 1970 Marrimpouey Jeune-Pau. Published by Éditions Marrimpouey Jeune et Cie., Pau. Translated by permission of Éditions Marrimpouey Jeune et Cie. (*pages 148, 159*).
Paradissis, Chrissa, *The Best Book of Greek Cookery.* Copyright © 1976 P. Efstathiadis & Sons. Published by P. Efstathiadis & Sons, Athens. By permission of P. Efstathiadis & Sons (*page 121*).
Peck, Paula, *Paula Peck's Art of Good Cooking.* Copyright © 1961, 1966 Paula Peck. Published by Simon & Schuster, New York. By permission of John Schaffner Agency (*page 97*).
Petersen, Bengt, *Delicious Fish Dishes.* © Bengt Petersen/Wezäta Förlag 1976. Published by Wezäta Förlag, Göteborg. By permission of Wezäta Förlag (*page 127*).
Les Petits Plats et les Grands, © 1977, by Éditions Denoël, Paris. Published by Éditions Denoël Sarl, Paris. Translated by permission of Éditions Denoël Sarl (*pages 133, 142*).
Petits Propos Culinaires (Vol. 1, February, 1979) © 1979, Prospect Books. Published by Prospect Books, London and Washington D.C. By permission of the publisher (*pages 102, 146*).
Pomiane, Édouard de, *Le Carnet d'Anna.* Published by Les Éditions Paul-Martial, Paris, 1938 (*page 109*).
Portinari, Laura Gras, *Cucina e Vini del Piemonte e della Valle d'Aosta.* © Copyright 1971 Ugo Mursia Editore—Milan. Published by Ugo Mursia Editore S.p.A. Milano. Translated by permission of Ugo Mursia Editore (*pages* 114, 140).
Les Princes de la Gastronomie. © 1.2.1975—Les Éditions Mondiales. Published by Modes de Paris. Translated by permission of Les Éditions Mondiales (*pages 128, 143*).
Progneaux, Jean E., *Les Spécialités et Recettes Gastronomiques Bordelaises et Girondines.* Published by Quartier Latin, La Rochelle. Translated by permission of Quartier Latin (*page 105*).
Reboul, J. B., *La Cuisinière Provençale.* Published by Tacussel, Marseilles. Translated by permission of Tacussel, Éditeur (*pages 154, 162*).
Renaudet, B., *Les Secrets de la Bonne Table.* Published by Éditions Albin Michel, Paris. Translated by

permission of Éditions Albin Michel (*pages 95, 96 and 139*).
Robaglia, Suzanne, *Margaridou: Journal et Recettes d'une Cuisinière au Pays d'Auverne.* Published by Éditions Creer, F6334 Nonette. Translated by permission of Éditions Creer (*pages 98, 139*).
Root, Waverley, *The Best of Italian Cooking.* Copyright © 1974 by Edita S.A. Published by André Deutsch Limited, London. By permission of André Deutsch Limited (*page 158*).
Ross, Janet and Waterfield, Michael, *Leaves from our Tuscan Kitchen.* Copyright © Michael Waterfield, 1973. Published by John Murray, London 1973 and Penguin Books Ltd., 1977. By permission of John Murray (Publishers) Ltd. (*pages 95, 142*).
Saint-Ange, Madame, *La Cuisine de Madame Saint-Ange.* © Éditions Chaix. Published by Éditions Chaix, Grenoble. Translated by permission of Éditions Chaix (*pages 100, 114 and 140*).
Sarvis, Shirley, *Simply Stews.* Published by Signet. By permission of Shirley Sarvis (*page 152*).
Savarin, Jeanne Mme. (Editor in Chief), *La Cuisine des Familles,* (Magazine). No. 19 October 29 1905, No. 7 August 6 1905, No. 131 December 22 1907, No. 12 September 10 1905 (*pages 95, 110, 136 and 147*).
Scott, Jack Denton, *The Complete Book of Pasta.* Copyright © 1968 by Jack Denton Scott. Published by William Morrow & Company, Inc., New York. Reprinted by permission of Jack Denton Scott and William Morrow & Company, Inc. (*pages 121, 150*).
Sigurdardóttir, Helga, *Matur Og Drykkur.* Published by Isafoldarprentsmidja H. F. Reykjavik. 4th edition 1966. Translated by permission of Isafoldarprentsmidja (*page 132*).
Skipwith, Sofka, *Eat Russian.* © Sofka Skipwith 1973. Published by David and Charles (Holdings) Ltd., Devon. By permission of David and Charles (Holdings) Ltd. (*pages 145, 158*).
Szathmary, Louis, *The Chef's Secret Cookbook.* Copyright © 1971 by Louis Szathmary. Published by Quadrangle Books, Chicago. Reprinted by permission of Times Books, A Division of Quadrangle/The New York Times Book Co. (*page 109*).
Tarr, Yvonne Young, *The New York Times Bread and Soup Cookbook.* Copyright © 1972 by Yvonne Young Tarr. Published by Quadrangle/New York Times. Reprinted by permission of Times Books, A Division of Quadrangle/The New York Times Book Co. (*page 131*).
Tobias, Doris and Merris, Mary, *The Golden Lemon.* Copyright © 1978 by Doris Tobias & Mary Merris. Published by Atheneum Publishers, New York. By permission of Atheneum Publishers (*page 141*).
Varenne, La, *Le Vray Cuisinier François,* 1651 (*pages 93, 161*).
Venesz, Jozsef, *Hungarian Cuisine.* © Jozsef Venesz, 1958. Published by Corvina Press (*pages 91, 92, 122*).
Wason, Betty, *The Art of German Cooking.* © Elizabeth Wason Hall 1967. First published in Great Britain by Allen & Unwin 1971. By permission of George Allen & Unwin (Publishers) Ltd., Hemel Hempstead (*page 136*).
Willinsky, Grete, *Kochbuch der Büchergilde.* © Büchergilde Gutenberg, Frankfurt am Main 1958. Published by Büchergilde Gutenberg. Translated by permission of Büchergilde Gutenberg (*pages 88, 93, 98 and 109*).
Witwicka, H. and Soskine, S., *La Cuisine Russe Classique.* © Éditions Albin Michel, 1968 et 1978. Published by Éditions Albin Michel, Paris. Translated by permission of Éditions Albin Michel (*pages 118, 122*).
Wright, Carol, *Portuguese Food.* Copyright © 1969 by Carol Wright. Published by J. M. Dent & Sons Ltd., Publishers, London. By permission of Deborah Rogers Ltd. on behalf of Carol Wright (*page 136*).

Acknowledgements and Picture Credits

The Editors of this book are particularly indebted to Jeremiah Tower, San Francisco; Elizabeth Lambert Ortiz, London; Alan Davidson, London, and Pat Alburey, Royston, Hertfordshire.

They also wish to thank the following: Sue Crowther, London; Jennifer Davidson, London; Pamela Davidson, London; Dorothy Frame, London; Diana Grant, London; Maggie Heinz, London; Marion Hunter, Sutton, Surrey; Brenda Jayes, London; John Leslie, London; Agneta Munktell, London; Jo Oxley, Morden, Surrey; Joanna Roberts, London; Alice Salmon, London; Eileen Turner, Brighton, Sussex.

Photographs by Tom Belshaw: 4, 10—top, 11—top, 12, 13, 14—second row centre, 16—top and bottom, 17—top and centre, 18—centre, 19—centre, 21, 22, 26, 27, 28—bottom, 29—bottom, 30 to 33, 42, 46 to 51, 52—bottom, 54, 56—bottom, 57—bottom, 58 to 62, 64, 65, 68—top, bottom centre and right, 69, 73, 78, 79, 80—top and bottom right, 81 to 85.
Photographs by Alan Duns: 8, 9, 10—bottom, 11—bottom, 14—top, centre left, bottom left and centre, 15, 16—centre, 17—bottom, 18—top and bottom, 19—top and bottom, 20, 24, 25, 28—top, 29—top, 34 to 37, 40, 44, 45, 52—top, 53, 56—top, 57—top, 66, 67, 70 to 72, 74, 76, 77, 80—left.

Other photographers: Gina Harris, 14—centre right, bottom right, 43, 68—bottom left, 86. Richard Jeffery, Cover. Louis Klein, 2.

Illustrations: 8 and 9—Basil Smith; all line cuts from Mary Evans Picture Library and private sources.

Colour separations by Gilchrist Ltd.—Leeds, England
Typesetting by Camden Typesetters—London, England
Printed and bound by Brepols S.A.—Turnhout, Belgium.